The Oxford Book of Children's Verse

Iona and Peter Opie, widely admired for their pioneering work on children's lore and literature, are the authors of: *The Oxford Dictionary of Nursery Rhymes*, *The Oxford Nursery Rhyme Book*, *The Lore and Language of Schoolchildren*, *Children's Games in Street and Playground*, *Classic Fairy Tales*, *A Nursery Companion*, *The Oxford Book of Narrative Verse*, and *The Singing Game* (which Iona Opie completed after her husband's death in 1982). Her most recent publication is *People in the Playground* (1993).

The Oxford Book of Children's Verse

Chosen and Edited, with Notes, by

Iona and Peter Opie

Oxford New York

OXFORD UNIVERSITY PRESS

Oxford University Press, Walton Street, Oxford OX2 6DP
Oxford New York
Athens Auckland Bangkok Bombay
Calcutta Cape Town Dar es Salaam Delhi
Florence Hong Kong Istanbul Karachi
Kuala Lumpur Madras Madrid Melbourne
Mexico City Nairobi Paris Singapore
Taipei Tokyo Toronto

and associated companies in
Berlin Ibadan

Oxford is a trade mark of Oxford University Press

First published by Oxford University Press 1973
First issued as an Oxford University Press paperback 1994

British Library Cataloguing in Publication Data
Data available

Library of Congress Cataloging in Publication Data
The Oxford book of children's verse / chosen and edited, with notes, by Iona and Peter Opie.
p. cm.
Includes index.
1. Children's poetry. I. Opie, Iona Archibald. II. Opie, Peter.
PN6110.C409 1994 821.008'09282—dc20 94-18386

ISBN 0-19-282349-3

5 7 9 10 8 6

Printed in Great Britain by
Biddles Ltd
Guildford and King's Lynn

Twice five years
Or less I might have seen, when first my mind
With conscious pleasure opened to the charm
Of words in tuneful order, found them sweet
For their own *sakes*, a passion, and a power;
And phrases pleased me chosen for delight,
For pomp, or love.

Wordsworth,
The Prelude, Bk. v.

Twice five years
Or less I might have seen, when first my mind
With conscious pleasure opened to the charm
Of words in tuneful order, found them sweet
For their own sakes, a passion, and a power;
And phrases pleased me chosen for delight,
For pomp, or love.

Wordsworth,
The Prelude, v

PREFACE

THE more precise an anthologist can be about his intentions the less likely is he to disappoint by his performance. This book is a gathering of verses that have been written for children, or written with children prominently in mind, which either were cherished in their own day, or which have stood the test of time. Its object is thus to make available in one place the classics of children's poetry: that small satchelful of verse whose existence constitutes one of the pleasing advantages of being born to the English tongue. In this respect, if in no other, the volume may be seen to be the child, or rather grandchild, of *The Oxford Book of English Verse*. When Quiller-Couch ranged over the centuries so that he should include all of the best that the English language had to offer, he was resolved that no piece should be omitted simply because it had appeared in other anthologies, and become familiar. 'The best is the best,' he protested, 'though a hundred judges have declared it so.' And Palgrave before him was of like mind when (under Tennyson's guidance) he amassed his *Golden Treasury*, asserting he would regard as his fittest readers 'those who love poetry so well' he could offer them 'nothing not already known and valued'.

In the present work no conscious effort has been made to seek out the unfamiliar, or to arrive at fresh assessments. An anthologist for the young intent on bringing distinction to his collection by the novelties he offers or the startling juxtapositions he contrives, may easily forget that children, despite their cheerful pretensions to the contrary, have not been born with the knowledge of former generations already in their heads. Children cannot be surprised by the extraordinary who have not been made aware of what is ordinary. A generation knowing top hats only as props for conjurors does not think it so remarkable when rabbits emerge from them, as when a man is seen in the street wearing one on his head. And no matter how well known certain poems may be to the rest of us, a new generation is not going to become acquainted with them unless somebody plays host and makes the introductions.

For novelty in this work, if novelty is a requirement, we must rely on our terms of reference; hoping that by our concentration upon verse written for children, the writing of verse for the young can be appreciated as an art-form; and that by our chronological arrangement—spanning, as it does, half a millennium—a view may be had of man's many, and occasionally successful, attempts to make aesthetic contact with his descendants.

Distinguishing the verse that was always for children from that subsequently adopted for children has been the principal difficulty, as also the perpetual interest, in the preparation of this work. Until the middle of the eighteenth century children were seldom regarded as they are today, as different creatures from the rest of us, requiring preferential treatment, a special dietary, and a separate literature. Before 1740 there was little writing for children as such, only exhortation. Few of our nursery rhymes, for instance, were originally compositions for the young; and no single one of the traditional ballads, so far as is known, such as were composed about Robin Hood and Johnny Armstrong, was conceived for juvenile wonder. The old tale of the 'Children in the Wood', it will be remembered, was addressed not to children but to 'you parents dear'; while the renowned nonsense-songs of the seventeenth century were designed for tipplers rather than toddlers. Even as late as 1784 it did not occur to Cowper to publish 'John Gilpin' as an amusement for the young; and only a little earlier Goldsmith, although serving in the heart of the juvenile book-trade, little thought he had the nucleus of a successful children's book in compositions such as 'Mrs. Mary Blaize' and 'An Elegy on the Death of a Mad Dog'. For a poem to be considered suitable for a child it was thought necessary that it should be edifying. Bunyan's emblems and Watts's songs, which in some ways mark the beginning of writing for children at their own level, were nevertheless produced strictly in the spirit of George Herbert:

> A verse may find him, who a sermon flies,
> And turn delight into a sacrifice.

In consequence any verse prior to the eighteenth century not didactic or divine was doubtfully intended for the young (Thomas Newbery's book *Dives Pragmaticus* was a reader); and, however affectionately expressed the verses may be that were addressed to individual children, such as those of John Hoskyns to his son

Benedict, Richard Corbet to his son Vincent, and Abraham Chear to his young kinsman 'R. L.', their motive, it will be seen, is admonitory. Thus poems purportedly addressed to the young, but not persuasive in tone, are almost always found to be attempts by the authors to ingratiate themselves with one or other of the parents, on the well-known principle that 'he who wipes the child's nose, kisseth the mother's cheek'. Ambrose Philips's notorious odes to the Carteret and Pulteney children are undoubtedly cases in point; and so, probably, is Horace Walpole's offering to little Anne Fitzpatrick.[1] The difference between the two types of verse readily appears if, for instance, comparison is made between Prior's arch lines 'To a Child of Quality, Five Years Old', composed, one suspects, for the gratification of the Earl of Jersey's household:

> Lords, knights, and squires, the numerous band
> That wear the fair Miss Mary's fetters,
> Were summoned by her high command
> To show their passions by their letters . . .[2]

and the lovely letter he addressed to 'little Peggy', the five-year-old Lady Margaret Cavendish Holles-Harley, a composition that conveys the genuine solicitude of an aging poet for a small friend.

Naturally, the more pure the poetry, the more difficult it can be to say for whom the poet is writing. Blake, 'piping songs of pleasant glee', performs not only for the young but for the innocence in all mankind; and so, in their own way, do Christina Rossetti and de la Mare, even when claiming only the young for their audience. Wordsworth, explicitly, addresses the world; and to have excluded 'Lucy Gray' and 'We are Seven' and 'The Pet Lamb' would have been to have excluded poems that are integral to the story of verse-writing for children. Indeed it will be seen how neatly Wordsworth's ballads link the eighteenth century to the new awareness of childhood in the nineteenth century. Included, too, are a few pieces which, though not written directly for children, feature in tales or dramas as specimens of verse addressed to the young, for instance the counsel the Manciple received from his mother, which he recalls in his

[1] See, *The Oxford Book of Eighteenth-Century Verse*, pp. 145–46 and 483–4.

[2] Ibid., p. 18.

Canterbury tale; the lullaby Janicolo sings while Babulo rocks the cradle in *Patient Grissill*; and the children's songs that Tennyson inserted, or wrote for insertion, in *The Princess*. For the most part, however, our choice comes from the mainstream of children's literature, the nature of the verse being our first consideration, and the publication in which it appears being our confirmation—attention also being given to what the writer himself has said about his verse.

The chronological arrangement has had its problems too; but its rewards are obvious. Chronological arrangement allows us to hold hands with history and meet old friends in their own surroundings. It enables us to see at a glance the type of verse being written for children at any particular period; and makes possible a review of the verse already current when a new poet appears, so that we can judge how fresh was his voice. Indeed, since verse for children tends to be intimately related to the period in which it was written, and since one author may take to writing for children early in life and another not until he is a grandparent, the poets are arranged here not by date of birth but by the date of publication (occasionally, the date of composition) of the earliest of their pieces to be included here. Had the poets been arranged by order of birth, as in other Oxford anthologies, Ann and Jane Taylor (born 1782 and 1783) would have appeared to have been imitators of Elizabeth Turner (born about 1775), when the contrary was the case; Mrs. Dorset's 'The Peacock "At Home"' would have seemed to have preceded William Roscoe's 'The Butterfly's Ball', to which it was a sequel; and C. H. Ross's *Comical Rhymes* would not have been seen to have anticipated the verse in *Alice in Wonderland*. With this arrangement, too, we have been able to place each of the anonymous pieces (and anonymous verse is endemic in juvenile literature) more exactly where it belongs in publishing history, thus letting at least one poetic hand, hitherto unsuspected, show itself as a precursor of William Blake. We are able to see, too, how the worldly counsel of early times gives place to the heavenly pleadings of the Puritans in the seventeenth century; and how humanity emerges in the eighteenth century, followed by the strange levity and surface morality of the early decades of the nineteenth century.

The influence of individual authors, too, will be apparent, as of Bunyan on Watts, and of Watts on nearly everyone in his century.

In fact we know how conscious of Watts were the Taylors in the nineteenth century—had not their great-grandmother, when a child, been taken on to the revered man's knee?—and how the Taylors gave rise to a whole manufactory of little books for children each hoping, and all failing, to be as successful as *Original Poems for Infant Minds*; just as, in the twenties and thirties of the present century, a proliferation of verse-makers attempted to emulate *When We Were Very Young*. We are able to observe how Seager's bedtime prayer preceded Coleridge's by more than two centuries, and how Smart's morning prayer foreran Ogden Nash's. We come upon a Johnny Head-in-Air ('The Stargazer') a century before Hoffmann; and find collections of limerick-style verses that pre-date Lear's *Book of Nonsense*. We listen to a minister, soon to settle in America, telling children of the defeat of the Spanish Armada when it was still within living memory; and a stay-at-home spinster evoking the perils of arctic exploration with a tale that stirred the boy Rudyard Kipling 'to the deeps', but which in later life he was unable to trace. We find Southey, when he wrote 'The Old Man's Comforts', adopting a metre used in his childhood by Dorothy Kilner; and are reminded that it was Southey's poem that Lewis Carroll was to eclipse with a parody which, a lifetime later, Eleanor Farjeon adapted for her tribute to the 'wise Mr. Dodgson'. We can appreciate more easily, perhaps, the shock that must have preceded glee when the Liddell children found their father's shy friend was making fun of the poetry they had been brought up to learn and love; yet may remark how, despite Christ Church levity, Watts and Southey and the Taylors continued to be part of children's normal repertoire at least to the end of the nineteenth century, so that all writers up to the recent past—the generation to which de la Mare and Eleanor Farjeon belonged—can be said to have been brought up on their rhythms. Bearing this in mind it will be appreciated why we have thought it fitting to pause here for the time being, and to include no writer who is still living, and whose work cannot be viewed as a whole.

The notes have been kept to the end of the volume so that, if desired, they can be disregarded in comfort. Our own recollection is that while nobody at school ever bothered to read a preface, we felt downright deprived if our poetry book had no notes in it. Whether poetry was too rich for the stomach, at that time, if unaccompanied by dry prose, or whether our attention was over-ready to be diverted by details of the personalities of literature, we possessed a genuine affection for the notes in our books, and would return to them again and again. Indeed without notes some children are unable to imagine that a poem or a hymn ever had a point of origin. They seem to have as much difficulty appreciating that a poem was the creation of a particular person at a particular time, as have some adults in accepting that a folksong commenced with one man's exertion. 'I always remember the look of surprise on a child's face,' said a teacher, 'after we had read one of Dylan Thomas's poems, and I remarked he had been broadcasting that week. She gazed at the name below the poem and said "Is he a real person?" ' We feel it can make all the difference, too, to one's attitude to some poems if one knows the circumstances in which they were written: that the tale of the naughty boy who ran away to Scotland is not so much a production of the great John Keats as an elder brother's waggery for a beloved sister cooped in London; that Mrs. Barbauld's 'Mouse's Petition' is said to have been written about a mouse made captive by Joseph Priestley for one of his experiments; that Robert Smith really was in prison and about to be burnt at the stake when he wrote his selfless exhortation to his children. Such, anyway, is our excuse for admitting notes to this volume, even if only discreetly by the back door; and we hope they will not distract from what has been our foremost care, the verse itself.

Our resolve has been that no less attention should be given to the editing of verse that is for children than has been given to the verse in the other volumes in this series, which are recognized works of scholarship. Rather, since poems for children are usually taken on trust—one anthologist copying from another—and the reliability of some of the texts was becoming increasingly doubtful, the need to verify them had become essential. So far as has been within our power we have sought out the original printing of each poem; and have then seen whether the author subsequently revised it, and revised it for the better. Sometimes our texts have been established only after collating four or more printings, an undertaking that would have been arduous, if not impractical, had we not (with a foresight which now amazes us) made our permanent home within a library of early children's books.

However, since this anthology is intended to give present pleasure as well as to satisfy historical curiosity, and to be a companion to the mature of all ages, no matter how young, our policy has been to modernize spelling and punctuation throughout; to assist with accents and glosses where without them a reader might momentarily hesitate; and, like Quiller-Couch, to excise the occasional weak stanza or to give an extract only of a lengthy work —provided it will stand on its own—just as we have sometimes restored attractive stanzas that for some reason are now usually omitted. It can thus be claimed that virtually the whole of this work, other than the medieval section, stems from a re-examination of the original sources. Indeed it has the benefit, as have we ourselves, of an extensive re-reading of this branch of literature; and we can only trust that not many pieces truly worthwhile have escaped us; yet at the same time hope that any splendid find will be brought to our notice.

'In poetry,' said Matthew Arnold, 'which is thought and art in one, it is the glory, the eternal honour, that charlatanism shall find no entrance.' We believe no verse is here that is not the clear expression of its begetter. It has also seemed to us that voice after voice speaks in unison. But our business is at an end when the voices have been assembled. As to whether this anthology has a message, and if it has, what that message may be, we leave to the wisdom of the reader.

I.O. & P.O.

West Liss in Hampshire
1972

However, since this anthology is intended to give present pleasure as well as to satisfy historical curiosity, and to be recommended to the reader of all ages, no matter how young, our policy has been to modernize spelling and punctuation throughout, to assist with accents and glosses where without them a reader might momentarily flounder, and, like Quiller-Couch, to revise the [illegible] word [illegible] —provided it will stand on its own—just as we have sometimes preferred alternative stanzas [illegible] are now usually [illegible]. It may thus be claimed that [illegible] work, other than the medieval section, stems from a re-examination of the original sources. Indeed it has the benefit, as have its forebears, of an extensive re-reading of this branch of literature; and we can only trust that not many pieces truly worth while have escaped us, at the same time hoping that any so [illegible] will be brought to our notice.

"In poetry," said Matthew Arnold, "which is thought and art in one, it is the glory, the eternal honour, that charlatanism shall find no entrance." We believe no charlatan here; this is not the place for exposition of that belief. It has also seemed to us that [illegible] voice speaks in unison. But our business is at an end when the voices have been assembled. As to whether this anthology has a message, and if it has, what that message may be, we leave to the wisdom of the reader.

[illegible]

ACKNOWLEDGEMENTS

It would be convenient to say, if it were not a simplification, that for the medieval period we have been guided by Brown, Robbins, and Cutler's *Index of Middle English Verse* and Furnivall's artificially named *Babees Book*; for the sixteenth and seventeenth centuries by William Sloane's *Children's Books in England and America in the Seventeenth Century*; for the eighteenth century by our own contribution to volume II of *The New Cambridge Bibliography of English Literature*; and for the nineteenth century by John Mackay Shaw's *Childhood in Poetry*, the catalogue of the Shaw Collection in Florida State University Library. But indispensable as these works have been, they have on the whole been used not so much to see what to include, as to ensure that everything qualified for inclusion has been considered; and if, for some reason, we had to make use only of one book as a guide to children's literature our choice would undoubtedly be F. J. Harvey Darton's *Children's Books in England*, a social and critical history which, despite the greater amount of information now available, remains the superlative work on its subject.

An anthologist, as well as being a borrower of other men's achievements, and a burrower in his predecessor's works of reference, is liable to be a bore to his friends whose opinions he is forever canvassing, and a badgerer of his colleagues for special information. In addition to our family, and those close to us, whose interest in the work has had more influence than they themselves may be aware, we are grateful to the following for specific kindnesses: Mr. E. F. Bleiler, editor of the Dover reprint of *Mother Goose's Melodies*, for sending us the earliest version so far found of 'I like little pussy'; Lady Bonham-Carter, for presenting us with a number of children's books that have proved invaluable; Mr. Arthur F. Bryce, Sandeman Librarian, Perth, for information about James Ferguson; The Director of Bath Municipal Libraries, for information about Henry Dixon; Lady Elton and Mr. Raisley Moorsom, for unveiling the identity of 'Aunt Effie'; Miss Carrol Jenkins, for the complete works of Mrs. Ewing, and for suggestions over many years; Mr. Roland Knaster, for making available children's books from his collection; Dr. Edgar Osborne, for sending the catalogue of his extensive collection of children's books at Toronto Public Library, expertly compiled by Miss Judith St. John; The Revd. Dr. Erik Routley, for advice about Julia Carney and hymn writing; Mr. Robert Scott, for digging deeply into his own collection of children's books for us; Mr. John Mackay Shaw, already referred to, for meticulous answers to inquiries; Mrs. Myfanwy Thomas, for confirming that it was for her sister and herself, respectively, that her father Edward Thomas wrote 'If I Should Ever by Chance' and 'What Shall I Give?'; and the late and gallant Dr. d'Alté A. Welch of Cleveland Heights, Ohio, for sending his massive *Bibliography of American Children's Books Printed Prior to 1821*, and for a willingness to answer queries put to him. Finally we are indebted, once again, to Miss F. Doreen Gullen, our mentor for more than twenty years, whose knowledge and energy seems always to extend beyond our own. Her friendship is reflected throughout these pages.

In addition we gratefully acknowledge the permission we have received to include copyright poems in this book.

Laurence Alma-Tadema: from *Realms of Unknown Kings*. Reprinted by permission of the Garnstone Press.

Sabine Baring-Gould: 'Now the Day is Over'. Reprinted by permission of Gordon Hitchcock on behalf of the Executors of the late Baring-Gould.

Hilaire Belloc: 'The Yak' and 'The Frog' from *The Bad Child's Book of Beasts*; 'The Python' and 'The Vulture' from *More Beasts for Worse Children*; and 'Jim' and 'Matilda' from *Cautionary Tales for Children*. Reprinted by permission of Gerald Duckworth & Co. Ltd. In the U.S., reprinted by permission of Alfred A. Knopf, Inc., from *Cautionary Verses*, 1941.

Walter de la Mare: from *Complete Poems*. Reprinted by permission of the Literary Trustees of Walter de la Mare, and The Society of Authors as their representative.

T. S. Eliot: from *Old Possum's Book of Practical Cats*. Reprinted by permission of Faber and Faber Ltd. In the U.S.: Copyright 1939 by T. S. Eliot, copyright 1967 by Esme Valerie Eliot. Reprinted by permission of Harcourt Brace Jovanovich, Inc.

Eleanor Farjeon: 'Blackfriars' from *Nursery Rhymes of London Town*. Reprinted by permission of Gerald Duckworth & Co.

Ltd. 'Tailor' from *Cherrystones*; 'Mrs. Malone' from *Mrs. Malone*; and 'The Night will Never Stay' from *Silver-Sand and Snow* (Michael Joseph Ltd.). 'Lewis Carroll' from *The New Book of Days* (Oxford University Press). Reprinted by permission of David Higham Associates, Ltd.

Rose Fyleman: 'Fairies', 'A Fairy Went A-Marketing', 'The Fairies Have Never a Penny to Spend', and 'I Don't Like Beetles' from *Fairies and Chimneys*; 'Mrs. Brown' from *The Fairy Green*; and 'Temper' from *The Fairy Flute* (all Methuen & Co. Ltd.). Reprinted by permission of The Society of Authors as the literary representative of the Estate of Rose Fyleman. In the U.S.: from *Fairies and Chimneys*, copyright 1918, 1920 by George H. Doran Company; *The Fairy Green*, copyright 1923 by George H. Doran Company; *The Fairy Flute*, copyright 1923 by Doubleday & Company, Inc. All reprinted by permission of Doubleday & Company, Inc.

Kenneth Grahame: from *The Wind in the Willows*. Reprinted by permission of The Bodleian Library, Oxford, and Methuen & Co. Ltd. In the U.S. and Canada 'Ducks' Ditty' is reprinted by permission of Charles Scribner's Sons.

John Hoskyns: from *Life, Letters, and Writings of John Hoskyns, 1566–1638*, by Louise Brown Osborn. Reprinted by permission of Yale University Press.

Peter Idley: from *Peter Idley's Instructions to his Son*, edited by Charlotte D'Evelyn. By permission of the Editor and The Modern Language Association of America.

Rudyard Kipling: 'The Hump' from *Just So Stories*; 'Puck's Song' (definitive version) and 'A Smuggler's Song' from *Puck of Pook's Hill*; 'The Way through the Woods' and 'If—?' from *Rewards and Fairies*. Reprinted by permission of A. P. Watt & Son on behalf of Mrs. George Bambridge, Macmillan & Co. Ltd., London, and The Macmillan Company of Canada Ltd. All the above poems are also reprinted by permission of Doubleday & Company, Inc. from their *Rudyard Kipling's Verse: Definitive Edition*.

A. A. Milne: 'Buckingham Palace', 'The Three Foxes', 'The King's Breakfast', and 'Vespers' from *When We Were Very Young*; 'Us Two' from *Now We Are Six*. Reprinted by permission of Mr. C. R. Milne and Methuen & Co. Ltd. In the U.S.: from *When We Were Very Young*, copyright 1924 by

E. P. Dutton & Co., Inc. and from *Now We Are Six*, copyright 1927 by E. P. Dutton & Co., Inc. Renewal copyrights 1952 by A. A. Milne. Published by E. P. Dutton & Co., Inc., and reprinted with their permission. Also reprinted by permission of the Canadian publishers, McClelland and Stewart Ltd., Toronto.

Ogden Nash: from *The New Nutcracker Suite and Other Innocent Verses*, copyright © 1961, 1962 by Ogden Nash. Reprinted by permission of Little, Brown and Company; and also by A. P. Watt & Son on behalf of the Estate of the late Ogden Nash.

E. Nesbit: from *A Pomander of Verse*. Reprinted by permission of John Farquharson Ltd.

Edward Abbott Parry: 'Pater's Bathe' and 'I would like you for a Comrade' from *Katawampus*; and 'The Jam Fish' from *The Scarlet Herring*. 'Oh, I have four children' (on p. 377) is from *Butterscotia*. Reprinted by permission of Christy & Moore Ltd.

Laura E. Richards: from *Tirra Lirra*. Reprinted by permission of Little, Brown and Company.

For permission to reproduce illustrations, we are indebted to the Trustees of the British Museum for the detail from the title-page of the *Grammatica Nova* of Nicolaus Perrottus (an edition of c. 1491), and for the illustration from the *Orbis Pictus* of John Amos Comenius, 1659. Also to the artist, and to Messrs Curtis Brown Ltd., for the illustration by Ernest H. Shepard from A. A. Milne's *Now We Are Six*, 1927, which in the U.S. is reproduced by permission of E. P. Dutton & Co, Inc.; and in Canada by permission of McClelland and Stewart Ltd., Toronto.

The remaining illustrations, all from items in our own collection, are from a wood-engraving by John Bewick on a reading card, c. 1790; from a drawing by William Mulready engraved on copper in Roscoe's *The Butterfly's Ball*, 1807; from a drawing by Arthur Hughes, engraved by Dalziel, in Christina Rossetti's *Sing-Song*, 1872; and from a pen-and-ink drawing by Kate Greenaway reproduced in G. E. Brunefille's *Topo*, 1878.

The picture on the jacket is a detail from George Romney's painting of the Gower family, reproduced by courtesy of the Lake District Art Gallery Trust.

CONTENTS

Medieval and Sixteenth Century

Seventeenth Century

CONTENTS

CONTENTS

Eighteenth Century

CONTENTS

CONTENTS

CONTENTS

CONTENTS

CONTENTS

CONTENTS

CONTENTS

MEDIEVAL AND SIXTEENTH CENTURY

GEOFFREY CHAUCER

*c.*1343–1400

Controlling the Tongue

MY son, keep well thy tongue, and keep thy friend.
A wicked tongue is worse than a fiend;
My son, from a fiend men may them bless.
My son, God of his endless goodness
Walled a tongue with teeth and lips eke,
For man should him avise what he speak.
My son, full oft, for too much speech
Hath many a man been spilt, as clerkès teach;
But for little speech avisely
Is no man shent, to speak generally.
My son, thy tongue shouldst thou restrain
At all time, but when thou dost thy pain
To speak of God, in honour and prayer.
The first virtue, son, if thou wilt lere,
Is to restrain and keep well thy tongue;
Thus learn children when that they been young.
My son, of muckle speaking evil-avised,
Where less speaking had enough sufficed,
Cometh muckle harm; thus was me told and taught.
In muckle speech sin wanteth nought.
Wost thou whereof a rakel tongue serveth?
Right as a sword forcutteth and forcarveth
An arm a-two, my dear son, right so
A tongue cutteth friendship all a-two.

bless, protect by making the sign of the cross ***eke***, also
avise, consider ***spilt***, spoilt, ruined ***clerkès***, clerics
avisely, prudently ***shent***, harmed ***dost thy pain***, takest pains
lere, learn ***muckle***, much ***evil-avised***, ill-considered
Wost, knowest ***rakel***, rash, hasty ***a-two***, in two

JOHN LYDGATE

1370?–1450

2 *The Boy Serving at Table*

MY dear child, first thyself enable
With all thine heart to virtuous discipline;
Afore thy sovereign, standing at the table,
Dispose thou thee after my doctrine
To all nurture thy courage to incline.
First, when thou speakest be not reckless,
Keep feet and fingers still in peace.
Be simple of cheer, cast not thine eye aside,
Gaze not about, turning thy sight over all.
Against the post let not thy back abide,
Neither make thy mirror of the wall.
Pick not thy nose, and, most especial,
Be well ware, and set hereon thy thought,
Before thy sovereign scratch nor rub thee nought.

***courage*, mind** ***sovereign*, lord, master**

PETER IDLEY

d. 1473?

3 *Sources of Good Counsel*

FIRST of God by whom all grace is spread
His counsel thou ask, for that is sure.
Secondly of thyself with good mind and sad,
For thyself of thyself hast most cure.
Think such counsel as will longest endure
And most best God and man to please,
It will grow to the most heart's ease.

***sad*, serious** ***cure*, care**

The third counsellor that thou have shall,
Choose thee a man of noble fame,
Proved in his works among other all,
That loveth worship and dreadeth shame,
And in his works not slow nor lame:
Good son, have this well in mind
And to thy great profit thou shalt it find.

Youth's counsel seldom availeth
Where wisdom is not the mean.
Many a man his works he waileth;
Know thyself, therefore, while thou art green,
That when age cometh crooked and lean
Thou live restfully, aye serving God,
And be not beaten with thine own rod.

4 *Covetousness*

Covetousness hath never end,
And where is no end, is no rest;
Where is no rest, peace doth wend;
Where is no peace, God is a guest;
For God himself made his nest
Where peace made his bower,
And there he dwelleth, our Saviour.

***guest*, stranger**

ANONYMOUS

c. 1478

5 *A Goodly Child*

It is to a goodly child well fitting
To use disports of mirth and pleasance,
To harp, or lute, or lustily to sing,
Or in the press right mannerly to dance.
When men see a child of such governance
They say, 'Glad may this child's friends be
To have a child so mannerly as he.'

press, crowd, throng *governance*, manner

6 *Customs Change*

Little child, I counsel you that ye
Take heed unto the nurture that men use,
New-found or ancient whether it be,
So shall no man your courtesy refuse;
The guise and custom shall you, my child, excuse.
Men's works have often interchange,
What now is nurture, sometime hath been strange.

Things whilom used be now laid aside,
And new feats daily be contrived;
Men's acts can in no plight abide,
They be changeable and oft moved:
Things sometime allowed be now reproved;
And after this shall things uprise
That men set now but at little price.

nurture, code of manners *guise*, style *whilom*, some time in the past
feats, actions *can in no plight abide*, cannot remain the same

c. 1480

7 *Manners at Table when away from Home*

LITTLE children, here ye may lere,
Much courtesy that is written here.

Look thine hands be washen clean,
That no filth in thy nails be seen.
Take thou no meat till grace be said
And till thou see all things arrayed.
Look, my son, that thou not sit
Till the ruler of the house thee bid.
And at thy meat, in the beginning,
Look on poor men that thou think:
For the full stomach ever fails
To understand what the hungry ails.
Eat not thy meat too hastily,
Abide and eat easily.
Carve not thy bread too thin,
Nor break it not in twain:
The morsels that thou beginnest to touch
Cast them not in thy pouch.
Put not thy fingers in thy dish,
Neither in flesh, neither in fish;
Put not thy meat into the salt
(Into thy cellar that thy salt halt)
But lay it fair on thy trencher
Before thee, that is honour.

Pick not thine ears nor thy nostrils,
If thou do, men will say thou com'st of churls.
And while thy meat in thy mouth is
Drink thou not—forget not this.
Eat thy meat by small morsels,
Fill not thy mouth as doeth rascals.
Pick not thy teeth with thy knife;
In no company begin thou strife.

lere, learn ***halt***, holds ***churls***, peasants

And when thou hast thy pottage done,
Out of thy dish put thou thy spoon.
Nor spit thou not over the table
Nor thereupon—for it is not able.
Lay not thine elbow nor thy fist
Upon the table whilst thou eat'st.
Bulk not, as a bean were in thy throat,
As a churl that comes out of a cot.
And if thy meat be of great price
Be ware of it, or thou art not wise.

Bite not thy meat, but carve it clean:
Be well ware no drop be seen.
When thou eatest gape not too wide,
That thy mouth be seen on every side.
And son, be ware, I rede, of one thing,
Blow neither in thy meat nor in thy drink.

And cast not thy bones unto the floor,
But lay them fair on thy trencher.
Keep clean thy cloth before all
And sit thou still, whatso befall,
Till grace be said unto the end,
And till thou have washen with thy friend.
And spit not in thy basin,
My sweet son, that thou washest in;
And arise up soft and still,
And jangle neither with Jack nor Jill,
But take thy leave of thy host lowly,
And thank him with thine heart highly.
Then men will say thereafter
That 'A gentleman was here.'

able, seemly ***Bulk***, belch ***cot***, cottage, particularly a humble one ***rede***, advise

c. 1500

8 *Symon's Lesson of Wisdom for all Manner of Children; or, How to become a Bishop*

CHILD, I warn thee in all wise
That thou tell truth and make no lies.
Child, be not froward, be not proud,
But hold up thy head and speak aloud.
And when any man speaketh to thee,
Doff thy hood and bow thy knee.
And wash thy hands and wash thy face,
And be courteous in every place.
And where thou comest, with good cheer,
In hall or bower, bid 'God be here!'
Look thou cast at no man's dog,
With staff nor stone at horse nor hog;
Look that thou not scorn nor jape
Neither with man, maiden, nor ape.
Let no man of thee make plaint,
Swear thou not by God, neither by saint;
Look thou be courteous, standing at meat,
And that men giveth thee, thou take and eat;
And look that thou neither cry nor crave,
And say, 'That and that would I have';
But stand thou still before the board,
And look thou speak no loud word.
And, child, worship thy father and thy mother,
And look thou grieve neither one nor other;
But ever among thou shalt kneel adown,
And ask their blessing and their benison.

And, child, keep thy clothes fair and clean,
And let no foul filth on them be seen.
Child, climb thou not over house nor wall,
For no fruit, birds, nor ball.

froward, perverse

And, child, cast no stones over men's house,
Nor cast no stones at no glass windows;
Nor make no crying, japes, nor plays
In holy church on holy days.
And, child, when thou goest to play,
Look thou come home by light of day.
And, child, I warn thee of another matter,
Look thou keep thee well from fire and water;
And be ware and wise how that thou look
Over any brink, well, or brook.

Child, when thou goest in any street,
If thou any good man or woman meet,
Avale thy hood to him or to her,
And bid, 'God speed, dame or sir!'
And be they small or great,
This lesson that thou not forget—
For it is seemly to every man's child—
Namely, to clerks to be meek and mild.
And, child, rise betimes and go to school,
And fare not as a wanton fool,
And learn as fast as thou may and can,
For our bishop is an old man;
And therefore thou must learn fast
If thou wouldst be bishop when he is past.

Avale, take off, doff *clerks*, clerics

c. 1525

9 *Demeanour*

Busy in study be thou, child,
And in the hall, meek and mild,
And at the table, merry and glad,
And at bed, soft and sad.

soft and sad, easy and settled

ANONYMOUS

10 *The Unhappy Schoolboy*

Hey! hey! by this day!
What availeth it me though I say nay?

I would fain be a clerk,
But yet it is a strange work;
The birchen twigs be so sharp,
It maketh me have a faint heart.
What availeth it me though I say nay?

On Monday in the morning when I shall rise
At six of the clock, it is the guise
To go to school without advice—
I would rather go twenty miles twice!
What availeth it me though I say nay?

My master looketh as he were mad:
'Where hast thou been, thou sorry lad?'
'Milking ducks, as my mother bade':
It was no marvel that I were sad.
What availeth it me though I say nay?

My master peppered my tail with good speed,
It was worse than fennel seed,
He would not leave till it did bleed.
Much sorrow have he for his deed!
What availeth it me though I say nay?

I would my master were a hare,
And all his books greyhounds were,
And I myself a jolly huntèr;
To blow my horn I would not spare,
For if he were dead I would not care!
What availeth it me though I say nay?

clerk, **scholar** ***guise***, **practice** ***without advice***, **without being told**

HUGH RHODES

fl. 1540

11 *Rising in the Morning*

A PLANT without moisture sweet
Can bring forth no good flower;
If in youth ye lack virtue,
In age ye shall want honour.
First dread you God, and fly from sin,
Earthly things are mortal;
Be thou not haughty in thy looks
For pride will have a fall.
Rise you early in the morning,
For it hath properties three:
Holiness, health, and happy wealth,
As my father taught me.
At six of the clock, without delay,
Accustom thee to rise,
And give God thanks for thy good rest
When thou openest thine eyes.
Pray him also to prosper thee
And thine affairs in deed:
All the day after, assure thyself,
The better shalt thou speed.

FRANCIS SEAGER

fl. 1550

12 *A Prayer to be said when thou goest to Bed*

O MERCIFUL God, hear this our request,
And grant unto us this night quiet rest.
Into thy tuition O Lord do us take:
Our bodies sleeping, our minds yet may wake.

tuition, care

Forgive the offences this day we have wrought
Against thee and our neighbour, in word, deed, and thought.
And grant us thy grace henceforth to fly sin
And that a new life we may now begin.
Deliver and defend us this night from all evil,
And from the danger of our enemy, the Devil,
Which goeth about seeking his prey
And by his craft whom we may betray.
Assist us, O Lord, with thy holy sprite,
That valiantly against him we may ever fight;
And winning the victory, may lift up our voice,
And in thy strength faithfully rejoice,
Saying, 'To the Lord be all honour and praise
For his defence both now and always!'

ROBERT SMITH

d. 1555

13 *The Exhortation of a Father to his Children*

YE are the temples of the Lord,
For ye are dearly bought;
And they that do defile the same,
Shall surely come to nought.

Possess not pride in any wise,
Build not your house too high;
But have always before your eyes,
That ye be born to die.

Defraud not him that hired is,
Your labour to sustain;
But give him always out of hand,
His penny for his pain.

out of hand, immediately

And as you would that other men
 Against you should proceed,
Do you the same to them again,
 When they do stand in need.

And part your portion with the poor,
 In money and in meat;
And feed the fainted feeble soul,
 With that which ye should eat.

Ask counsel always at the wise,
 Give ear unto the end;
Refuse not you the sweet rebuke
 Of him that is your friend.

Be thankful always to the Lord,
 With prayer and with praise,
Desiring him in all your works
 For to direct your ways.

THOMAS NEWBERY

fl. 1563

14 *The Great Merchant, Dives Pragmaticus, Cries his Wares*

WHAT lack you, sir? What seek you? What will you buy?
Come hither to me, look what you can spy:
I have to sell of all things under the sky,
What lack you, my masters? Come hither to me.

I have to sell books, for men of divine,
And books of all laws, most pleasant and fine:
Of all arts and stories, as men will incline,
What lack you, gentleman? Come hither to me.

men of divine, men of divinity, i.e. churchmen

THOMAS NEWBERY

I have ink, paper, and pens, to load with a barge,
Inkhorns, and penners: fine, small, and large;
Primers and ABCs, and books of small charge,
What lack you, scholars? Come hither to me.

I have fine gowns, cloaks, jackets, and coats,
Fine jerkins, doublets, and hose without motes;
Fine daggers, and knives, bags, purses for groats,
What lack you, my friend? Come hither to me.

I have of all things plenty to furnish a house,
Racks for cheese, and traps for a mouse;
Fine pans for milk, and trim tubs for souse,
First cheap, and then buy. Come hither to me.

I have ladles, skimmers, andirons and spits,
Dripping pans, pot hooks, old cats and kits;
And pretty fine dogs, without fleas or nits,
What lack you, my friend? Come hither to me.

I have fine moulds for cooks, and fine cutting knives,
Axes for butchers, and fine glasses for wives;
Medicines for rats to shorten their lives,
What lack you? What buy you? Come hither to me.

I have rollingpins, battledores, washbowls, and broom,
Wild beasts and puppets, sent from beyond Rome;
Fine, gay, and strange garlands, for bride and for groom,
What lack you, fair maidens? Come hither to me.

I have ornaments, implements, fit for the church,
Fine rods for children, of willow and birch;
If I have not quick sale, I shall have a lurch,
What do you lack, sir? Come hither to me.

penners, pencases *motes*, faults *souse*, pickled pork
cheap, ask the price, bargain for *andirons*, fire-dogs
lurch, setback, disappointment

WILLIAM BULLOKAR

c. 1520–*c.* 1590

15 *To his Child*

WHOSO in harvest mindeth to reap
  The fruits that good and pleasant be,
In the springtime he must them sow,
  The hot summer may else them dry:

So, that their profit may grow small
  When that the crop may chance to fail
Of the increase much looked for,
  The bulk being slight, the gain as small.

So he that wisheth in elder years
  To have wisdom, he must begin
To learn the same in tender years,
  Else may he miss that he would win.

Soon bendeth the twig that new is sprung,
  The for-sprung branch men may yet wield,
But seld they may the grown bough,
  Old stems will rather break than yield.

wield, control ***seld***, seldom

THOMAS DEKKER

1572?–1632

16

A Cradle Song

GOLDEN slumbers kiss your eyes,
Smiles awake you when you rise.
Sleep, pretty wantons, do not cry,
And I will sing a lullaby:
Rock them, rock them, lullaby.

Care is heavy, therefore sleep you;
You are care, and care must keep you.
Sleep, pretty wantons, do not cry,
And I will sing a lullaby:
Rock them, rock them, lullaby.

THOMAS DEKKER

(1572–1632)

A Cradle Song

Golden slumbers kiss your eyes,
Smiles awake you when you rise;
Sleep, pretty wantons, do not cry,
And I will sing a lullaby,
Rock them, rock them, lullaby.

Care is heavy, therefore sleep you,
You are care, and care must keep you;
Sleep, pretty wantons, do not cry,
And I will sing a lullaby:
Rock them, rock them, lullaby.

SEVENTEENTH CENTURY

JOHN HOSKYNS

1566–1638

17 *To his little Son Benedict*
from the Tower of London

SWEET Benedict, whilst thou art young,
And know'st not yet the use of tongue,
Keep it in thrall whilst thou art free:
Imprison it or it will thee.

in thrall, in bondage

ANONYMOUS

c. 1625

18 *A Schoolmaster's Admonition*

GOOD children, refuse not these lessons to learn,
The pathway to virtue you here may discern;
In keeping them truly you shall be most sure
The praise of all people thereby to procure.

Let God first be served, who all things doth give,
That by his good blessing thou long time mayst live;
And then to thy parents thy duty unfold,
Who keepeth thee daily from hunger and cold.

To all men be courteous, yea, and mannerly both,
For fear lest thy betters thy presence do loathe;
For youth without manners no man can abide,
Much like a poor beggar possessèd with pride.

Thy garments unbuttoned delight not to wear,
Lest slovenly nickname fall unto thy share;
Thy hose if ungartered deserveth like shame,
Whereby thou wilt purchase thy tutor much blame.

Be comely and decent in all thy array,
Not wantonly given to sport and to play;
But labour by virtue, in youth, to obtain
The love of thy betters, their friendship to gain.

I likewise command thee this lesson to keep,
No longer than due time delight not to sleep,
Lest sloth in thy bosom such harbour do find
As will cause thee be termed a sluggard by kind.

The morning appearing, rise thou with speed,
Wash hands and face cleanly before thou go feed;
Let shoes be fast tied both, close to thy feet,
The better to travel all day in the street.

Thy shirt-band most comely about thy neck wear,
Have handkerchief likewise both cleanly and fair;
With hat ready brushed, that people may say,
'There goes a child cleanly in all his array'.

Go never untrussed, for fear of the cold,
For it doth endanger both the young and old;
Thy girdle forget not, I put thee in mind,
'No girdle, no blessing,' that day thou shalt find.

If thou be a scholar, to school make good haste,
For he is a truant that cometh there last;
For if thou dost loiter and play by the way,
Be sure with thy master it will cause a fray.

But being there placed, I charge thee to look
Thou lose not thy inkhorn, thy pen, nor thy book,
Thy garters, thy girdle, thy band, nor thy hat,
For fear lest thy parents be grievèd thereat.

Swear not, nor curse not; delight not to steal;
Thy master obey thou; his secrets conceal;
Take heed of false lying; set no man at strife;
Nor be thou too desperate to strike with a knife.

ANONYMOUS

Amongst thy companions be gentle and kind,
If that thou their favours dost look for to find;
For gentleness gaineth thee love from a foe,
And getteth thee glory wherever thou go.

Play not, nor laugh not, thy master to fret,
When thou amongst scholars art orderly set;
For silence is virtue, and virtue is grace,
Which ought to be used to thy betters in place.

Thus, you good children, and scholars each one,
Here in good order your follies are shown:
In following these precepts you purchase always
The love of your parents, and schoolmaster's praise.

But if that in idleness you do delight,
Refusing these lessons here plainly in sight;
Look then for no kindness, no favour, nor love,
But your master's displeasure, if thus you him move.

Therefore be wary you do not offend
Your parents, your master, nor injure your friend;
Lest stripes do reward you, and make you to say,
'Your precepts I'll follow, your words I'll obey.'

And now, to conclude, bear this well in mind,
A diligent scholar much favour shall find;
But such as will loiter, and lazy will bc,
Shall for their labour be brought on their knee.

JOHN WILSON
1588–1677

19 *The Armada, 1588*

OUR little fleet in July first,
Their mighty fleet did view:
She came but with a softly course,
Though winds behind her blew.
Her front much like the moon was crook'd,
(The horns seven miles asunder)
Her masts like stately towers looked,
The ocean groaning under.
And now, behold, they were at hand,
Daring our English borders,
Making full sure to bring our land
Under their Spanish orders.
But God above, laughing to scorn
Their wicked wile, and wealth,
To his annointed raised an horn
Of hope and saving health.
Prince, prophets, people, jointly cried
To Christ alone for aid;
Whose power invincible was tried
With banner all displayed.
That noble Drake drove on apace,
And made the Spaniard dive;
And Hawkins followed hard the chase
(As hawk doth covey drive).
With these, well furbished Frobisher
Their navy did assail:
All at her back did thunder her
And swept away her tail.
Those were the worthies three, which first
(Next to their Admiral)
Ventured the hostile ranks to burst
(Spite of their Don Recalde);

covey, brood of partridges *Don Recalde* was the Spanish vice-admiral

And many more of great renown
   Did bravely play their part,
In skill and valour putting down
   The Spanish strength and art.
But why do I record the men,
   That fought with such as braved us?
I said, and so I say again,
   It was the Lord that saved us.

RICHARD CORBET
1582–1635

20 *To his Son, Vincent Corbet, on his Birthday, November 10, 1630, being then Three Years old*

WHAT I shall leave thee none can tell,
But all shall say I wish thee well;
I wish thee, Vin, before all wealth,
Both bodily and ghostly health:
Nor too much wealth, nor wit, come to thee,
So much of either may undo thee.
I wish thee learning, not for show,
Enough for to instruct, and know;
Not such as gentlemen require,
To prate at table, or at fire.
I wish thee all thy mother's graces,
Thy father's fortunes, and his places.
I wish thee friends, and one at Court.
Not to build on, but support;
To keep thee, not in doing many
Oppressions, but from suffering any.
I wish thee peace in all thy ways,
Nor lazy nor contentious days;
And when thy soul and body part,
As innocent as now thou art.

JOHN PENKETHMAN

fl. 1630

21 *A Schoolmaster's Precepts*

My little scholar, to thy book inclined,
Come near, and print my sayings in thy mind.
Leave thy bed early, let not sleep invade thee;
Haste thee to church, and worship him that made thee:
Yet first thy hands and visage wash thou fair,
Let all thy clothes be neat, and comb thy hair;
And when my school shall bid thee come away,
Be there without excuse of loitering stay.
When there thou seest thy master, him salute,
And to thy mates in order be not mute.
Sit where I set thee, and in any case,
Unless I countermand it, keep thy place;
And as more learning every one doth get,
So in a higher place he shall be set.
And for thy studies have thou ready still,
Books, with a penknife, paper, ink and quill.
If aught to thee I dictate or allot,
Write thou it rightly, without fault or spot;
But such thy writings do thou not commit
To papers loose, for which a book is fit.
Record thy lessons more than once or twice,
And if thou doubt'st, of others take advice:
Who doubts and often asks, my charge retaineth,
But he that nothing doubts, no profit gaineth.
Learn, boy, nor let forgetfulness abuse thee,
Lest that a guilty mind of sloth accuse thee.
And mark me well, for what avail my pains,
Unless thou fix my sayings in thy brains:
'The hardest things through diligence are known;
Be painful, and the glory is thine own.
For as the earth yields neither seeds nor flowers,
Unless manured in seasonable hours,

painful, painstaking

So he that doth not exercise his wit
Doth lose, with precious time, the hope of it.'
Let order likewise in thy speech commend thee,
Lest by uncivil babbling thou offend me;
Speak low, when thou thy lesson dost apply,
But to me saying, let thy voice be high.
To me, when thou repeatest *ad unguem*, look
Thou hast all ready, laying by thy book.
And let none prompt thee, when thou art repeating,
For that much hurts thee, and deserves a beating.
If aught I question, answer to the same,
As thou thereby mayst merit praise and fame.
Instructions asked, unto thy fellows grant;
And help (to my desire) the ignorant:
'Those that want learning, he that seeks to teach,
Himself (though most unlearned) may all outreach.'

ad unguem, exactly

22

Some Boys

SOME boys (their minds denying virtue room),
The time do love in trifles to consume;
Others their fellows trouble, making sport
With hands or feet, or in some other sort;
And those there are that boasting of their stocks,
Disparage others with unsavoury mocks.
Such evil patterns do not thou regard,
Lest that thy deeds at length have just reward.
Nor buy, nor sell, nor changing give or take,
By others' loss do thou no profit make.
Let money go, which many hath defiled—
Nothing but what is chaste becomes a child.

stocks, lineage

GEORGE WITHER

1588–1667

23

A Rocking Hymn

SWEET baby, sleep: what ails my dear?
  What ails my darling thus to cry?
Be still, my child, and lend thine ear,
  To hear me sing thy lullaby.
My pretty lamb, forbear to weep;
Be still, my dear; sweet baby, sleep.

Thou blessèd soul, what can'st thou fear,
  What thing to thee can mischief do?
Thy God is now thy father dear,
  His holy Spouse thy mother too.
Sweet baby, then, forbear to weep;
Be still, my babe; sweet baby, sleep.

Whilst thus thy lullaby I sing,
  For thee great blessings ripening be;
Thine Eldest Brother is a king,
  And hath a kingdom bought for thee.
Sweet baby, then, forbear to weep;
Be still, my babe; sweet baby, sleep.

Sweet baby, sleep, and nothing fear;
  For whosoever thee offends
By thy protector threatened are,
  And God and angels are thy friends.
Sweet baby, then, forbear to weep;
Be still, my babe; sweet baby, sleep.

24 *For Scholars and Pupils*

THOUGH knowledge must be got with pain,
  And seemeth bitter at the root,
It brings, at last, a matchless gain,
  And yieldeth forth most pleasant fruit.
It is the richest kind of trim,
  That noble persons can put on;
It reason keeps from growing dim,
  It sets a lustre thereupon.
And raiseth princes, now and then,
Out of the lowest ranks of men.

But such as do this gem neglect,
  Or seek it not whilst they are young,
Grow old in years without respect,
  And perish in the vulgar throng.
Like brutish beasts they little know,
  Save how their bellies they may fill.
When others rise they sit below,
  They see no choice 'twixt good and ill;
And that which best commends their state
Is, they repent when 'tis too late.

I therefore now do sing thy praise,
  And give thee thanks, thrice-blessed Lord,
That thou in these my youthful days,
  The means of knowledge doth afford.
Compellèd many others are
  (That knowing men they might become)
To pay great sums, and travel far,
  For that which I may gain at home;
Or where supplied all things are,
As well as if at home I were.

Vouchsafe me, therefore, so much grace
  As to endeavour what I may;
Whilst I have leisure, means, and space,
  And wits, to bear this prize away.

Be pleased, likewise, to reason so
The knowledge which I shall attain,
That puffèd up I may not grow,
Nor foolèd be, with science vain;
But let my chief endeavours be,
To know my self, thy will, and Thee.

to reason, to govern with reason

ROBERT HERRICK

1591–1674

25 *A Child's Present*

Go pretty child, and bear this flower
Unto thy little Saviour;
And tell Him, by that bud now blown,
He is the Rose of Sharon known:
When thou hast said so, stick it there
Upon His bib, or stomacher:
And tell Him (for good handsel too)
That thou hast brought a whistle new,
Made of a clean straight oaten reed,
To charm His cries (at time of need):
Tell Him, for coral, thou hast none;
But if thou hadst, He should have one;
But poor thou art, and known to be
Even as moneyless, as He.
Lastly, if thou canst win a kiss
From those mellifluous lips of His;
Then never take a second on,
To spoil the first impression.

good handsel, a luck-bringing gift
coral, sprig of polished coral, for an infant to cut his teeth on

26 *A Grace for Children*

WHAT God gives, and what we take,
'Tis a gift for Christ His sake:
Be the meal of beans and peas,
God be thanked for those, and these:
Have we flesh, or have we fish,
All are fragments from His dish.
He His Church save, and the King,
And our peace here, like a spring,
Make it ever flourishing.

27 *Another Grace*

HERE a little child I stand
Heaving up my either hand;
Cold as paddocks though they be,
Here I lift them up to Thee,
For a benison to fall
On our meat and on us all.

paddocks, frogs

28 *God to be First Served*

HONOUR thy parents; but good manners call
Thee to adore thy God, the first of all.

SAMUEL CROSSMAN

1624?–1684

29 *My Song is Love Unknown*

My song is love unknown,
  My Saviour's love to me;
Love to the loveless shown,
  That they might lovely be.
    O who am I,
    That for my sake
    My Lord should take
    Frail flesh, and die?

He came from his blest throne,
  Salvation to bestow;
But men made strange, and none
  The longed-for Christ would know.
    But O, my friend,
    My friend indeed,
    Who at my need
    His life did spend!

Sometimes they strew his way,
  And his sweet praises sing,
Resounding all the day
  Hosannas to their King.
    Then 'Crucify!'
    Is all their breath,
    And for his death
    They thirst and cry.

Why, what hath my Lord done?
  What makes this rage and spite?
He made the lame to run,
  He gave the blind their sight:

Sweet injuries!
Yet they are these
Themselves displease,
And 'gainst him rise.

They rise, and needs will have
My dear Lord made away;
A murderer they save,
The Prince of Life they slay.
Yet cheerful he
To suffering goes,
That he his foes
From thence might free.

In life no house, no home,
My Lord on earth might have;
In death no friendly tomb,
But what a stranger gave.
What may I say?
Heaven was his home;
But mine the tomb
Wherein he lay.

Here might I stay and sing,
No story so divine;
Never was love, dear King,
Never was grief like thine!
This is my friend,
In whose sweet praise
I all my days
Could gladly spend.

ABRAHAM CHEAR

d. 1668

30 *To My Youngest Kinsman, R. L.*

My little cousin, if you'll be
  Your Uncle's dearest boy,
You must take heed of every deed
  That would your soul destroy.
You must not curse, nor fight, nor steal,
  Nor spend your time in games,
Nor make a lie, whate'er you ail,
  Nor call ungodly names.
With wicked children do not play,
  For such to hell will go;
The Devil's children sin all day,
  But you must not do so.
Begin, I pray, to learn that way
  That doth to heaven tend:
O learn a little, day by day,
  Which leadeth to that end.
For God and good men love such boys,
  And will them good things give;
Father and mother will rejoice,
  And I in comfort live.

THOMAS KEN

1637–1711

31 *An Evening Hymn*

All praise to thee, my God, this night,
For all the blessings of the light;
Keep me, O keep me, King of Kings,
Beneath thy own almighty wings.

Forgive me, Lord, for thy dear son,
The ill that I this day have done;
That with the world, myself, and thee,
I, ere I sleep, at peace may be.

O may my soul on thee repose,
And may sweet sleep my eyelids close:
Sleep that may me more vigorous make
To serve my God when I awake.

JOHN BUNYAN

1628–1688

32 *Of the Boy and Butterfly*

Behold, how eager this our little boy
Is for a butterfly, as if all joy,
All profits, honours, yea, and lasting pleasures,
Were wrapped up in her, or the richest treasures
Found in her would be bundled up together,
When all her all is lighter than a feather.

He halloos, runs, and cries out, 'Here, boys, here!'
Nor doth he brambles or the nettles fear:
He stumbles at the molehills, up he gets,
And runs again, as one bereft of wits;
And all his labour and his large outcry
Is only for a silly butterfly.

Comparison

This little boy an emblem is of those
Whose hearts are wholly at the world's dispose.
The butterfly doth represent to me
The world's best things at best but fading be.
All are but painted nothings and false joys,
Like this poor butterfly to these our boys.

His running through nettles, thorns, and briers,
To gratify his boyish fond desires,
His tumbling over molehills to attain
His end, namely, his butterfly to gain,
Doth plainly show what hazards some men run
To get what will be lost as soon as won.

33 *Upon the Swallow*

THIS pretty bird, oh, how she flies and sings!
But could she do so if she had not wings?
Her wings bespeak my faith, her songs my peace;
When I believe and sing, my doubtings cease.

34 *Upon a Snail*

SHE goes but softly, but she goeth sure,
  She stumbles not, as stronger creatures do;
Her journey's shorter, so she may endure
  Better than they which do much further go.

She makes no noise, but stilly seizeth on
  The flower or herb appointed for her food;
The which she quietly doth feed upon,
  While others range, and glare, but find no good.

And though she doth but very softly go,
  However slow her pace be, yet 'tis sure;
And certainly they that do travel so,
  The prize which they do aim at, they procure.

Comparison

Although they seem not much to stir or go,
  For Christ that hunger, or from wrath that flee;
Yet what they seek for, quickly they come to,
  Though it doth seem the furthest off to be.

One act of faith doth bring them to that flower
  They so long for, that they may eat and live;
Which to attain is not in others' power,
  Though for it a king's ransom they would give.

Then let none faint, nor be at all dismayed,
  That life by Christ do seek: they shall not fail
To have it; let them nothing be afraid;
  The herb, the flower, is eaten by the snail.

35 *Upon the Weathercock*

BRAVE weathercock, I see thou'lt set thy nose
Against the wind, which way soe'er it blows:
So let a Christian in any wise
Face Antichrist in each disguise.

36 *Of the Child with the Bird on the Bush*

MY little bird, how canst thou sit
  And sing amidst so many thorns?
Let me but hold upon thee get,
  My love with honour thee adorns.

Thou art at present little worth:
  Five farthings none will give for thee;
But prithee little bird come forth,
  Thou of more value art to me.

'Tis true it is sunshine today,
  Tomorrow birds will have a storm;
My pretty one, come thou away,
  My bosom then shall keep thee warm.

Thou subject art to cold o' nights,
  When darkness is thy covering;
By day thy danger's great by kites,
  How canst thou then sit there and sing?

Thy food is scarce and scanty too,
'Tis worms and trash which thou dost eat;
Thy present state I pity do,
Come, I'll provide thee better meat.

I'll feed thee with white bread and milk,
And sugar-plums, if thou them crave;
I'll cover thee with finest silk,
That from the cold I may thee save.

My father's palace shall be thine,
Yea, in it thou shalt sit and sing;
My little bird, if thou'lt be mine,
The whole year round should be thy spring.

I'll teach thee all the notes at court;
Unthought-of music thou shalt play;
And all that thither do resort
Shall praise thee for it every day.

I'll keep thee safe from cat and cur,
No manner o' harm shall come to thee:
Yea, I will be thy succourer,
My bosom shall thy cabin be.

But lo, behold, the bird is gone!
These charmings would not make her yield:
The child's left at the bush alone,
The bird flies yonder o'er the field.

37

Upon the Horse and his Rider

THERE'S one rides very sagely on the road,
Showing that he affects the gravest mode;
Another rides tantivy, or full trot,
To show such gravity he matters not.

Lo! here comes one amain, he rides full speed,
Hedge, ditch, or miry bog, he doth not heed.
One claws it up hill, without stop or check;
Another down, as if he'd break his neck.
  Now every horse has his especial guider:
  Then by his going you may know the rider.

Comparison

Now let us turn our horse into the man,
The rider to a spirit, if we can;
Then let us, by the methods of the guider,
Tell every horse how he should know his rider.

Some go as men direct, in a right way,
Nor are they suffered e'er to go astray:
As with a bridle they are governed well,
And kept from paths which lead them unto hell.
  Now this good man has his especial guider;
  Then by his going let him know his rider.

Some go as if they did not greatly care
Whether of heaven or hell they should be heir:
The rein, it seems, is laid upon their neck,
They seem to go their way without a check.
  Now this man, too, has his especial guider;
  And by his going he may know his rider.

Again, some run as if resolved to die,
Body and soul to all eternity.
Good counsel they by no means can abide,
They'll have their course, whatever them betide.
  Now these poor men have their especial guider:
  Were they not fools, they soon might know their rider.

There's one makes head against all godliness,
Those, too, that do profess it he'll distress:
He'll taunt and flout if goodness doth appear,
And at its countenancers mock and jeer.
  Now this man, too, has his especial guider;
  And by his going he may know his rider.

ANONYMOUS

1687

38 *The Maiden's Best Adorning*

DEAR child, these words which briefly I declare,
Let them not hang like jewels in thine ear;
But in the secret closet of thine heart,
Lock them up safe, that they may ne'er depart.

Give first to God the flower of thy youth;
Take Scripture for thy guide, that word of truth;
Adorn thy soul with grace; prize wisdom more
Than all the pearls upon the Indian shore.
Think not to live still free from grief and sorrow:
That man who laughs today, may weep tomorrow.
Nor dream of joys unmixèd, here below:
No roses here, but what on thorns do grow.

Let not thy wingèd days be spent in vain;
When gone, no gold will call them back again.
Strive to subdue thy sin, when first beginning;
Custom (when once confirmed) is strangely winning.
Be much in prayer: it is the begging-trade
By which true Christians are the richest made.

Be loving, patient, courteous, and kind:
So doing, thou shalt praise and honour find
Here upon earth; and when all-conquering death
Thy body shall dissolve, and stop thy breath,
Upon the golden wings of faith and love
Thy soul shall fly to paradise above.

NATHANIEL CROUCH

1632?–1725?

39 *David and Goliath*

WHEN Israel against Philistia
War wagèd under Saul,
A giant in their host they saw,
Whom they Goliath call.

In height he others did surpass,
In strength he did excel;
He had a head-piece all of brass,
And he with pride did swell.

Who marching to their tents doth boast
And insolently cry,
With the best captains in their host
His courage he will try.

The Israelites were in great fear,
And trembling at his voice,
Which made their enemies scoff and jeer,
And over them rejoice.

Thus proud Goliath oft doth vaunt,
And challenge them to fight,
But Israel's generals courage want,
To meet this man of might.

When David came into the host,
And heard his blasphemies,
Displeased he should thus huff and boast
'I'll fight with him,' he cries.

Goliath doth this youth despise,
  Swears he will have his life;
David as valiantly replies,
  His death shall end the strife.

Goliath came with sword and spear,
  But David with a sling;
And though the giant rage and swear,
  Down David doth him bring.

He only slings a little stone,
  And therewith lays him dead;
Which done, he bravely marches on,
  And then cuts off his head.

40 *The Tower of Babel*

AFTER the dreadful Flood was past,
  And Mankind did abound,
A Tower they built, for fear the earth
  Should once again be drowned,

And that they to posterity
  Might leave a lasting name.
The Almighty saw it and was much
  Displeasèd with the same.

And to prevent this vain attempt,
  Their language did confound
That what they to each other speak
  Was but an empty sound.

So that one cries, 'Come bring me here
  A trowel quickly, quick';
But he a hammer reaches him.
  One he cries 'Hew this brick';

Instead of which he busy is
  To cleave in two a tree.
'Make fast this rope,' another bids;
  And then they let it flee.

One loudly calls for planks and boards,
  Another mortar lacks;
But to the first a stone they bring,
  And to the last an axe.

One in great haste does nails require,
  And him a spade they give.
Another for a saw doth ask,
  And him they bring a sieve.

Thus being crossly crossed they fret
  And vex but all in vain;
For what one with much pains hath made
  Another spoils again.

This makes them leave their work undone,
  And like mad men, or fools,
They scatter all their stuff abroad,
  And tumble down their tools.

ANONYMOUS

c. 1700

41 *A was an Archer*

A WAS an Archer, and shot at a frog,
B was a Blindman, and led by a dog.
C was a Cutpurse, and lived in disgrace,
D was a Drunkard, and had a red face.
E was an Eater, a glutton was he,
F was a Fighter, and fought with a flea.

Cutpurse, thief

G was a Giant, and pulled down a house,
H was a Hunter, and hunted a mouse.
I was an Ill man, and hated by all,
K was a Knave, and he robbed great and small.
L was a Liar, and told many lies,
M was a Madman, and beat out his eyes.
N was a Nobleman, nobly born,
O was an Ostler, and stole horses' corn.
P was a Pedlar, and sold many pins,
Q was a Quarreller, and broke both his shins.
R was a Rogue, and ran about town,
S was a Sailor, a man of renown.
T was a Tailor, and knavishly bent,
U was a Usurer, took ten per cent.
W was a Writer, and money he earned,
X was one Xenophon, prudent and learn'd.
Y was a Yeoman, and worked for his bread,
Z was one Zeno the Great, but he's dead.

Ill man, bad man

EIGHTEENTH CENTURY

ANONYMOUS

1708

42 *To Theodora*

WOULD'ST be happy, little child,
Be thou innocent and mild:
Like the patient lamb and dove,
Full of meekness, full of love;
Modestly thy looks compose,
Sweet and blushing like the rose.

When in gardens thou dost play,
In the pleasant flowery May,
And art driven by sudden showers
From the fresh and fragrant flowers,
Think how short that pleasure is
Which the world esteemeth bliss.

When the fruits are sour and green,
Come not near them, be not seen
Touching, tasting, till the sun
His sweet ripening work hath done;
Think how harsh thy nature is
Till heaven ripen thee for bliss.

Or lest thou should'st drop away,
Like the leaf that fell today,
Still be ready to depart,
Love thy God with all thy heart;
Then thou wilt ascend on high,
From time to eternity.

Paradise is sweeter there,
Than the flowers and roses here;
Here's a glimpse, and then away,
There 'twill be forever day;
Where thou ever in heaven's spring
Shalt with saints and angels sing.

WILLIAM RONKSLEY

fl. 1712

43 *To Cheer our Minds*

To cheer our minds
Such crowds and kinds
Of charms all round us are;
That if we were
All eye or ear
Each sense would have full share.

Birds in the spring
Do chirp and sing,
With clear, shrill, and sweet throats:
Some hop, some fly,
Some soar on high,
Each of them knows its notes.

With bills and breasts
They build their nests,
Then lay and hatch their young;
They feed them too,
All this they do,
And spare some time for song.

Hear you a lark?
Tell me what clerk
Can match her! He that beats
The next thorn bush,
May raise a thrush
Would put down all our waits.

clerk, choir man
Would put down all our waits, Would surpass all our carol-singers

ISAAC WATTS
1674–1748

44 *Against Quarrelling and Fighting*

LET dogs delight to bark and bite,
  For God hath made them so:
Let bears and lions growl and fight,
  For 'tis their nature, too.

But, children, you should never let
  Such angry passions rise:
Your little hands were never made
  To tear each other's eyes.

Let love through all your actions run,
  And all your words be mild:
Live like the blessed Virgin's Son,
  That sweet and lovely child.

His soul was gentle as a lamb;
  And as his nature grew,
He grew in favour both with man,
  And God his Father, too.

Now, Lord of all, he reigns above,
  And from his heavenly throne
He sees what children dwell in love,
  And marks them for his own.

45 *Against Idleness and Mischief*

HOW doth the little busy bee
  Improve each shining hour,
And gather honey all the day
  From every opening flower!

How skilfully she builds her cell!
  How neat she spreads the wax!
And labours hard to store it well
  With the sweet food she makes.

In works of labour or of skill
  I would be busy too;
For Satan finds some mischief still
  For idle hands to do.

In books, or work, or healthful play,
  Let my first years be passed,
That I may give for every day
  Some good account at last.

46 *For the Lord's Day Evening*

LORD, how delightful 'tis to see
A whole assembly worship thee!
At once they sing, at once they pray;
They hear of heaven, and learn the way.

I have been there, and still would go:
'Tis like a little heaven below!
Not all my pleasure and my play
Shall tempt me to forget this day.

O write upon my memory, Lord,
The text and doctrines of thy Word;
That I may break thy laws no more,
But love thee better than before.

With thoughts of Christ and things divine
Fill up this foolish heart of mine;
That, hoping pardon through his blood,
I may lie down, and wake with God.

47 *Our Saviour's Golden Rule*

BE you to others kind and true,
As you'd have others be to you;
And neither do nor say to men
Whate'er you would not take again.

48 *The Sluggard*

'TIS the voice of the Sluggard: I heard him complain,
'You have waked me too soon, I must slumber again.'
As the door on its hinges, so he on his bed
Turns his sides and his shoulders and his heavy head.

'A little more sleep, and a little more slumber',
Thus he wastes half his days, and his hours without number;
And when he gets up, he sits folding his hands,
Or walks about saunt'ring, or trifling he stands.

I passed by his garden, and saw the wild brier,
The thorn and the thistle grow broader and higher;
The clothes that hang on him are turning to rags;
And his money still wastes, till he starves or he begs.

I made him a visit, still hoping to find
That he took better care for improving his mind;
He told me his dreams, talked of eating and drinking,
But he scarce reads his Bible, and never loves thinking.

Said I then to my heart: 'Here's a lesson for me;
That man's but a picture of what I might be;
But thanks to my friends for their care in my breeding,
Who taught me betimes to love working and reading.'

49 *Cradle Hymn*

HUSH! my dear, lie still and slumber,
  Holy angels guard thy bed!
Heavenly blessings without number
  Gently falling on thy head.

Sleep, my babe; thy food and raiment,
  House and home, thy friends provide;
All without thy care or payment,
  All thy wants are well supplied.

How much better thou'rt attended
  Than the Son of God could be,
When from heaven He descended,
  And became a child like thee!

Soft and easy is thy cradle:
  Coarse and hard thy Saviour lay,
When His birthplace was a stable,
  And His softest bed was hay.

Was there nothing but a manger
  Cursèd sinners could afford
To receive the heavenly stranger?
  Did they thus affront their Lord?

See the kinder shepherds round Him,
  Telling wonders from the sky;
Where they sought Him, there they found Him,
  With His Virgin mother by.

See the lovely babe a-dressing;
  Lovely infant, how He smiled!
When He wept, the mother's blessing
  Soothed and hushed the holy child.

Lo, He slumbers in His manger,
  Where the hornèd oxen fed;
Peace, my darling; here's no danger,
  Here's no ox a-near thy bed.

May'st thou live to know and fear Him,
  Trust and love Him all thy days;
Then go dwell for ever near Him,
  See His face, and sing His praise!

MATTHEW PRIOR

1664–1721

50

A Letter to the Child
Lady Margaret Cavendish Holles-Harley

My noble, lovely, little Peggy,
Let this my First Epistle beg ye,
At dawn of morn and close of even,
To lift your heart and hands to Heaven.
In double beauty say your prayer:
'Our Father' first, then 'Notre Père'.
And, dearest child, along the day,
In every thing you do and say,
Obey and please my lord and lady,
So God shall love, and angels aid ye.

If to these precepts you attend,
No second letter need I send,
And so I rest your constant friend.

HENRY DIXON

1675–1760

51 *The Description of a Good Boy*

THE boy that is good,
Does learn his book well;
And if he can't read,
Will strive for to spell.

His school he does love,
And when he is there,
For play and for toys,
No time can he spare.

His mind is full bent,
On what he is taught;
He sits in the school,
As one full of thought.

Though not as a mope,
Who quakes out of fear
The whip or the rod
Should fall on his rear.

But like a good lad
Who aims to be wise,
He thinks on his book,
And not on his toys.

His mien will be grave,
Yet, if you would know,
He plays with an air,
When a dunce dare not so.

His aim is to learn,
His task is his play;
And when he has learned,
He smiles and looks gay.

THOMAS FOXTON

c. 1695–1740

52 *Upon Boys Diverting Themselves in the River*

How swift along the winding way
The beauteous river rolls,
Whilst sunbeams on the waters play
And fishes swim in shoals.

Thither the boys fatigued with heat,
With glad consent repair,
To plunge in waters cool and sweet,
And find refreshment there.

Soft winds breathed o'er the neighbouring meads,
Rich with the spoils of flowers,
And gently sporting round their heads,
Refreshed their drooping powers.

Each youth was fond of this delight,
And in the river played:
Some active lads could dive downright,
And others only wade.

While thus they passed their time away,
The cheerful day was gone;
Some left the river fresh and gay,
And others ventured on.

But those who rashly stayed too late
Received a chilling air,
Which sharp distempers did create;
They bought their pleasures dear.

Let moderation still be used
In softest scenes of joy,
The greatest comforts, if abused,
Will torture and destroy.

53 *On a Little Boy's Endeavouring to Catch a Snake*

WHEN gardens shone with flowery pride,
And fruit with crimson streaks was dyed,
And every bush in green attire
With ripened berries raised desire.

A master did indulge his boys
A free pursuit of country joys,
Upon a day with mirth o'erspread
And marked in almanacks with red.

Through lofty woods they wandering run
Where boughs kept off the scorching sun,
And merry birds with tuneful airs
Flew round the trees in gentle pairs.

Young Henry wandered from the rest,
In hopes to find a pretty nest,
Where birds just feathered he might seize,
That would his childish fancy please.

But as he rambled pert and gay,
A snake shot 'cross the flowery way,
And proudly drew upon the plain
The glossy honours of his train.

He saw the speckled creature pass
In wanton curls along the grass;
Its gaudy colours struck his eyes
And gave him pleasure with surprise.

He followed hard to overtake
And in the thicket catch the snake,
Charmed with the beauties of his crest,
And burnished spots that graced his breast.

But all in vain the boy essayed
To find it in the thicker shade;
It soon deceived his eager sight,
And robbed him of his new delight.

The child his fortune did deplore,
That he should never see it more;
No more for ever should behold
Its glittering sides that shone like gold.

Had he but known its hurtful sting,
Swift as a bird of active wing,
From painted poison he had fled,
From tempting green, and burning red.

Thus hapless mortals, prone to vice
(Whose flattering colours soon entice),
Pursue their ruin, dote on death,
And lose their honour and their breath.

ANONYMOUS

1731

54 *The Ten Commandments*

I. HAVE thou no other gods but me,
II. And to no image bow thy knee.
III. Take not the name of God in vain:
IV. The sabbath day do not profane.
V. Honour thy father and mother too;
VI. And see that thou no murder do.
VII. Abstain from words and deeds unclean;
VIII. Nor steal, though thou art poor and mean.
IX. Bear not false witness, shun that blot;
X. What is thy neighbour's covet not.

These laws, O Lord, write in my heart, that I,
May in thy faithful service live and die.

COLLEY CIBBER

1671–1757

55

The Blind Boy

O SAY, what is that thing called light,
Which I can ne'er enjoy?
What is the blessing of the sight?
O tell your poor blind boy!

You talk of wondrous things you see,
You say the sun shines bright;
I feel him warm, but how can he
Then make it day or night?

My day or night myself I make
Whene'er I sleep or play;
And could I ever keep awake
With me 'twere always day.

With heavy sighs I often hear
You mourn my hapless woe;
But sure with patience I may bear
A loss I ne'er can know.

Then let not what I cannot have
My cheer of mind destroy;
Whilst thus I sing, I am a king,
Although a poor blind boy.

CHARLES WESLEY

1707–1788

56 *Gentle Jesus, Meek and Mild*

GENTLE Jesus, meek and mild,
Look upon a little child;
Pity my simplicity,
Suffer me to come to thee.

Fain I would to thee be brought,
Dearest God, forbid it not;
Give me, dearest God, a place
In the kingdom of thy grace.

Put thy hands upon my head,
Let me in thine arms be stayed,
Let me lean upon thy breast,
Lull me, lull me, Lord, to rest.

Hold me fast in thine embrace,
Let me see thy smiling face,
Give me, Lord, thy blessing give,
Pray for me, and I shall live.

Lamb of God, I look to thee,
Thou shalt my example be;
Thou art gentle, meek, and mild,
Thou wast once a little child.

Fain I would be as thou art,
Give me thy obedient heart;
Thou art pitiful and kind,
Let me have thy loving mind.

Let me, above all, fulfil
God my heavenly Father's will,
Never his good Spirit grieve,
Only to his glory live.

Thou didst live to God alone,
Thou didst never seek thine own,
Thou thyself didst never please:
God was all thy happiness.

Loving Jesus, gentle Lamb,
In thy gracious hands I am;
Make me, Saviour, what thou art,
Live thyself within my heart.

I shall then show forth thy praise,
Serve thee all my happy days;
Then the world shall always see
Christ, the holy Child, in me.

ANONYMOUS

1744?

57 *Tumbling*

In jumping and tumbling
  We spend the whole day,
Till night by arriving
  Has finished our play.

What then? One and all,
  There's no more to be said,
As we tumbled all day,
  So we tumble to bed.

JOHN MARCHANT

1749

58 ### *The English Succession*

THE Norman Conquest all historians fix
To the year of Christ, one thousand sixty-six.
Two Wills, one Henry, Stephen, Kings are reckoned;
Then rose Plantagenet in Henry second.
First Richard, John, third Henry, Edwards three,
And second Richard in one line we see.
Fourth, fifth, and sixth Lancastrian Henrys reign;
Then Yorkist Edwards two, and Richard slain.
Next Tudor comes in seventh Henry's right,
Who the red rose engrafted on the white.
Eighth Henry, Edward sixth, first Mary, Bess;
Then Scottish Stuart's right the peers confess.
James, double Charles, a second James expelled;
With Mary, Will; then Anne the sceptre held.
Last, Brunswick's issue has two Georges given;
Late may the second pass from earth to heaven!

JOHN MARCHANT

fl. 1751

59 ### *Little Miss and her Parrot*

PRETTY prating poll,
Answer to my call,
Thou art all in all
  My lovely bird;
Prithee give a kiss
To thine own dear Miss,
Thou can'st do no less
  Upon my word.

Perch upon my hand,
Take awhile thy stand,
Be at my command,
  Thy head recline;
I will stroke thy back,
Give thee nuts to crack,
Nothing shalt thou lack
  Of all that's mine.

Mimic now the cock,
Now the quacking duck,
Lisping Lettice mock,
  My wanton do;
Pleasant is thy voice,
Does my heart rejoice,
Never once annoys,
  I love thee so.

To thy perch away,
Chatter all the day,
While I work or play
  As I think fit;
Yet thy prittle-pattle
Is no more than rattle,
Without sense thy twattle,
  More noise than wit.

Well thou hast been taught,
Yet what hast thou got?
Tongue without a thought,
  Poor mimic fool!
Is it not absurd,
That a senseless bird,
Which knows not a word,
  My mind should rule?

Lettice, early form of the name Letitia

60 *Young Master's Account of a Puppet Show*

WHAT wondrous pretty things I've seen,
  How were my eyes delighted!
Fine lords and ladies, King and Queen,
  With gold and silver dighted.

The little creatures, how they spoke
  With voices shrill and squeaking!
Methinks I see their puny look,
  And still I hear them speaking.

Here's one in love o'er head and ears,
  Tries every way to move her;
While with a scorn the lady hears
  Her sighing, dying lover.

The wretch, despairing to obtain
  Her favour or her graces,
With sword or halter ends his pain,
  And kinder death embraces.

The lady, when she's told his fate,
  Distracted with her passion,
Curses her scorn, alas! too late,
  And dies with mere vexation.

Next Punch, a bragging rogue, appears,
  With huge and strutting belly;
Talks big and swaggers, huffs and stares,
  And who but he, he'll tell you.

To show his valour, takes a switch,
  And trims poor Cherry's jacket;
She cries and scolds; he kicks her breech,
  And vows the jade does lack it.

dighted, clad

His wit and jokes, and jibing jeers,
 Made all who heard him merry;
Yet I could lug him by the ears
 For beating honest Cherry.

NATHANIEL COTTON

1705–1788

61 *Contentment*

THOSE my friendships most obtain,
Who prize their duty more than gain;
Soft flow the hours whene'er we meet,
And conscious virtue is our treat;
Our harmless breasts no envy know,
And hence we fear no secret foe;
Our walks ambition ne'er attends,
And hence we ask no powerful friends;
We wish the best to Church and State,
But leave the steerage to the great;
Careless who rises or who falls,
And never dream of vacant stalls;
Much less, by pride or interest drawn,
Sigh for the mitre and the lawn.

Observe the secrets of my art,
I'll fundamental truths impart;
And if you'll my advice pursue,
I'll quit my hut, and dwell with you.

The passions are a numerous crowd,
Imperious, positive, and loud:
Curb these licentious sons of strife;
Hence chiefly rise the storms of life:
If they grow mutinous, and rave,
They are thy masters, thou their slave.

stalls, seats of church dignitaries
the mitre and the lawn, the head-dress and fine linen of a bishop

Regard the world with cautious eye,
Nor raise your expectation high.
See that the balanced scales be such,
You neither fear nor hope too much.
For disappointment's not the thing,
'Tis pride and passion point the sting.
Life is a sea, where storms must rise,
'Tis folly talks of cloudless skies:
He who contracts his swelling sail
Eludes the fury of the gale.

62 *Early Thoughts of Marriage*

THOSE awful words 'Till death do part'
May well alarm the youthful heart:
No after-thought when once a wife;
The die is cast, and cast for life;
Yet thousands venture every day,
As some base passion leads the way.

Pert Sylvia talks of wedlock-scenes,
Though hardly entered on her teens;
Smiles on her whining spark, and hears
The sugared speech with raptured ears;
Impatient of a parent's rule,
She leaves her sire, and weds a fool;
Want enters at the guardless door,
And Love is fled, to come no more.

Attend, my fair, to wisdom's voice,
A better fate shall crown thy choice.
A married life, to speak the best,
Is all a lottery contest:
Yet if my fair-one will be wise,
I will ensure my girl a prize;
Though not a prize to match thy worth,
Perhaps thy equal's not on earth.

'Tis an important point to know,
There's no perfection here below.
Man's an odd compound after all,
And ever has been since the Fall.
Say, that he loves you from his soul,
Still Man is proud, nor brooks control.
And though a slave in love's soft school,
In wedlock claims his right to rule.
The best, in short, has faults about him,
If few those faults, you must not flout him.

63 *To a Child Five Years Old*

FAIREST flower, all flowers excelling,
  Which in Eden's garden grew;
Flowers of Eve's embowered dwelling
  Are, my fair one, types of you.
Mark, my Polly, how the roses
  Emulate thy damask cheek;
How the bud its sweets discloses—
  Buds thy opening bloom bespeak.
Lilies are, by plain direction,
  Emblems of a double kind;
Emblems of thy fair complexion,
  Emblems of thy fairer mind.
But, dear girl, both flowers and beauty
  Blossom, fade, and die away;
Then pursue good sense and duty,
  Evergreens that ne'er decay.

64 *The Bee, the Ant, and the Sparrow*

A Fable, Addressed to Phoebe and Kitty C. at Boarding School

My dears, 'tis said in days of old,
That beasts could talk, and birds could scold;
But now, it seems the human race
Alone engross the speaker's place.
Yet lately, if report be true
(And much the tale relates to you),
There met a Sparrow, Ant, and Bee,
Which reasoned and conversed as we.

Who reads my page will doubtless grant
That Phe's the wise industrious Ant;
And all with half an eye may see
That Kitty is the busy Bee.
Here then are two—but where's the third?
Go search the school, you'll find the bird.
Your school! I ask your pardon fair,
I'm sure you'll find no sparrow there.

Now to my tale—One summer's morn
A Bee ranged o'er the verdant lawn,
Studious to husband every hour,
And make the most of every flower.
Nimble from stalk to stalk she flies,
And loads with yellow wax her thighs,
With which the artist builds her comb,
And keeps all tight and warm at home;
Or from the cowslips' golden bells
Sucks honey, to enrich her cells;
Or every tempting rose pursues,
Or sips the lily's fragrant dews;
Yet never robs the shining bloom,
Or of its beauty or perfume.
Thus she discharged in every way
The various duties of the day.

It chanced a frugal Ant was near,
Whose brow was wrinkled o'er by care:
A great economist was she,
Nor less laborious than the Bee;
By pensive parents often taught
What ills arise from want of thought;
That poverty on sloth depends,
On poverty the loss of friends.
Hence every day the Ant is found
With anxious steps to tread the ground;
With curious search to trace the grain,
And drag the heavy load with pain.

The active Bee with pleasure saw
The Ant fulfil her parents' law.
'Ah! sister-labourer,' says she,
'How very fortunate are we!
Who, taught in infancy to know
The comforts which from labour flow,
Are independent of the great,
Nor know the wants of pride and state.
Why is our food so very sweet?
Because we earn before we eat.'

A wanton Sparrow longed to hear
Their sage discourse, and straight drew near.
The bird was talkative and loud,
And very pert and very proud;
As worthless and as vain a thing,
Perhaps, as ever wore a wing.
She found, as on a spray she sat,
The little friends were deep in chat;
That virtue was their favourite theme,
And toil and probity their scheme:
Such talk was hateful to her breast;
She thought them arrant prudes at best.

When, to display her naughty mind,
Hunger with cruelty combined,
She viewed the Ant with savage eyes,
And hopped and hopped to snatch her prize.
The Bee, who watched her opening bill,
And guessed her fell design to kill,
Asked her from what her anger rose,
And why she treated Ants as foes.

The Sparrow her reply began,
And thus the conversation ran:
'Whenever I'm disposed to dine,
I think the whole creation mine;
That I'm a bird of high degree,
And every insect made for me.
Hence oft I search the emmet-brood
(For emmets are delicious food),
And oft, in wantonness and play,
I slay ten thousand in a day.
For truth it is, without disguise,
That I love mischief as my eyes.'

'Oh fie!' the honest Bee replied,
'I fear you make base man your guide;
Of every creature sure the worst,
Though in creation's scale the first.
Ungrateful man! 'tis strange he thrives,
Who burns the bees to rob their hives.
I hate his vile administration,
And so do all the emmet nation.
What fatal foes to birds are men,
Quite to the eagle from the wren!
Oh, do not men's example take,
Who mischief do for mischief's sake;
But spare the Ant—her worth demands
Esteem and friendship at your hands.
A mind with every virtue blest,
Must raise compassion in your breast.'

'Virtue!' rejoined the sneering bird,
'Where did you learn that Gothic word?
Since I was hatched, I never heard
That virtue was at all revered.
Trust me, Miss Bee—to speak the truth
I've copied man from earliest youth;
The same our taste, the same our school,
Passion and appetite our rule;
And call me bird, or call me sinner,
I'll ne'er forego my sport or dinner.'

A prowling cat the miscreant spies,
And wide expands her amber eyes:
Near and more near Grimalkin draws;
She wags her tail, extends her claws,
Then, springing on her thoughtless prey,
She bore the vicious bird away.

ANONYMOUS

1751

65 *The Happy Nightingale*

THE nightingale, in dead of night,
On some green hawthorn hid from sight,
  Her wondrous art displays;
While all the feathered choir's at rest,
Nor fowler's snares her joys molest,
  She sings melodious lays.

The groves her warbling notes repeat,
The silence makes her music sweet,
  And heightens every note.
Benighted travellers admire
To hear her thus exert her fire,
  And swell her little throat.

No fear of phantoms, frightful noise,
Nor hideous form her bliss destroys;
Darkness no terror brings;
But each returning shade of night
Affords the songster new delight;
Unawed she sits and sings.

So children who are good and wise,
Hobgoblin stories will despise,
And all such idle tales;
Virtue can fortitude instil,
And ward off all impending ill
Which over vice prevails.

CHRISTOPHER SMART

1722–1771

66 *A Morning Hymn*

O THOU, who lately closed my eyes,
And calmed my soul to rest,
Now the dull blank of darkness flies,
Be thanked, be praised, and blest!

And as thou sav'st me in the night,
From anguish and dismay,
Lead through the labours of the light,
And dangers of the day.

Though from thy laws I daily swerve,
Yet still thy mercy grant;
Shield me from all that I deserve,
And grant me all I want.

Howe'er she's tempted to descend,
Keep reason on her throne;
From all men's passions me defend,
But chiefly from my own.

Give me a heart to assist the poor,
  E'en as thy hand bestows;
For thee and man a love most pure,
  And friendship for my foes.

This, through the merits, death and birth
  Of our blest Lord be given;
So shall I compass peace on earth,
  And endless bliss in heaven.

67 *Mirth*

IF you are merry sing away,
  And touch the organs sweet;
This is the Lord's triumphant day,
Ye children in the galleries gay,
  Shout from each goodly seat.

It shall be May tomorrow's morn,
  A-field then let us run,
And deck us in the blooming thorn,
Soon as the cock begins to warn,
  And long before the sun.

I give the praise to Christ alone,
  My pinks already show;
And my streaked roses fully blown,
The sweetness of the Lord make known,
  And to his glory grow.

Ye little prattlers that repair
  For cowslips in the mead,
Of those exulting colts beware,
But blithe security is there,
  Where skipping lambkins feed.

With white and crimson laughs the sky,
  With birds the hedgerows ring;
To give the praise to God most high,
And all the sulky fiends defy,
  Is a most joyful thing.

68 *Praise*

THOUGH conscience void of all offence
  Is man's divinest praise,
A godly heart-felt innocence,
Which does at first by grace commence,
  By supplication stays.

Yet I do love my brother's laud,
  In each attempt to please;
O may he frequently applaud,
'Good child, thou soon shalt go abroad,
  Or have such things as these:

'This silver coined by sweet Queen Anne,
  This nosegay, and these toys,
Thou this gilt Testament shalt scan,
This pictured hymnbook on a plan
  To make good girls and boys.'

O may they give before I ask,
  Suggest before desire,
While in the summer-house I bask,
The little labourer at his task
  Is worthy of his hire.

69 *Consideration for Others*

SOME think that in the Christian scheme
  Politeness has no part;
That manners we should disesteem,
  And look upon the heart.

The heart the Lord alone can read,
  Which left us this decree,
That men alternate take the lead
  In sweet complacency.

When his Disciples' great dispute
  Christ Jesus reconciled,
He made their sharp contention mute,
  By showing them a child.

If I have got the greater share
  Of talents—I should bow
To Christ, and take the greater care
  To serve and to allow.

This union with thy grace empower
  More influence to supply;
Hereafter, he that lacks this hour,
  May be as great as I.

70 *Hymn for Saturday*

Now's the time for mirth and play,
Saturday's an holiday;
Praise to heaven unceasing yield,
I've found a lark's nest in the field.

A lark's nest, then your playmate begs
You'd spare herself and speckled eggs;
Soon she shall ascend and sing
Your praises to the eternal King.

ANONYMOUS

1757

71 *The Bald Cavalier*

When periwigs came first in wear,
  Their use was to supply
And cover the bald pate with hair,
  To keep it warm and dry.

For this good end, our Cavalier
  Determined one to buy,
Which did so natural appear
  That it deceived the eye.

But riding out one windy day,
  Behold! a sudden squall
Soon blew his feathered hat away,
  And periwig and all.

He joined the laugh with noddle bare,
  And sang in concert tone,
'How should I save another's hair,
  Who could not keep my own?'

Moral

To take upon oneself a joke,
  Good humour shows and wit,
Which may a second laugh provoke,
  And leave the biter bit.

72 *The Father and his Children*

As round their dying father's bed
His sons attend, the peasant said:
'Children, deep hid from prying eyes,
A treasure in my vineyard lies;
When you have laid me in the grave,
Dig, search—and your reward you'll have.'
'Father,' cries one, 'but where's the spot?'
—He sighs! he sinks! but answers not.

The tedious burial service o'er,
Home hie his sons, and straight explore
Each corner of the vineyard round,
Dig up, beat, break, and sift the ground;
Yet though to search so well inclined,
Nor gold, nor treasure could they find;
But when the autumn next drew near,
A double vintage crowned the year.
'Now,' quoth the peasant's wisest son,
'Our father's legacy is known,
In yon rich purple grapes 'tis seen,
Which, but for digging, ne'er had been.

'Then let us all reflect with pleasure,
That labour is the source of treasure.'

73 *The Stargazer*

A STARGAZER out late at night,
With eyes and thoughts turned both upright,
Tumbled by chance into a well
(A dismal story this to tell);
He roared and sobbed, and roared again,
And cursed the 'Bear' and 'Charles's Wain'.

His woeful cries a neighbour brought,
Less learned, but wiser far in thought:
'My friend,' quoth he, 'you're much misled,
With stars to trouble thus your head;
Since you with these misfortunes meet,
For want of looking to your feet.'

1765

74 *Epitaph on a Dormouse, which some Children were to bury*

IN paper case,
Hard by this place,
Dead a poor dormouse lies;
And soon or late,
Summoned by fate,
Each prince, each monarch dies.

Ye sons of verse,
While I rehearse,
Attend instructive rhyme;
No sins had Dor
To answer for,
Repent of yours in time.

JOHN HUDDLESTONE WYNNE

1743–1788

75 *Time*

TIME'S an hand's-breadth; 'tis a tale;
'Tis a vessel under sail;
'Tis an eagle in its way,
Darting down upon its prey;
'Tis an arrow in its flight,
Mocking the pursuing sight;
'Tis a short-lived fading flower;
'Tis a rainbow on a shower;
'Tis a momentary ray,
Smiling in a winter's day;
'Tis a torrent's rapid stream;
'Tis a shadow; 'tis a dream;
'Tis the closing watch of night,
Dying at the rising light;
'Tis a bubble; 'tis a sigh:
Be prepared, O Man! to die.

76 *The Horse and the Mule*

THE pampered steed, of swiftness proud,
Pranced o'er the plains, and neighed aloud.
A Mule he met, of sober pace,
And straight defied her to a race.
Long she declined to try the course;
How could *she* match in speed the horse?
At length, while pawing side by side,
A precipice the Mule espied,
And in her turn the Horse defied.
Near to its foot there stood a tree,
Which both agreed the goal should be.
Hasty rushed on the bounding steed,
And slowly sees the Mule proceed:
He sees, he scorns; but as they bend
From the rough mountain to descend,
He finds his boasted swiftness vain,
For footing here he can't maintain.
The steady Mule the toil abides,
And skilful down the hill she slides,
Reaching the goal, well pleased to find
The vaunting Horse creep slow behind;
Who, tumbling from the mountain's brow,
Came battered to the vale below;
Too late convinced, by what had passed,
That 'slow and sure goes far at last'.

ANNA LAETITIA BARBAULD
1743–1825

77

The Mouse's Petition

Found in the trap, where he had been confined all night

O HEAR a pensive prisoner's prayer,
For liberty that sighs;
And never let thine heart be shut
Against the wretch's cries!

For here forlorn and sad I sit
Within the wiry grate;
And tremble at the approaching morn,
Which brings impending fate.

If e'er thy breast with freedom glowed
And spurned a tyrant's chain,
Let not thy strong oppressive force
A free-born mouse detain.

O do not stain with guiltless blood
Thy hospitable hearth;
Nor triumph that thy wiles betrayed
A prize so little worth!

The scattered gleanings of a feast
My frugal meals supply:
But if thine unrelenting heart
That slender boon deny,

The cheerful light, the vital air,
Are blessings widely given;
Let nature's commoners enjoy
The common gifts of heaven.

The well-taught philosophic mind
  To all compassion gives,
Casts round the world an equal eye,
  And feels for all that lives.

ANONYMOUS

1773

78 *A Guinea-pig Song*

THERE was a little guinea-pig,
Who, being little, was not big;
He always walked upon his feet,
And never fasted when he eat.

When from a place he run away,
He never at the place did stay;
And while he run, as I am told,
He ne'er stood still for young or old.

He often squeaked, and sometimes violent,
And when he squeaked he ne'er was silent.
Though ne'er instructed by a cat,
He knew a mouse was not a rat.

One day, as I am certified,
He took a whim and fairly died;
And as I am told by men of sense,
He never has been living since.

79 *The Song of the Reed Sparrow*

WHERE the waters gently flow,
There I always love to go;
As the waters gently glide,
Sweet I sing in all my pride.

Mounted on a bending reed,
Chanting as my fancies lead,
Tender tales I oft repeat,
Clear, harmonious, soft, and sweet.

Thus myself I entertain,
Free from sorrow, free from pain;
Free from care, and free from strife,
Thus I pass my harmless life.

When the gentle swelling breeze,
Mildly whistles through the trees,
Though my pipe is clear and strong,
Mild and gentle is my song.

When in spring refreshing showers
Fall to glad the opening flowers,
Sweetly I in song complain
Of the gently falling rain.

When nature wears an angry form,
And reeds are broken by the storm,
Then in each note the thing is told,
Then my song is fierce and bold.

Be the weather foul or fine,
Let it rain, or hail, or shine;
Prove the weather how it will,
I can sing about it still.

Reed Sparrow, reed-bunting

80 *The Wren*

THE little Wren of tender mind,
To every other bird is kind;
It ne'er to mischief bends its will,
But sings and is good-humoured still.
Whoe'er has mixed in childish play
Must sure have heard the children say,
'The Robin and the Jenny Wren
Are God Almighty's cock and hen.'
Hence 'tis from all respect they meet,
Hence all in kindly manner treat;
For none would use with disrespect,
Whom Heaven thinks proper to protect.

DOROTHY KILNER

1755–1836

81 *Henry's Secret*

SAYS William to Henry, 'I cannot conceive,
  What method, my friend, you pursue;
For though you at all times are first of the class,
  Yet you seem to have nothing to do.

'While I scarce find a moment for pleasure or sport,
  Still I suffer with shame and disgrace;
Am chid for a dunce, and no honour obtain,
  And keep always the lowest in place.'

'I'll tell you,' quoth Hal, as he twisted the cord,
  And cast down his top on the ground;
'I'll tell you, but do for the present survey
  How nicely it spins itself round.

'My days, my dear Will, are much longer than yours,
  Why, you start with amaze and surprise!
But two hours in the morn while you snore in your bed,
  I to learning with industry rise.

'That period the fittest for study I find,
  And it forwards the work of the day;
Since my exercise done, I am ever prepared,
  And have leisure remaining for play.'

JOHN OAKMAN

1748?–1793

82 *The Glutton*

THE voice of the glutton I heard with disdain:
'I've not eaten this hour, I must eat again;
O give me a pudding, a pie, or a tart,
A duck, or a fowl, which I love from my heart!
    How sweet is the picking
    Of capon or chicken,
    A turkey and chine,
    Is most charming and fine;
To eat and to drink, all my pleasure is still,
I care not what 'tis, if I have but my fill'.

O let me not be like the glutton inclined,
In feasting my body and starving my mind!
With moderate viands be thankful, and pray
That the Lord may supply me with food the next day;
    Not always a-craving,
    With hunger still raving;
    But little and sweet
    Be the food that I eat.
To learning and wisdom, O let me apply,
And leave to the glutton his pudding and pie.

WILLIAM BLAKE
1757–1827

83 *The Piper*

PIPING down the valleys wild,
Piping songs of pleasant glee,
On a cloud I saw a child,
And he laughing said to me:

'Pipe a song about a lamb!'
So I piped with merry cheer.
'Piper, pipe that song again;'
So I piped: he wept to hear.

'Drop thy pipe, thy happy pipe;
Sing thy songs of happy cheer.'
So I sung the same again,
While he wept with joy to hear.

'Piper, sit thee down and write
In a book that all may read.'
So he vanished from my sight,
And I plucked a hollow reed.

And I made a rural pen,
And I stained the water clear,
And I wrote my happy songs
Every child may joy to hear.

84 *The Lamb*

LITTLE lamb, who made thee?
Dost thou know who made thee?
Gave thee life, and bid thee feed
By the stream and o'er the mead;
Gave thee clothing of delight,
Softest clothing, woolly, bright;
Gave thee such a tender voice,
Making all the vales rejoice?
Little lamb, who made thee?
Dost thou know who made thee?

Little lamb, I'll tell thee,
Little lamb, I'll tell thee:
He is callèd by thy name,
For he calls himself a lamb.
He is meek, and he is mild;
He became a little child.
I a child, and thou a lamb,
We are callèd by his name.
Little lamb, God bless thee!
Little lamb, God bless thee!

85 *The Little Black Boy*

MY mother bore me in the southern wild,
And I am black, but O my soul is white!
White as an angel is the English child,
But I am black, as if bereaved of light.

My mother taught me underneath a tree,
And sitting down before the heat of day,
She took me on her lap and kissèd me,
And pointing to the east, began to say:

'Look on the rising sun: there God does live,
And gives his light, and gives his heat away;
And flowers and trees and beasts and men receive
Comfort in morning, joy in the noonday.

'And we are put on earth a little space,
That we may learn to bear the beams of love;
And these black bodies and this sunburnt face
Is but a cloud, and like a shady grove.

'For when our souls have learned the heat to bear,
The cloud will vanish; we shall hear his voice,
Saying, "Come out from the grove, my love and care,
And round my golden tent like lambs rejoice." '

Thus did my mother say, and kissèd me;
And thus I say to little English boy.
When I from black and he from white cloud free,
And round the tent of God like lambs we joy,

I'll shade him from the heat, till he can bear
To lean in joy upon our father's knee;
And then I'll stand and stroke his silver hair,
And be like him, and he will then love me.

86 *The Chimney Sweeper*

WHEN my mother died I was very young,
And my father sold me while yet my tongue
Could scarcely cry ' 'weep! 'weep! 'weep! 'weep!'
So your chimneys I sweep, and in soot I sleep.

There's little Tom Dacre, who cried when his head,
That curled like a lamb's back, was shaved: so I said,
'Hush, Tom! never mind it, for when your head's bare
You know that the soot cannot spoil your white hair.'

And so he was quiet, and that very night,
As Tom was a-sleeping, he had such a sight!
That thousands of sweepers, Dick, Joe, Ned, and Jack,
Were all of them locked up in coffins of black.

And by came an Angel who had a bright key,
And he opened the coffins and set them all free;
Then down a green plain leaping, laughing, they run,
And wash in a river and shine in the sun.

Then naked and white, all their bags left behind,
They rise upon clouds, and sport in the wind;
And the Angel told Tom, if he'd be a good boy,
He'd have God for his father, and never want joy.

And so Tom awoke; and we rose in the dark,
And got with our bags and our brushes to work.
Though the morning was cold, Tom was happy and warm;
So if all do their duty they need not fear harm.

87 *Laughing Song*

WHEN the green woods laugh with the voice of joy,
And the dimpling stream runs laughing by;
When the air does laugh with our merry wit,
And the green hill laughs with the noise of it;

When the meadows laugh with lively green,
And the grasshopper laughs in the merry scene;
When Mary and Susan and Emily
With their sweet round mouths sing 'Ha, ha, he!'

When the painted birds laugh in the shade,
When our table with cherries and nuts is spread:
Come live, and be merry, and join with me
To sing the sweet chorus of 'Ha, ha, he!'

88 *Nurse's Song*

WHEN the voices of children are heard on the green,
And laughing is heard on the hill,
My heart is at rest within my breast,
And everything else is still.

'Then come home, my children, the sun is gone down,
And the dews of night arise;
Come, come, leave off play, and let us away
Till the morning appears in the skies.'

'No, no, let us play, for it is yet day,
And we cannot go to sleep;
Besides, in the sky the little birds fly,
And the hills are all covered with sheep.'

'Well, well, go and play till the light fades away,
And then go home to bed.'
The little ones leaped and shouted and laughed
And all the hills echoèd.

89 *Night*

THE sun descending in the west,
The evening star does shine;
The birds are silent in their nest,
And I must seek for mine.
The moon, like a flower
In heaven's high bower,
With silent delight
Sits and smiles on the night.

Farewell green fields and happy groves,
Where flocks have took delight.
Where lambs have nibbled, silent moves
The feet of angels bright;
Unseen they pour blessing
And joy without ceasing
On each bud and blossom,
And each sleeping bosom.

They look in every thoughtless nest
Where birds are covered warm;
They visit caves of every beast,
To keep them all from harm.
If they see any weeping
That should have been sleeping,
They pour sleep on their head,
And sit down by their bed.

When wolves and tigers howl for prey,
They pitying stand and weep,
Seeking to drive their thirst away,
And keep them from the sheep.
But if they rush dreadful,
The angels, most heedful,
Receive each mild spirit,
New worlds to inherit.

And there the lion's ruddy eyes
Shall flow with tears of gold,
And pitying the tender cries,
And walking round the fold,
Saying, 'Wrath, by his meekness,
And, by his health, sickness
Is driven away
From our immortal day.

'And now beside thee, bleating lamb,
I can lie down and sleep;
Or think on him who bore thy name,
Graze after thee and weep.
For, washed in life's river,
My bright mane for ever
Shall shine like the gold,
As I guard o'er the fold.'

JOHN AIKIN

1747–1822

90 *Tit for Tat: A Tale*

A LAW there is of ancient fame,
By nature's self in every land implanted,
Lex Talionis is its Latin name;
But if an English term be wanted,
Give your next neighbour but a pat
He'll give back as good, and tell you 'tit for tat'.

This 'tit for tat', it seems, not men alone,
But elephants, for legal justice own;
In proof of this a story I shall tell ye,
Imported from the famous town of Delhi.

A mighty elephant that swelled the state
Of Aurengzebe the Great,
One day was taken by his driver
To drink and cool him in the river;
The driver on his neck was seated,
And as he rode along,
By some acquaintance in the throng,
With a ripe coconut was treated.

A coconut's a pretty fruit enough,
But guarded by a shell, both hard and tough.
  The fellow tried, and tried, and tried,
    Working and sweating,
    Tutting and fretting,
  To find out its inside,
And pick the kernel for his eating.

At length, quite out of patience grown,
'Who'll reach me up (he cries) a stone
    To break this plaguy shell?
  But stay, I've here a solid bone
    May do perhaps as well.'
  So half in earnest, half in jest,
He banged it on the forehead of his beast.

An elephant, they say, has human feeling,
  And, full as well as we, he knows
  The difference between words and blows,
Between horse-play and civil dealing.
  Use him but well, he'll do his best,
And serve you faithfully and truly;
  But insults unprovoked he can't digest,
He studies o'er them, and repays them duly.

'To make my head an anvil (thought the creature)
Was never, certainly, the will of nature;
  So, master mine, you may repent!'
Then, shaking his broad ears, away he went.
  The driver took him to the water,
  And thought no more about the matter;
But elephant within his memory hid it;
He *felt* the wrong—the other only *did* it.

A week or two elapsed, one market day
Again the beast and driver took their way;
  Through rows of shops and booths they passed,
With eatables and trinkets stored,
  Till to a gardener's stall they came at last,
Where coconuts lay piled upon the board.
  'Ha!' thought the elephant, ' 'tis now my turn
To show this method of nut-breaking;
  My friend above will like to learn,
Though at the cost of a head-aching.'

Then in his curling trunk he took a heap,
And waved it o'er his neck with sudden sweep,
  And on the hapless driver's sconce
    He laid a blow so hard and full,
  That cracked the nuts at once,
    But with them cracked his skull.

Young folks, whene'er you feel inclined
  To rompish sports and freedoms rough,
Bear 'tit for tat' in mind,
  Nor give an elephant a cuff,
    To be repaid in kind.

ROBERT BURNS

1759–1796

91 *Wee Willie Gray*

Wee Willie Gray, and his leather wallet,
Peel a willow wand to be him boots and jacket;
The rose upon the brier will be him trouse an' doublet,
The rose upon the brier will be him trouse an' doublet.

Wee Willie Gray, and his leather wallet,
Twice a lily-flower will be him sark and cravat;
Feathers of a flee wad feather up his bonnet,
Feathers of a flee wad feather up his bonnet.

sark, shirt

ROBERT SOUTHEY

1774–1843

92 *The Old Man's Comforts and How He Gained Them*

'You are old, Father William,' the young man cried,
'The few locks which are left you are grey;
You are hale, Father William, a hearty old man,
Now tell me the reason, I pray.'

'In the days of my youth,' Father William replied,
'I remembered that youth would fly fast,
And abused not my health and my vigour at first,
That I never might need them at last.'

'You are old, Father William,' the young man cried,
'And pleasures with youth pass away;
And yet you lament not the days that are gone,
Now tell me the reason, I pray.'

'In the days of my youth,' Father William replied,
'I remembered that youth could not last;
I thought of the future, whatever I did,
That I never might grieve for the past.'

'You are old, Father William,' the young man cried,
'And life must be hastening away;
You are cheerful, and love to converse upon death,
Now tell me the reason, I pray.'

'I am cheerful, young man,' Father William replied,
'Let the cause thy attention engage;
In the days of my youth I remembered my God,
And He hath not forgotten my age.'

93 *The Cataract of Lodore*

'How does the Water
Come down at Lodore?'
My little boy asked me
Thus, once on a time;
And moreover he tasked me
To tell him in rhyme.
Anon at the word,
There first came one daughter
And then came another,
To second and third
The request of their brother,
And to hear how the water
Comes down at Lodore,
With its rush and its roar,
As many a time
They had seen it before.
So I told them in rhyme,
For of rhymes I had store:
And 'twas in my vocation
For their recreation
That so I should sing;
Because I was Laureate
To them and the King.

From its sources which well
In the Tarn on the fell;
From its fountains
In the mountains,
Its rills and its gills;
Through moss and through brake,
It runs and it creeps
For awhile, till it sleeps
In its own little lake.
And thence at departing,
Awakening and starting,
It runs through the reeds
And away it proceeds,

Through meadow and glade,
In sun and in shade,
And through the wood-shelter,
Among crags in its flurry,
Helter-skelter,
Hurry-scurry.
Here it comes sparkling,
And there it lies darkling;
Now smoking and frothing
Its tumult and wrath in,
Till in this rapid race
On which it is bent,
It reaches the place
Of its steep descent.

The Cataract strong
Then plunges along,
Striking and raging
As if a war waging
Its caverns and rocks among:
Rising and leaping,
Sinking and creeping,
Swelling and sweeping,
Showering and springing,
Flying and flinging,
Writhing and ringing,
Eddying and whisking,
Spouting and frisking,
Turning and twisting,
Around and around
With endless rebound!
Smiting and fighting,
A sight to delight in;
Confounding, astounding,
Dizzying and deafening the ear with its sound.

Collecting, projecting,
Receding and speeding,
And shocking and rocking,
And darting and parting,
And threading and spreading,
And whizzing and hissing,
And dripping and skipping,
And hitting and splitting,
And shining and twining,
And rattling and battling,
And shaking and quaking,
And pouring and roaring,
And waving and raving,
And tossing and crossing,
And flowing and going,
And running and stunning,
And foaming and roaming,
And dinning and spinning,
And dropping and hopping,
And working and jerking,
And guggling and struggling,
And heaving and cleaving,
And moaning and groaning;

And glittering and frittering,
And gathering and feathering,
And whitening and brightening,
And quivering and shivering,
And hurrying and scurrying,
And thundering and floundering;

Dividing and gliding and sliding,
And falling and brawling and sprawling,
And driving and riving and striving,
And sprinkling and twinkling and wrinkling,
And sounding and bounding and rounding,
And bubbling and troubling and doubling,
And grumbling and rumbling and tumbling,
And clattering and battering and shattering;

Retreating and beating and meeting and sheeting,
Delaying and straying and playing and spraying,
Advancing and prancing and glancing and dancing,
Recoiling, turmoiling and toiling and boiling,
And gleaming and streaming and steaming and beaming,
And rushing and flushing and brushing and gushing,
And flapping and rapping and clapping and slapping,
And curling and whirling and purling and twirling,
And thumping and plumping and bumping and jumping,
And dashing and flashing and splashing and clashing;
And so never ending, but always descending,
Sounds and motions for ever and ever are blending,
All at once and all o'er, with a mighty uproar,
And this way the Water comes down at Lodore.

ANONYMOUS

c. 1800

94 *The Babes in the Wood*

My dear, do you know,
How a long time ago,
    Two poor little children,
Whose names I don't know,
Were stolen away
On a fine summer's day,
    And left in a wood,
As I've heard people say.

Among the trees high
Beneath the blue sky
    They plucked the bright flowers
And watched the birds fly;
Then on blackberries fed,
And strawberries red,
    And when they were weary
'We'll go home,' they said.

And when it was night
So sad was their plight,
 The sun it went down,
And the moon gave no light.
They sobbed and they sighed
And they bitterly cried,
 And long before morning
They lay down and died.

And when they were dead,
The robins so red
 Brought strawberry leaves
And over them spread;
And all the day long,
The green branches among,
 They'd prettily whistle
And this was their song—
'Poor babes in the wood!
Sweet babes in the wood!
 Oh the sad fate of
The babes in the wood!'

WILLIAM WORDSWORTH

1770–1850

95 *Lucy Gray; or, Solitude*

OFT I had heard of Lucy Gray:
And, when I crossed the wild,
I chanced to see at break of day
The solitary child.

No mate, no comrade Lucy knew;
She dwelt on a wide moor,
—The sweetest thing that ever grew
Beside a human door!

You yet may spy the fawn at play,
The hare upon the green;
But the sweet face of Lucy Gray
Will never more be seen.

'Tonight will be a stormy night—
You to the town must go;
And take a lantern, child, to light
Your mother through the snow.'

'That, Father, will I gladly do:
'Tis scarcely afternoon—
The minster-clock has just struck two,
And yonder is the moon!'

At this the father raised his hook,
And snapped a faggot-band;
He plied his work; and Lucy took
The lantern in her hand.

Not blither is the mountain roe:
With many a wanton stroke
Her feet disperse the powdery snow,
That rises up like smoke.

The storm came on before its time:
She wandered up and down;
And many a hill did Lucy climb:
But never reached the town.

The wretched parents all that night
Went shouting far and wide;
But there was neither sound nor sight
To serve them for a guide.

At daybreak on a hill they stood
That overlooked the moor;
And thence they saw the bridge of wood,
A furlong from their door.

They wept—and, turning homeward, cried,
'In heaven we all shall meet';
—When in the snow the mother spied
The print of Lucy's feet.

Then downwards from the steep hill's edge
They tracked the footmarks small;
And through the broken hawthorn hedge,
And by the long stone-wall;

And then an open field they crossed:
The marks were still the same;
They tracked them on, nor ever lost;
And to the bridge they came.

They followed from the snowy bank
Those footmarks, one by one,
Into the middle of the plank;
And further there were none!

—Yet some maintain that to this day
She is a living child;
That you may see sweet Lucy Gray
Upon the lonesome wild.

O'er rough and smooth she trips along,
And never looks behind;
And sings a solitary song
That whistles in the wind.

96 *We are Seven*

——A SIMPLE child,
That lightly draws its breath,
And feels its life in every limb,
What should it know of death?

I met a little cottage girl:
She was eight years old, she said;
Her hair was thick with many a curl
That clustered round her head.

She had a rustic, woodland air,
And she was wildly clad:
Her eyes were fair, and very fair;
—Her beauty made me glad.

'Sisters and brothers, little maid,
How many may you be?'
'How many? Seven in all,' she said,
And wondering looked at me.

'And where are they? I pray you tell.'
She answered, 'Seven are we;
And two of us at Conway dwell,
And two are gone to sea.

'Two of us in the churchyard lie,
My sister and my brother;
And, in the churchyard cottage, I
Dwell near them with my mother.'

'You say that two at Conway dwell,
And two are gone to sea,
Yet ye are seven! I pray you tell,
Sweet maid, how this may be.'

Then did the little maid reply,
'Seven boys and girls are we;
Two of us in the churchyard lie,
Beneath the churchyard tree.'

'You run about, my little maid,
Your limbs they are alive;
If two are in the churchyard laid,
Then ye are only five.'

'Their graves are green, they may be seen,'
The little maid replied,
'Twelve steps or more from my mother's door,
And they are side by side.

'My stockings there I often knit,
My kerchief there I hem;
And there upon the ground I sit,
And sing a song to them.

'And often after sunset, sir,
When it is light and fair,
I take my little porringer,
And eat my supper there.

'The first that died was sister Jane;
In bed she moaning lay,
Till God released her of her pain,
And then she went away.

'So in the churchyard she was laid;
And, when the grass was dry,
Together round her grave we played,
My brother John and I.

'And when the ground was white with snow,
And I could run and slide,
My brother John was forced to go,
And he lies by her side.'

'How many are you, then,' said I,
'If they two are in heaven?'
Quick was the little maid's reply,
'O master, we are seven.'

'But they are dead; those two are dead!
Their spirits are in heaven!'
'Twas throwing words away; for still
The little maid would have her will,
And said, 'Nay, we are seven!'

97 *The Pet Lamb*

THE dew was falling fast, the stars began to blink;
I heard a voice, it said, 'Drink, pretty creature, drink!'
And looking o'er the hedge, before me I espied
A snow-white mountain-lamb with a maiden at its side.

Nor sheep nor kine were near: the lamb was all alone,
And by a slender cord was tethered to a stone;
With one knee on the grass did the little maiden kneel,
While to that mountain-lamb she gave its evening meal.

The lamb, while from her hand he thus his supper took,
Seemed to feast with head and ears; and his tail with pleasure shook.
'Drink, pretty creature, drink,' she said in such a tone
That I almost received her heart into my own.

'Twas little Barbara Lewthwaite, a child of beauty rare!
I watched them with delight, they were a lovely pair.
Now with her empty can the maiden turned away:
But ere ten yards were gone her footsteps did she stay.

Right towards the lamb she looked; and from a shady place
I unobserved could see the workings of her face:
If Nature to her tongue could measured numbers bring,
Thus, thought I, to her lamb that little maid might sing:

'What ails thee, young one? what? Why pull so at thy cord?
Is it not well with thee? well both for bed and board?
Thy plot of grass is soft, and green as grass can be;
Rest, little young one, rest; what is't that aileth thee?

'What is it thou wouldst seek? What is wanting to thy heart?
Thy limbs, are they not strong? And beautiful thou art:
This grass is tender grass; these flowers they have no peers;
And that green corn all day is rustling in thy ears!

'If the sun be shining hot, do but stretch thy woollen chain,
This beech is standing by, its covert thou canst gain;
For rain and mountain storms—the like thou needst not fear,
The rain and storm are things that scarcely can come here.

'Rest, little young one, rest; thou hast forgot the day
When my father found thee first in places far away;
Many flocks were on the hills, but thou wert owned by none,
And thy mother from thy side for evermore was gone.

'He took thee in his arms, and in pity brought thee home:
A blessèd day for thee! then whither wouldst thou roam?
A faithful nurse thou hast; the dam that did thee yean
Upon the mountain tops no kinder could have been.

'Thou know'st that twice a day I have brought thee in this can
Fresh water from the brook, as clear as ever ran;
And twice in the day, when the ground is wet with dew,
I bring thee draughts of milk, warm milk it is and new.

'Thy limbs will shortly be twice as stout as they are now,
Then I'll yoke thee to my cart like a pony in the plough;
My playmate thou shalt be; and when the wind is cold
Our hearth shall be thy bed, our house shall be thy fold.

'It will not, will not rest!—Poor creature, can it be
That 'tis thy mother's heart which is working so in thee?
Things that I know not of belike to thee are dear,
And dreams of things which thou canst neither see nor hear

'Alas, the mountain-tops that look so green and fair!
I've heard of fearful winds and darkness that come there;
The little brooks that seem all pastime and all play,
When they are angry, roar like lions for their prey.

'Here thou need'st not dread the raven in the sky;
Night and day thou art safe,—our cottage is hard by.
Why bleat so after me? Why pull so at thy chain?
Sleep—and at break of day I will come to thee again!'

yean, bring forth

—As homeward through the lane I went with lazy feet,
This song to myself did I oftentimes repeat;
And it seemed, as I retraced the ballad line by line,
That but half of it was hers, and one half of it was *mine*.

Again, and once again, did I repeat the song;
'Nay,' said I, 'more than half to the damsel must belong,
For she looked with such a look, and she spake with such a tone,
That I almost received her heart into my own.'

98 *Written in the Album of a Child*

SMALL service is true service while it lasts;
Of friends, however humble, scorn not one:
The daisy, by the shadow that it casts,
Protects the lingering dew-drop from the sun.

NINETEENTH CENTURY
FIRST HALF

LUCY AIKIN

1781–1864

99 *The Beggar Man*

AROUND the fire one wintry night
  The farmer's rosy children sat;
The faggot lent its blazing light,
  And jokes went round, and careless chat.

When, hark! a gentle hand they hear
  Low tapping at the bolted door,
And thus, to gain their willing ear,
  A feeble voice was heard t'implore:

'Cold blows the blast across the moor,
  The sleet drives hissing in the wind;
Yon toilsome mountain lies before,
  A dreary treeless waste behind.

'My eyes are weak and dim with age,
  No road, no path, can I descry,
And these poor rags ill stand the rage
  Of such a keen inclement sky.

'So faint I am—these tottering feet
  No more my palsied frame can bear;
My freezing heart forgets to beat,
  And drifting snows my tomb prepare.

'Open your hospitable door,
  And shield me from the biting blast:
Cold, cold it blows across the moor,
  The weary moor that I have passed.'

With hasty step the farmer ran,
  And close beside the fire they place
The poor half-frozen beggar man
  With shaking limbs and blue, pale face.

The little children flocking came
  And chafed his frozen hands in theirs,
And busily the good old dame
  A comfortable mess prepares.

Their kindness cheered his drooping soul,
  And slowly down his wrinkled cheek
The big round tears were seen to roll,
  And told the thanks he could not speak.

The children too began to sigh,
  And all their merry chat was o'er;
And yet they felt, they knew not why,
  More glad than they had done before.

100 *The Swallow*

SWALLOW, that on rapid wing
Sweep'st along in sportive ring,
Now here, now there, now low, now high,
Chasing keen the painted fly—
Could I skim away with thee
Over land and over sea,
What streams would flow, what cities rise,
What landscapes dance before mine eyes!
First from England's southern shore
'Cross the channel we would soar,
And our vent'rous course advance
To the lively plains of France;
Sport among the feathered choir
On the verdant banks of Loire,

Skim Garonne's majestic tide,
Where Bordeaux adorns his side;
Cross the towering Pyrenees,
'Mid orange groves and myrtle trees;
Entering then the wild domain
Where wolves prowl round the flocks of Spain,
Where silkworms spin, and olives grow,
And mules plod surely on and slow.
Steering then for many a day
Far to south our course away,
From Gibraltar's rocky steep
Dashing o'er the foaming deep,
On sultry Afric's fruitful shore
We'd rest at length, our journey o'er,
Till vernal gales should gently play
To waft us on our homeward way.

SAMUEL TAYLOR COLERIDGE

1772–1834

101 *Answer to a Child's Question*

Do you ask what the birds say? The sparrow, the dove,
The linnet and thrush say, 'I love and I love!'
In the winter they're silent—the wind is so strong;
What it says, I don't know, but it sings a loud song.
But green leaves, and blossoms, and sunny warm weather,
And singing, and loving—all come back together.
But the lark is so brimful of gladness and love,
The green fields below him, the blue sky above,
That he sings, and he sings; and for ever sings he—
'I love my Love, and my Love loves me!'

102 *A Child's Evening Prayer*

ERE on my bed my limbs I lay,
God grant me grace my prayers to say:
O God! preserve my mother dear
In strength and health for many a year;
And, O! preserve my father too,
And may I pay him reverence due;
And may I my best thoughts employ
To be my parents' hope and joy;
And O! preserve my brothers both
From evil doings and from sloth,
And may we always love each other
Our friends, our father, and our mother:
And still, O Lord, to me impart
An innocent and grateful heart,
That after my great sleep I may
Awake to thy eternal day! Amen.

103 *Metrical Feet*

TRŌCHĒ̆E trīps frŏm lōng tŏ shōrt;
From long to long in solemn sort
Slōw Spōndēe stālks; strōng fo͞ot! yet ill able
Ē̆vĕr tŏ cōme ŭp wĭth Dāctȳ̆l trĭsȳllăblĕ.
Ī̆āmbĭcs mārch frŏm shōrt tŏ lōng;—
Wĭth ă le͞ap ănd ă bo͞und thĕ swĭft Ā̆năpăests thrōng;
One syllable long, with one short at each side,
Ā̆mphībrăchȳ̆s hāstes wĭth ă stātelȳ̆ stride;—
Fīrst ănd lāst bēĭng lōng, mīddlĕ shōrt, A͞mphĭmācer
Strīkes hĭs thūndērĭng ho͞ofs līke ă pro͞ud hīgh-brĕd Rācer.

CHARLOTTE SMITH

1749–1806

104 *Invitation to the Bee*

CHILD of patient industry,
Little active busy bee,
Thou art out at early morn,
Just as the opening flowers are born,
Among the green and grassy meads
Where the cowslips hang their heads;
Or by hedgerows, while the dew
Glitters on the harebell blue.

Then on eager wing art flown
To thymy hillocks on the down;
Or to revel on the broom;
Or suck the clover's crimson bloom;
Murmuring still, thou busy bee,
Thy little ode to industry.

Go while summer suns are bright,
Take at large thy wandering flight;
Go and load thy tiny feet
With every rich and various sweet;
Cling around the flowering thorn,
Dive in the woodbine's honeyed horn,
Seek the wild rose that shades the dell,
Explore the foxglove's freckled bell,
Or in the heath flower's fairy cup
Drink the fragrant spirit up.

But when the meadows shall be mown,
And summer's garlands overblown;
Then come, thou little busy bee,
And let thy homestead be with me;
There, sheltered by thy straw-built hive,
In my garden thou shalt live,
And that garden shall supply
Thy delicious alchemy.

ANN TAYLOR

1782–1866

105 *My Mother*

WHO fed me from her gentle breast,
And hushed me in her arms to rest,
And on my cheek sweet kisses prest?
My Mother.

When sleep forsook my open eye,
Who was it sung sweet hushaby,
And rocked me that I should not cry?
My Mother.

Who sat and watched my infant head,
When sleeping on my cradle bed,
And tears of sweet affection shed?
My Mother.

When pain and sickness made me cry,
Who gazed upon my heavy eye,
And wept, for fear that I should die?
My Mother.

Who dressed my doll in clothes so gay,
And fondly taught me how to play,
And minded all I had to say?
My Mother.

Who ran to help me when I fell,
And would some pretty story tell,
Or kiss the place to make it well?
My Mother.

Who taught my infant lips to pray,
And love God's holy book and day,
And walk in wisdom's pleasant way?
My Mother.

And can I ever cease to be
Affectionate and kind to thee,
Who was so very kind to me,
My Mother?

Ah no! the thought I cannot bear,
And if God please my life to spare,
I hope I shall reward thy care,
My Mother.

When thou art feeble, old, and grey,
My healthy arm shall be thy stay,
And I will soothe thy pains away,
My Mother.

And when I see thee hang thy head,
'Twill be my turn to watch thy bed,
And tears of sweet affection shed,
My Mother.

For could our Father in the skies
Look down with pleased or loving eyes,
If ever I could dare despise
My Mother?

106 *Meddlesome Matty*

ONE ugly trick has often spoiled
The sweetest and the best;
Matilda, though a pleasant child,
One ugly trick possessed,
Which, like a cloud before the skies,
Hid all her better qualities.

Sometimes she'd lift the tea-pot lid,
To peep at what was in it;
Or tilt the kettle, if you did
But turn your back a minute.
In vain you told her not to touch,
Her trick of meddling grew so much.

Her grandmamma went out one day,
  And by mistake she laid
Her spectacles and snuff-box gay
  Too near the little maid;
'Ah well,' thought she, 'I'll try them on,
As soon as grandmamma is gone.'

Forthwith she placed upon her nose
  The glasses large and wide;
And looking round, as I suppose,
  The snuff-box too she spied:
'Oh, what a pretty box is this,
I'll open it,' said little Miss.

'I know that grandmamma would say,
  "Don't meddle with it, dear";
But then she's far enough away,
  And no one else is near;
Besides, what can there be amiss
In opening such a box as this?'

So thumb and finger went to work
  To move the stubborn lid,
And presently a mighty jerk
  The mighty mischief did;
For all at once, ah! woeful case,
The snuff came puffing in her face.

Poor eyes, and nose, and mouth, and chin,
  A dismal sight presented;
And as the snuff got further in,
  Sincerely she repented.
In vain she ran about for ease,
She could do nothing else but sneeze.

She dashed the spectacles away,
  To wipe her tingling eyes,
And as in twenty bits they lay,
  Her grandmamma she spies.
'Heyday! and what's the matter now?'
Cried grandmamma, with lifted brow.

Matilda, smarting with the pain,
  And tingling still, and sore,
Made many a promise to refrain
  From meddling evermore;
And 'tis a fact, as I have heard,
She ever since has kept her word.

107 *The Pin*

'DEAR me! what signifies a pin,
  Wedged in a rotten board?
I'm certain that I won't begin,
  At ten years old, to hoard!
I never will be called a miser;
That I'm determined,' said Eliza.

So onward tripped the little maid,
  And left the pin behind,
Which very snug and quiet laid,
  To its hard fate resigned;
Nor did she think (a careless chit)
'Twas worth her while to stop for it.

Next day a party was to ride
  To see an air balloon;
And all the company beside,
  Were dressed and ready soon:
But she a woeful case was in,
For want of just a single pin.

In vain her eager eyes she brings
  To every darksome crack,
There was not one! and yet her things
  Were dropping off her back.
She cut her pincushion in two,
But no! not one had slidden through.

At last, as hunting on the floor,
  Over a crack she lay,
The carriage rattled to the door,
  Then rattled fast away;
But poor Eliza was not in,
For want of just—a single pin!

There's hardly any thing so small,
  So trifling, or so mean,
That we may never want at all,
  For service unforeseen;
And wilful waste, depend upon't,
Brings, almost always, woeful want.

108 *The Notorious Glutton*

A DUCK who had got such a habit of stuffing,
That all the day long she was panting and puffing,
And by every creature who did her great crop see,
Was thought to be galloping fast for a dropsy;

One day, after eating a plentiful dinner,
With full twice as much as there should have been in her,
While up to her forehead still greedily roking,
Was greatly alarmed by the symptoms of choking.

Now there was an old fellow, much famed for discerning
(A drake, who had taken a liking for learning),
And high in repute with his feathery friends,
Was called Dr. Drake—for this doctor she sends.

In a hole of the dunghill was Dr. Drake's shop,
Where he kept a few simples for curing the crop;
Small pebbles, and two or three different gravels,
With certain famed plants he had found in his travels.

roking, poking about

So taking a handful of suitable things,
And brushing his topple and pluming his wings,
And putting his feathers in apple-pie order,
He went to prescribe for the lady's disorder.

'Dear sir,' said the duck, with a delicate quack,
Just turning a little way round on her back,
And leaning her head on a stone in the yard,
'My case, Dr. Drake, is exceedingly hard.

'I feel so distended with wind, and opprest,
So squeamish and faint, such a load at my chest;
And, day after day, I assure you it *is* hard,
To suffer with patience these pains in my gizzard.'

'Give me leave,' said the Doctor, with medical look,
As her cold flabby paw in his fingers he took;
'By the feel of your pulse, your complaint, I've been thinking,
Must surely be owing to eating and drinking.'

'Oh no, sir, believe me!' the lady replied
(Alarmed for her stomach, as well as her pride),
'I'm sure it arises from nothing I eat,
But I rather suspect I got wet in my feet.

'I've only been raking a bit in the gutter,
Where cook has been pouring some cold melted butter,
And a slice of green cabbage, and scraps of cold meat,
Just a trifle or two, that I thought I could eat.'

The Doctor was just to his business proceeding,
By gentle emetics, a blister, and bleeding,
When all on a sudden she rolled on her side,
Gave a terrible quack, and a struggle, and died!

Her remains were interred in a neighbouring swamp,
By her friends with a great deal of funeral pomp;
But I've heard, this inscription her tombstone displayed,
'Here poor Mrs. Duck, the great glutton, is laid';
And all the young ducklings are brought by their friends,
To learn the disgrace in which gluttony ends.

109
The Baby's Dance

DANCE, little baby, dance up high,
Never mind baby, mother is by;
Crow and caper, caper and crow,
There little baby, there you go:
Up to the ceiling, down to the ground,
Backwards and forwards, round and round.
Then dance, little baby, and mother shall sing,
With the merry gay coral, ding, ding, a-ding, ding.

JANE TAYLOR

1783–1824

110
The Gleaner

BEFORE the bright sun rises over the hill,
  In the cornfield poor Mary is seen,
Impatient her little blue apron to fill,
  With the few scattered ears she can glean.

She never leaves off, or runs out of her place,
  To play, or to idle and chat;
Except now and then, just to wipe her hot face,
  And fan herself with her broad hat.

'Poor girl, hard at work in the heat of the sun,
  How tired and hot you must be;
Why don't you leave off, as the others have done,
  And sit with them under the tree?'

'O no! for my mother lies ill in her bed,
  Too feeble to spin or to knit;
And my poor little brothers are crying for bread,
  And yet we can't give them a bit.

'Then could I be merry, and idle, and play,
  While they are so hungry and ill?
O no, I would rather work hard all the day,
  My little blue apron to fill.'

111 *Greedy Richard*

'I THINK I want some pies this morning,'
Said Dick, stretching himself and yawning;
So down he threw his slate and books,
And sauntered to the pastry-cook's.

And there he cast his greedy eyes,
Round on the jellies and the pies,
So to select, with anxious care,
The very nicest that was there.

At last the point was thus decided:
As his opinion was divided
'Twixt pie and jelly, he was loath
Either to leave, so took them both.

Now Richard never could be pleased
To stop when hunger was appeased,
But he'd go on to eat and stuff,
Long after he had had enough.

'I shan't take any more,' said Dick,
'Dear me, I feel extremely sick:
I cannot eat this other bit;
I wish I had not tasted it.'

Then slowly rising from his seat,
He threw his cheesecake in the street,
And left the tempting pastry-cook's,
With very discontented looks.

Just then a man with wooden leg
Met Dick, and held his hat to beg;
And while he told his mournful case,
Looked at him with imploring face.

Dick, wishing to relieve his pain,
His pocket searched, but searched in vain,
And so at last he did declare,
He had not got a farthing there.

The beggar turned, with face of grief,
And look of patient unbelief,
While Richard, now completely tamed,
Felt inconceivably ashamed.

'I wish,' said he (but wishing's vain),
'I had my money back again,
And had not spent my last, to pay
For what I only threw away.

'Another time I'll take advice,
And not buy things because they're nice;
But rather save my little store
To give poor folks, who want it more.'

112 *The Star*

TWINKLE, twinkle, little star,
How I wonder what you are!
Up above the world so high,
Like a diamond in the sky.

When the blazing sun is gone,
When he nothing shines upon,
Then you show your little light,
Twinkle, twinkle, all the night.

Then the traveller in the dark,
Thanks you for your tiny spark,
He could not see which way to go,
If you did not twinkle so.

In the dark blue sky you keep,
And often through my curtains peep,
For you never shut your eye,
Till the sun is in the sky.

As your bright and tiny spark,
Lights the traveller in the dark—
Though I know not what you are,
Twinkle, twinkle, little star.

ANN AND JANE TAYLOR

113 *The Cow*

THANK you, pretty cow, that made
Pleasant milk, to soak my bread;
Every day, and every night,
Warm, and fresh, and sweet, and white.

Do not chew the hemlock rank,
Growing on the weedy bank;
But the yellow cowslips eat,
They will make it very sweet.

Where the purple violet grows,
Where the bubbling water flows,
Where the grass is fresh and fine,
Pretty cow, go there and dine.

114 *The Sheep*

'LAZY sheep, pray tell me why
In the pleasant fields you lie,
Eating grass, and daisies white,
From the morning till the night?
Every thing can something do,
But what kind of use are you?'

'Nay, my little master, nay,
Do not serve me so, I pray;
Don't you see the wool that grows
On my back, to make you clothes?
Cold, and very cold, you'd be
If you had not wool from me.

'True, it seems a pleasant thing,
To nip the daisies in the spring;
But many chilly nights I pass
On the cold and dewy grass,
Or pick a scanty dinner, where
All the common's brown and bare.

'Then the farmer comes at last,
When the merry spring is past,
And cuts my woolly coat away,
To warm you in the winter's day:
Little master, this is why
In the pleasant fields I lie.'

ADELAIDE O'KEEFFE
1776–1855

115 *Beasts and Birds*

THE dog will come when he is called,
  The cat will walk away;
The monkey's cheek is very bald,
  The goat is fond of play.
The parrot is a prate-apace,
  Yet knows not what she says;
The noble horse will win the race,
  Or draw you in a chaise.

The pig is not a feeder nice,
  The squirrel loves a nut,
The wolf would eat you in a trice,
  The buzzard's eyes are shut.
The lark sings high up in the air,
  The linnet in the tree;
The swan he has a bosom fair,
  And who so proud as he?

116 *The Kite*

My kite is three feet broad, and six feet long;
The standard straight, the bender tough and strong,
And to its milk-white breast five painted stars belong.

Grand and majestic soars my paper kite,
Through trackless skies it takes its lofty flight:
Nor lark nor eagle flies to such a noble height.

As in the field I stand and hold the twine,
Swift I unwind, to give it length of line,
Yet swifter it ascends, nor will to earth incline.

Like a small speck, so high I see it sail,
I hear its pinions flutter in the gale,
And, like a flock of wild geese, sweeps its flowing tail.

SARAH CATHERINE MARTIN

1768–1826

117 *The Comic Adventures of Old Mother Hubbard and Her Dog*

Old Mother Hubbard
Went to the cupboard,
To give the poor dog a bone;
When she came there
The cupboard was bare,
And so the poor dog had none.

She went to the baker's
  To buy him some bread;
When she came back
  The dog was dead.

She went to the undertaker's
  To buy him a coffin;
When she came back
  The dog was laughing.

She took a clean dish
  To get him some tripe;
When she came back
  He was smoking his pipe.

She went to the alehouse
  To get him some beer;
When she came back
  The dog sat in a chair.

She went to the tavern
  For white wine and red;
When she came back
  The dog stood on his head.

She went to the fruiterer's
  To buy him some fruit;
When she came back
  He was playing the flute.

She went to the tailor's
  To buy him a coat;
When she came back
  He was riding a goat.

She went to the hatter's
  To buy him a hat;
When she came back
  He was feeding the cat.

She went to the barber's
 To buy him a wig;
When she came back
 He was dancing a jig.

She went to the cobbler's
 To buy him some shoes;
When she came back
 He was reading the news.

She went to the seamstress
 To buy him some linen;
When she came back
 The dog was spinning.

She went to the hosier's
 To buy him some hose;
When she came back
 He was dressed in his clothes.

The dame made a curtsy,
 The dog made a bow;
The dame said 'Your servant',
 The dog said 'Bow-wow'.

DOROTHY WORDSWORTH

1771–1855

118 *The Cottager to her Infant*

THE days are cold, the nights are long,
The north wind sings a doleful song;
Then hush again upon my breast;
All merry things are now at rest,
 Save thee, my pretty love!

The kitten sleeps upon the hearth,
The crickets long have ceased their mirth;
There's nothing stirring in the house
Save one wee, hungry, nibbling mouse,
  Then why so busy thou?

Nay! start not at that sparkling light;
'Tis but the moon that shines so bright
On the window-pane bedropped with rain:
Then, little darling, sleep again,
  And wake when it is day!

119 *Address to a Child during a Boisterous Winter Evening*

WHAT way does the Wind come? What way does he go?
He rides over the water, and over the snow,
Through wood, and through vale; and o'er rocky height,
Which the goat cannot climb, takes his sounding flight;
He tosses about in every bare tree,
As, if you look up, you plainly may see;
But how he will come, and whither he goes,
There's never a scholar in England knows.

He will suddenly stop in a cunning nook,
And rings a sharp 'larum; but, if you should look,
There's nothing to see but a cushion of snow
Round as a pillow, and whiter than milk,
And softer than if it were covered with silk.
Sometimes he'll hide in the cave of a rock,
Then whistle as shrill as the buzzard cock.
Yet seek him—and what shall you find in his place?
Nothing but silence and empty space;
Save, in a corner, a heap of dry leaves,
That he's left, for a bed, to beggars or thieves!

As soon as 'tis daylight, tomorrow with me
You shall go to the orchard, and then you will see
That he has been there, and made a great rout,
And cracked the branches, and strewn them about:
Heaven grant that he spare but that one upright twig
That looked up at the sky so proud and big
All last summer, as well you know,
Studded with apples, a beautiful show!

Hark! over the roof he makes a pause,
And growls as if he would fix his claws
Right in the slates, and with a huge rattle
Drive them down, like men in a battle.
But let him range round; he does us no harm,
We build up the fire, we're snug and warm;
Untouched by his breath, see the candle shines bright,
And burns with a clear and steady light.
Books have we to read—but that half-stifled knell,
Alas! 'tis the sound of the eight o'clock bell.

Come, now we'll to bed! and when we are there
He may work his own will, and what shall we care?
He may knock at the door—we'll not let him in;
May drive at the windows—we'll laugh at his din.
Let him seek his own home, wherever it be:
Here's a cosy warm house for Edward and me.

120 *Loving and Liking*

THERE'S more in words than I can teach:
Yet listen, child!—I would not preach;
But only give some plain directions
To guide your speech and your affections.
Say not you *love* a roasted fowl,
But you may love a screaming owl,

And, if you can, the unwieldy toad
That crawls from his secure abode
Within the mossy garden wall
When evening dews begin to fall.
Oh! mark the beauty of his eye:
What wonders in that circle lie!
So clear, so bright, our fathers said
He wears a jewel in his head!
And when, upon some showery day,
Into a path or public way
A frog leaps out from bordering grass,
Startling the timid as they pass,
Do you observe him, and endeavour
To take the intruder into favour;
Learning from him to find a reason
For a light heart in a dull season.
And you may love him in the pool,
That is for him a happy school,
In which he swims as taught by nature,
Fit pattern for a human creature,
Glancing amid the water bright,
And sending upward sparkling light.

Nor blush if o'er your heart be stealing
A love of things that have no feeling:
The spring's first rose by you espied,
May fill your breast with joyful pride;
And you may love the strawberry-flower,
And love the strawberry in its bower;
But when the fruit, so often praised
For beauty, to your lip is raised,
Say not you *love* the delicate treat,
But *like* it, enjoy it, and thankfully eat.

WILLIAM ROSCOE

1753–1831

121 *The Butterfly's Ball*

COME take up your hats, and away let us haste,
To the Butterfly's Ball, and the Grasshopper's Feast.
The trumpeter Gadfly has summoned the crew,
And the revels are now only waiting for you.

On the smooth-shaven grass by the side of a wood,
Beneath a broad oak which for ages has stood,
See the children of earth and the tenants of air,
For an evening's amusement together repair.

And there came the Beetle, so blind and so black,
Who carried the Emmet, his friend, on his back.
And there came the Gnat, and the Dragonfly too,
And all their relations, green, orange, and blue.

And there came the Moth, with her plumage of down,
And the Hornet, with jacket of yellow and brown;
Who with him the Wasp, his companion, did bring,
But they promised that evening, to lay by their sting.

Then the sly little Dormouse crept out of his hole,
And led to the feast his blind cousin the Mole.
And the Snail, with his horns peeping out of his shell,
Came, fatigued with the distance, the length of an ell.

A mushroom their table, and on it was laid
A water-dock leaf, which a tablecloth made.
The viands were various, to each of their taste,
And the Bee brought the honey to sweeten the feast.

With steps most majestic the Snail did advance,
And he promised the gazers a minuet to dance;
But they all laughed so loud that he drew in his head,
And went in his own little chamber to bed.

Then, as evening gave way to the shadows of night,
Their watchman, the Glow-worm, came out with his light.
So home let us hasten, while yet we can see;
For no watchman is waiting for you and for me.

CATHERINE ANN DORSET

1750?–1817?

122 *The Peacock 'At Home'*

THE Butterfly's Ball and the Grasshopper's Feasts
Excited the spleen of the birds and the beasts:
For their mirth and good cheer—of the Bee was the theme,
And the Gnat blew his horn, as he danced in the beam;
'Twas hummed by the Beetle, 'twas buzzed by the Fly,
And sung by the myriads that sport through the sky.
The quadrupeds listened with sullen displeasure,
But the tenants of air were enraged beyond measure.

The Peacock displayed his bright plumes to the sun,
And, addressing his mates, thus indignant begun:
'Shall we, like domestic, inelegant fowls,
As unpolished as geese, and as stupid as owls,
Sit tamely at home, hum-drum with our spouses,
While crickets and butterflies open their houses?
Shall such mean little insects pretend to the fashion?
Cousin Turkey-cock, well may you be in a passion!
If I suffer such insolent airs to prevail,
May Juno pluck out all the eyes in my tail!
So a fête I will give, and my taste I'll display,
And send out my cards for St. Valentine's Day.'

This determined, six fleet Carrier Pigeons went out
To invite all the birds to Sir Argus's rout.
The nest-loving Turtle-dove sent an excuse;
Dame Partlet lay in, as did good Mrs. Goose.

rout, party

The Turkey, poor soul! was confined to the rip:
For all her young brood had just failed with the pip.
The Partridge was asked; but a neighbour hard by
Had engaged a snug party to meet in a pie;
And the Wheatear declined, recollecting her cousins,
Last year, to a feast were invited by dozens—
But, alas! they returned not; and she had no taste
To appear in a costume of vine-leaves or paste.
The Woodcock preferred his lone haunt on the moor;
And the traveller, Swallow, was still on his tour;
While the Cuckoo, who should have been one of the guests,
Was rambling on visits to other birds' nests.
But the rest all accepted the kind invitation,
And much bustle it caused in the plumèd creation.

Such ruffling of feathers, such pruning of coats,
Such chirping, such whistling, such clearing of throats,
Such polishing bills, and such oiling of pinions,
Had never been known in the biped dominions!
The Tailor-bird offered to make up new clothes
For all the young birdlings who wished to be beaux:
He made for the Robin a doublet of red,
And a new velvet cap for the Goldfinch's head;
He added a plume to the Wren's golden crest,
And spangled with silver the Guinea-fowl's breast;
While the Halcyon bent over the streamlet to view
How pretty she looked in her bodice of blue.

Thus adorned, they set off for the Peacock's abode
With the guide Indicator, who showed them the road;
From all points of the compass flocked birds of all feather,
And the Parrot can tell who and who were together.
There was Lord Cassowary and General Flamingo,
And Don Peroqueto, escaped from Domingo;
From his high rock-built eyrie the Eagle came forth,
And the Duchess of Ptarmigan flew from the north.

rip, coop ***pip***, poultry disease ***Halcyon***, kingfisher
Indicator, the honey-guide bird ***Peroqueto***, parakeet

The Grebe and the Eider-duck came up by water,
With the Swan, who brought out the young Cygnet, her daughter.
From his woodland abode came the Pheasant, to meet
Two kindred, arrived by the last India fleet:
The one, like a nabob, in habit most splendid,
Where gold with each hue of the rainbow was blended:
In silver and black, like a fair pensive maid
Who mourns for her love, was the other arrayed.
The Chough came from Cornwall, and brought up his wife;
The Grouse travelled south, from his lairdship in Fife;
The Bunting forsook her soft nest in the reeds;
And the Widow-bird came, though she still wore her weeds.
Sir John Heron, of the Lakes, strutted in a *grand pas*,
But no card had been sent to the pilfering Daw,
As the Peacock kept up his progenitor's quarrel,
Which Aesop relates, about cast-off apparel;
For birds are like men in their contests together,
And, in questions of right, can dispute for a feather.

The Peacock, imperial, the pride of his race,
Received all his guests with an infinite grace,
Waved high his blue neck, and his train he displayed,
Embroidered with gold, and with emeralds inlaid;
Then with all the gay troop to the shrubbery repaired,
Where the musical birds had a concert prepared.
A holly bush formed the orchestra, and in it
Sat the Blackbird, the Thrush, the Lark, and the Linnet;
A Bullfinch, a captive almost from the nest,
Now escaped from his cage, and with liberty blest,
In a sweet mellow tone joined the lessons of art
With the accents of nature which flowed from his heart.
The Canary, a much-admired foreign musician,
Condescended to sing to the fowls of condition;
While the Nightingale warbled and quavered so fine
That they all clapped their wings and declared it divine.
The Skylark, in ecstasy, sang from a cloud,
And Chanticleer crowed, and the Yaffil laughed loud.

habit, **garment** ***condition***, **social standing** ***Yaffil***, **woodpecker**

The dancing began when the singing was over:
A Dotterel first opened the ball with the Plover;
Baron Stork in a waltz was allowed to excel,
With his beautiful partner, the fair Demoiselle;
And a newly-fledged Gosling, so fair and genteel,
A minuet swam with the spruce Mr. Teal.
A London-bred Sparrow—a pert forward cit!
Danced a reel with Miss Wagtail, and little Tom Tit.
And the Sieur Guillemot next performed a *pas seul*,
While the elderly bipeds were playing a pool.
The Dowager Toucan was first to cut in,
With old Doctor Buzzard and Admiral Penguin;
From her ivy-bush tower came Dame Owlet the wise,
And Counsellor Crossbill sat by to advise.
Some birds past their prime, o'er whose heads it was fated
Should pass many St. Valentines—yet be unmated,
Sat by, and remarked that the prudent and sage
Were quite overlooked in this frivolous age,
When birds, scarce pen-feathered, were brought to a rout,
Forward chits! from the egg-shell but newly come out.
In their youthful days, they ne'er witnessed such frisking;
And how wrong in the Greenfinch to flirt with the Siskin!
So thought Lady Mackaw, and her friend Cockatoo;
And the Raven foretold that no good could ensue!
They censured the Bantam, for strutting and crowing
In those vile pantaloons, which he fancied looked knowing;
And a want of decorum caused many demurs
Against the Game Chicken, for coming in spurs.

Old Alderman Cormorant, for supper impatient,
At the eating-room door for an hour had been stationed,
Till a Magpie, at length, the banquet announcing,
Gave the signal, long wished for, of clamouring and pouncing:
At the well-furnished board all were eager to perch,
But the little Miss Creepers were left in the lurch.

Demoiselle, Numidian crane   *cit*, citizen, townsman
a pool, a session at cards

Description must fail, and the pen is unable
To recount all the luxuries that covered the table.
Each delicate viand that taste could denote,
Wasps *à la sauce piquante*, and flies *en compôte*;
Worms and frogs *en friture*, for the web-footed fowl,
And a barbecued mouse was prepared for the Owl;
Nuts, grains, fruit, and fish, to regale every palate,
And groundsel and chickweed served up in a salad.
The Razorbill carved for the famishing group,
And the Spoonbill obligingly ladled the soup;
So they filled all their crops with the dainties before 'em,
And the tables were cleared with the utmost decorum.

When they gaily had carolled till peep of the dawn,
The Lark gently hinted 'twas time to be gone;
And his clarion, so shrill, gave the company warning,
That Chanticleer scented the gales of the morning.
So they chirped, in full chorus, a friendly adieu;
And, with hearts beating light as the plumage that grew
On their merry-thought bosoms, away they all flew.

Then long live the Peacock, in splendour unmatched,
Whose ball shall be talked of by birds yet unhatched!
His praise let the Trumpeter loudly proclaim,
And the Goose lend her quill to transmit it to fame.

***Trumpeter*, South American bird which makes a sound like a trumpet**

ELIZABETH TURNER

1775?–1846

123 *The Canary*

MARY had a little bird,
With feathers bright and yellow
Slender legs—upon my word,
He was a pretty fellow!

Sweetest notes he always sung,
  Which much delighted Mary;
Often where his cage was hung,
  She sat to hear Canary.

Crumbs of bread and dainty seeds
  She carried to him daily,
Seeking for the early weeds,
  She decked his palace gaily.

This, my little readers, learn,
  And ever practice duly;
Songs and smiles of love return
  To friends who love you truly.

124 *Truth the Best*

YESTERDAY Rebecca Mason,
  In the parlour by herself,
Broke a handsome china basin,
  Placed upon the mantelshelf.

Quite alarmed, she thought of going
  Very quietly away,
Not a single person knowing
  Of her being there that day.

But Rebecca recollected
  She was taught deceit to shun;
And the moment she reflected,
  Told her mother what was done;

Who commended her behaviour,
Loved her better, and forgave her.

125 *How to Write a Letter*

MARIA intended a letter to write,
But could not begin (as she thought) to indite;
So went to her mother with pencil and slate,
Containing 'Dear Sister', and also a date.

'With nothing to say, my dear girl, do not think
Of wasting your time over paper and ink;
But certainly this is an excellent way,
To try with your slate to find something to say.

'I will give you a rule,' said her mother, 'my dear,
Just think for a moment your sister is here,
And what would you tell her? Consider, and then,
Though silent your tongue, you can speak with your pen.'

126 *The Two Little Miss Lloyds*

THE two Miss Lloyds were twins, and dressed
  In frocks and hats the same;
The friends who ought to know them best,
  Sometimes mistook their name!

And if in temper they had proved
  As much alike, they would
No doubt have been alike beloved,
  But it was understood,

That Sarah could not bear rebuke
  Without a sullen air,
Whilst Mary with a tearful look
  Would promise better care.

So by and by when taller grown
Their faces will be better known.

RICHARD SCRAFTON SHARPE

c. 1775–1852

127 *The Country Mouse and the City Mouse*

In a snug little cot lived a fat little mouse,
Who enjoyed, unmolested, the range of the house;
With plain food content, she would breakfast on cheese,
She dined upon bacon, and supped on grey peas.

A friend from the town to the cottage did stray,
And he said he was come a short visit to pay;
So the mouse spread her table as gay as you please,
And brought the nice bacon and charming grey peas.

The visitor frowned, and he thought to be witty:
Cried he, 'You must know, I am come from the city,
Where we all should be shocked at provisions like these,
For we never eat bacon and horrid grey peas.

'To town come with me, I will give you a treat:
Some excellent food, most delightful to eat.
With me shall you feast just as long as you please;
Come, leave this fat bacon and shocking grey peas.'

This kind invitation she could not refuse,
And the city mouse wished not a moment to lose;
Reluctant she quitted the fields and the trees,
The delicious fat bacon and charming grey peas.

They slily crept under a gay parlour door,
Where a feast had been given the evening before;
And it must be confessed they on dainties did seize,
Far better than bacon, or even grey peas.

Here were custard and trifle, and cheesecakes good store,
Nice sweetmeats and jellies, and twenty things more;
All that art had invented the palate to please,
Except some fat bacon and smoking grey peas.

They were nicely regaling, when into the room
Came the dog and the cat, and the maid with a broom:
They jumped in a custard both up to their knees;
The country mouse sighed for her bacon and peas.

Cried she to her friend, 'Get me safely away,
I can venture no longer in London to stay;
For if oft you receive interruptions like these,
Give me my nice bacon and charming grey peas.

'Your living is splendid and gay, to be sure,
But the dread of disturbance you ever endure;
I taste true delight in contentment and ease,
And I *feast* on fat bacon and charming grey peas.'

CHARLES AND MARY LAMB

1775–1834
1764–1847

128 *Envy*

THIS rose tree is not made to bear
The violet blue, nor lily fair,
Nor the sweet mignonette:
And if this tree were discontent,
Or wished to change its natural bent,
It all in vain would fret.

And should it fret, you would suppose
It ne'er had seen its own red rose,
Nor after gentle shower
Had ever smelled its rose's scent,
Or it could ne'er be discontent
With its own pretty flower.

Like such a blind and senseless tree
As I've imagined this to be,
    All envious persons are:
With care and culture all may find
Some pretty flower in their own mind,
    Some talent that is rare.

129 *Choosing a Name*

I HAVE got a new-born sister;
I was nigh the first that kissed her.
When the nursing woman brought her
To papa, his infant daughter,
How papa's dear eyes did glisten!—
She will shortly be to christen:
And papa has made the offer,
I shall have the naming of her.

Now I wonder what would please her,
Charlotte, Julia, or Louisa.
Ann and Mary, they're too common;
Joan's too formal for a woman;
Jane's a prettier name beside;
But we had a Jane that died.
They would say, if 'twas Rebecca,
That she was a little Quaker.
Edith's pretty, but that looks
Better in old English books;
Ellen's left off long ago;
Blanche is out of fashion now.
None that I have named as yet
Are so good as Margaret.
Emily is neat and fine.
What do you think of Caroline?
How I'm puzzled and perplexed
What to choose or think of next!
I am in a little fever.
Lest the name that I shall give her
Should disgrace her or defame her,
I will leave papa to name her.

130 *The Boy and the Snake*

HENRY was every morning fed
With a full mess of milk and bread.
One day the boy his breakfast took,
And ate it by a purling brook
Which through his mother's orchard ran.
From that time ever when he can
Escape his mother's eye, he there
Takes his food in th'open air.
Finding the child delight to eat
Abroad, and make the grass his seat,
His mother lets him have his way.
With free leave Henry every day
Thither repairs, until she heard
Him talking of a fine 'grey bird'.
This pretty bird, he said, indeed,
Came every day with him to feed,
And it loved him, and loved his milk,
And it was smooth and soft like silk.
His mother thought she'd go and see
What sort of bird this same might be.
So the next morn she follows Harry,
And carefully she sees him carry
Through the long grass his heaped-up mess.
What was her terror and distress,
When she saw the infant take
His bread and milk close to a snake!
Upon the grass he spreads his feast,
And sits down by his frightful guest,
Who had waited for the treat;
And now they both begin to eat.
Fond mother, shriek not! O beware
The least small noise, O have a care—
The least small noise that may be made,
The wily snake will be afraid—
If he hear the lightest sound,
He will inflict th'envenomed wound.
She speaks not, moves not, scarce does breathe,

As she stands the trees beneath;
No sound she utters; and she soon
Sees the child lift up its spoon,
And tap the snake upon the head,
Fearless of harm; and then he said,
As speaking to familiar mate,
'Keep on your own side, do, Grey Pate.'
The snake then to the other side,
As one rebuked, seems to glide;
And now again advancing nigh,
Again she hears the infant cry,
Tapping the snake, 'Keep further, do;
Mind, Grey Pate, what I say to you.'
The danger's o'er!—she sees the boy
(O what a change from fear to joy!)
Rise and bid the snake 'goodbye'.
Says he, 'Our breakfast's done, and I
Will come again tomorrow day',
Then lightly tripping, ran away.

131 *The First Tooth*

THROUGH the house what busy joy,
Just because the infant boy
Has a tiny tooth to show!
I have got a double row,
All as white, and all as small;
Yet no one cares for mine at all.
He can say but half a word,
Yet that single sound's preferred
To all the words that I can say
In the longest summer day.
He cannot walk, yet if he put
With mimic motion out his foot,
As if he thought he were advancing,
It's prized more than my best dancing.

132 *Cleanliness*

COME, my little Robert, near—
Fie! what filthy hands are here!
Who that e'er could understand
The rare structure of a hand,
With its branching fingers fine,
Work itself of hands divine,
Strong, yet delicately knit,
For ten thousand uses fit,
Overlaid with so clear skin
You may see the blood within,
And the curious palm, disposed
In such lines, some have supposed
You may read the fortunes there
By the figures that appear—
Who this hand would choose to cover
With a crust of dirt all over,
Till it looked in hue and shape
Like the forefoot of an ape?
Man or boy that works or plays
In the fields or the highways,
May, without offence or hurt,
From the soil contract a dirt,
Which the next clear spring or river
Washes out and out for ever—
But to cherish stains impure,
Soil deliberate to endure,
On the skin to fix a stain
Till it works into the grain,
Argues a degenerate mind,
Sordid, slothful, ill-inclined,
Wanting in that self-respect
Which does virtue best protect.

All-endearing cleanliness,
Virtue next to godliness,

Easiest, cheapest, needfull'st duty,
To the body, health and beauty;
Who that's human would refuse it,
When a little water does it?

133

Going into Breeches

Joy to Philip, he this day
Has his long coats cast away,
And (the childish season gone)
Puts the manly breeches on.
Officer on gay parade,
Redcoat in his first cockade,
Bridegroom in his wedding trim,
Birthday beau surpassing him,
Never did with conscious gait
Strut about in half the state,
Or the pride (yet free from sin)
Of my little manikin:
Never was there pride, or bliss,
Half so rational as his.
Sashes, frocks, to those that need 'em—
Philip's limbs have got their freedom—
He can run, or he can ride,
And do twenty things beside,
Which his petticoats forbad:
Is he not a happy lad?
Now he's under other banners,
He must leave his former manners;
Bid adieu to female games,
And forget their very names,
Puss-in-corners, hide and seek,
Sports for girls and punies weak!
Baste-the-bear he now may play at,
Leapfrog, football, sport away at,
Show his strength and skill at cricket,

Baste-the-bear, **a hitting and catching game**

Mark his distance, pitch his wicket,
Run about in winter's snow
Till his cheeks and fingers glow,
Climb a tree, or scale a wall,
Without any fear to fall.
If he get a hurt or bruise,
To complain he must refuse,
Though the anguish and the smart
Go unto his little heart,
He must have his courage ready,
Keep his voice and visage steady,
Brace his eyeballs stiff as drum,
That a tear may never come;
And his grief must only speak
From the colour in his cheek.
This and more he must endure,
Hero he in miniature!
This and more must now be done
Now the breeches are put on.

134 *Feigned Courage*

HORATIO, of ideal courage vain,
Was flourishing in air his father's cane,
And, as the fumes of valour swelled his pate,
Now thought himself *this* hero, and now *that*:
'And now,' he cried, 'I will Achilles be;
My sword I brandish: see, the Trojans flee!
Now I'll be Hector, when his angry blade
A lane through heaps of slaughtered Grecians made!
And now by deeds still braver, I'll evince,
I am no less than Edward the Black Prince—
Give way, ye coward French!' As thus he spoke,
And aimed in fancy a sufficient stroke
To fix the fate of Crecy or Poitiers
(The Muse relates the hero's fate with tears),
He struck his milk-white hand against a nail,
Sees his own blood, and feels his courage fail.

Ah! where is now that boasted valour flown,
That in the tented field so late was shown!
Achilles weeps, great Hector hangs his head,
And the Black Prince goes whimpering to bed.

SIR WALTER SCOTT

1771–1832

135 *Lullaby of an Infant Chief*

O HUSH thee, my baby, thy sire was a knight,
Thy mother a lady, both lovely and bright;
The woods and the glens, from the towers which we see,
They all are belonging, dear baby, to thee.

O fear not the bugle, though loudly it blows,
It calls but the warders that guard thy repose;
Their bows would be bended, their blades would be red,
Ere the step of a foeman drew near to thy bed.

O hush thee, my baby, the time soon will come,
When thy sleep shall be broken by trumpet and drum;
Then hush thee, my darling, take rest while you may,
For strife comes with manhood, and waking with day.

JOHN KEATS

1795–1821

136 *Meg Merrilies*

OLD Meg she was a gipsy,
    And lived upon the moors;
Her bed it was the brown heath turf,
    And her house was out of doors.
Her apples were swart blackberries,
    Her currants, pods o' broom;
Her wine was dew of the wild white rose,
    Her book a churchyard tomb.

Her brothers were the craggy hills,
  Her sisters larchen trees;
Alone with her great family
  She lived as she did please.
No breakfast had she many a morn,
  No dinner many a noon,
And, 'stead of supper, she would stare
  Full hard against the moon.

But every morn, of woodbine fresh
  She made her garlanding;
And, every night, the dark glen yew
  She wove, and she would sing.
And with her fingers, old and brown,
  She plaited mats of rushes,
And gave them to the cottagers
  She met among the bushes.

Old Meg was brave as Margaret Queen,
  And tall as Amazon:
An old red blanket cloak she wore,
  A chip-hat had she on.
God rest her aged bones somewhere—
  She died full long agone!

137 *There was a Naughty Boy*

THERE was a naughty boy,
  A naughty boy was he,
He would not stop at home,
  He could not quiet be—
    He took
    In his knapsack
    A book
    Full of vowels
    And a shirt
    With some towels,
    A slight cap
    For night cap,

A hair brush,
Comb ditto,
New stockings—
For old ones
Would split O!
This knapsack
Tight at 's back
He rivetted close
And followed his nose
To the North,
To the North,
And followed his nose
To the North.

There was a naughty boy,
And a naughty boy was he,
He ran away to Scotland
The people for to see—
There he found
That the ground
Was as hard,
That a yard
Was as long,
That a song
Was as merry,
That a cherry
Was as red—
That lead
Was as weighty
That fourscore
Was as eighty,
That a door
Was as wooden
As in England—
So he stood in his shoes
And he wondered,
He wondered,
He stood in his shoes
And he wondered.

JOHN HOOKHAM FRERE

1769–1846

138 *The Boy and the Parrot*

'PARROT, if I had your wings
I should do so many things:
The first thing I should like to do
If I had little wings like you,
I should fly to Uncle Bartle,
Don't you think 'twould make him startle,
If he saw me when I came,
Flapping at the window frame
Exactly like the parrot of fame?'

All this the wise old parrot heard,
The parrot was an ancient bird,
And paused and pondered every word;
First, therefore, he began to cough,
Then said, 'It is a great way off,
A great way off, my dear'; and then
He paused awhile, and coughed again:
'Master John, pray think a little,
What will you do for beds and victual?'

'Oh! parrot, Uncle John can tell—
But we should manage very well;
At night we'd perch upon the trees,
And so fly forward by degrees.'

'Does Uncle John', the parrot said,
'Put nonsense in his nephew's head?
Instead of telling you such things,
And teaching you to wish for wings,
I think he might have taught you better,
You might have learnt to write a letter:
That is the thing that I should do
If I had little hands like you.'

139

The Fable of the Piece of Glass and the Piece of Ice

ONCE on a time, it came to pass,
A piece of ice and a piece of glass
Were lying on a bank together.
There came a sudden change of weather,
The sun shone through them both.—The ice
Turned to his neighbour for advice.
The piece of glass made this reply:
'Take care by all means not to cry.'
The foolish piece of ice relied
On being pitied if he cried.
The story says—That he cried on
Till he was melted, and quite gone.

This may serve you for a rule
With the little boys at school;
If you weep, I must forewarn ye,
All the boys will tease and scorn ye.

ANONYMOUS
1820

140

Three Wonderful Old Women

i

THERE was an old woman named Towl,
Who went out to sea with her owl,
    But the owl was sea-sick,
    And screamed for physic;
Which sadly annoyed Mistress Towl.

ii

There lived an old woman at Lynn,
Whose nose very near touched her chin,
You may easy suppose
She had plenty of beaux;
This charming old woman of Lynn.

iii

There was an old woman in Surrey,
Who was morn, noon, and night in a hurry,
Called her husband a fool,
Drove her children to school;
The worrying old woman of Surrey.

c. 1821

141 *Anecdotes of Four Gentlemen*

i

THERE was an old soldier of Bicester
Was walking one day with his sister;
A bull, with one poke,
Tossed her into an oak,
Before the old gentleman missed her.

ii

As a little fat man of Bombay
Was smoking one very hot day,
A bird called a snipe
Flew away with his pipe,
Which vexed the fat man of Bombay.

iii

There was a sick man of Tobago
Lived long on rice-gruel and sago;
But at last, to his bliss,
The physician said this:
'To a roast leg of mutton you may go'.

iv

There was an old miser at Reading,
Had a house, and a yard with a shed in;
  'Twas meant for a cow,
  But so small, that I vow
The poor creature could scarce get her head in.

1823

142 *Dame Wiggins of Lee*

DAME WIGGINS of Lee was a worthy old soul
As e'er threaded a needle, or washed in a bowl;
She held mice and rats in such antipathy,
That seven fine cats kept Dame Wiggins of Lee.

The rats and mice scared by this fierce-whiskered crew,
The seven poor cats soon had nothing to do;
So, as anyone idle she ne'er wished to see,
She sent them to school, did Dame Wiggins of Lee.

But soon she grew tired of living alone,
So she sent for her cats from school to come home:
Each rowing a wherry, returning, you see—
The frolic made merry Dame Wiggins of Lee.

To give them a treat she ran out for some rice;
When she came back they were skating on ice.
'I shall soon see one down. Aye, perhaps two or three,
I'll bet half-a-crown,' said Dame Wiggins of Lee.

While, to make a nice pudding, she went for a sparrow,
They were wheeling a sick lamb home in a barrow.
'You shall all have some sprats for your humanity,
My seven good cats,' said Dame Wiggins of Lee.

While she ran to the field, to look for its dam,
They were warming the bed for the poor sick lamb;
They turned up the clothes as neat as could be:
'I shall ne'er want a nurse,' said Dame Wiggins of Lee.

She wished them good-night, and went up to bed;
When lo! in the morning the cats were all fled.
But soon—what a fuss! 'Where can they all be?
Here, pussy, puss, puss!' cried Dame Wiggins of Lee.

The Dame's heart was nigh broke, so she sat down to weep,
When she saw them come back, each riding a sheep;
She fondled and patted each purring Tommy:
'Ah, welcome, my dears!' said Dame Wiggins of Lee.

The Dame was unable her pleasure to smother,
To see the sick lamb jump up to its mother.
In spite of the gout, and a pain in her knee,
She went dancing about, did Dame Wiggins of Lee.

CLEMENT CLARKE MOORE
1779–1863

143 *A Visit from St. Nicholas*

'TWAS the night before Christmas, when all through the house
Not a creature was stirring, not even a mouse;
The stockings were hung by the chimney with care,
In hopes that St. Nicholas soon would be there;
The children were nestled all snug in their beds,
While visions of sugar-plums danced in their heads;
And mamma in her 'kerchief, and I in my cap,
Had just settled our brains for a long winter's nap—
When out on the lawn there arose such a clatter,
I sprang from my bed to see what was the matter.
Away to the window I flew like a flash,
Tore open the shutters, and threw up the sash.
The moon, on the breast of the new-fallen snow,
Gave the lustre of midday to objects below;
When, what to my wondering eyes should appear,
But a miniature sleigh and eight tiny reindeer,
With a little old driver, so lively and quick,
I knew in a moment it must be St. Nick.

More rapid than eagles his coursers they came,
And he whistled, and shouted, and called them by name:
'Now, *Dasher*! now, *Dancer*! now, *Prancer* and *Vixen*!
On, *Comet*! on, *Cupid*! on, *Donder* and *Blitzen*!
To the top of the porch! to the top of the wall!
Now dash away! dash away! dash away all!'
As dry leaves that before the wild hurricane fly,
When they meet with an obstacle, mount to the sky;
So up to the house-top the coursers they flew
With the sleigh full of toys, and St. Nicholas too.
And then, in a twinkling, I heard on the roof
The prancing and pawing of each little hoof—
As I drew in my head, and was turning around,
Down the chimney St. Nicholas came with a bound.
He was dressed all in fur, from his head to his foot,
And his clothes were all tarnished with ashes and soot;
A bundle of toys he had flung on his back,
And he looked like a pedlar just opening his pack.
His eyes—how they twinkled; his dimples, how merry!
His cheeks were like roses, his nose like a cherry!
His droll little mouth was drawn up like a bow,
And the beard of his chin was as white as the snow;
The stump of a pipe he held tight in his teeth,
And the smoke it encircled his head like a wreath;
He had a broad face and a little round belly
That shook, when he laughed, like a bowl full of jelly.
He was chubby and plump, a right jolly old elf,
And I laughed when I saw him, in spite of myself;
A wink of his eye and a twist of his head
Soon gave me to know I had nothing to dread;
He spoke not a word, but went straight to his work,
And filled all the stockings; then turned with a jerk,
And laying his finger aside of his nose,
And giving a nod, up the chimney he rose;
He sprang to his sleigh, to his team gave a whistle,
And away they all flew like the down of a thistle.
But I heard him exclaim, ere he drove out of sight,
'*Happy Christmas to all, and to all a good night!*'

JAMES HOGG

1770–1835

144 *A Boy's Song*

WHERE the pools are bright and deep,
Where the grey trout lies asleep,
Up the river and o'er the lea,
That's the way for Billy and me.

Where the blackbird sings the latest,
Where the hawthorn blooms the sweetest,
Where the nestlings chirp and flee,
That's the way for Billy and me.

Where the mowers mow the cleanest,
Where the hay lies thick and greenest;
There to trace the homeward bee,
That's the way for Billy and me.

Where the hazel bank is steepest,
Where the shadow falls the deepest,
Where the clustering nuts fall free,
That's the way for Billy and me.

Why the boys should drive away
Little sweet maidens from the play,
Or love to banter and fight so well,
That's the thing I never could tell.

But this I know, I love to play,
Through the meadow, among the hay;
Up the water and o'er the lea,
That's the way for Billy and me.

THEODORE HOOK

1788–1841

145 *Cautionary Verses to Youth of Both Sexes*

My little dears, who learn to read, pray early learn to shun
That very silly thing indeed which people call a pun.
Read Entick's rules, and 'twill be found how simple an offence
It is, to make the selfsame sound afford a double sense.

For instance, *ale* may make you *ail*, your *aunt* an *ant* may kill,
You in a *vale* may buy a *veil*, and *Bill* may pay the *bill*.
Or if to France your *bark* you steer, at Dover, it may be,
A *peer appears* upon the *pier*, who, blind, still goes to *sea*.

Thus one might say, when to a treat good friends accept our greeting,
'Tis *meet* that men who *meet* to eat should eat their *meat* when meeting.
Brawn on the board's no *bore* indeed, although from *boar* prepared;
Nor can the *fowl*, on which we feed, *foul* feeding be declared.

Thus *one* ripe fruit may be a *pear*, and yet be *pared* again,
And still be *one*, which seemeth rare until we do explain.
It therefore should be all your aim to speak with ample care;
For who, however fond of game, would choose to swallow *hair*?

A fat man's *gait* may make us smile, who has no *gate* to close,
The farmer sitting on his *stile* no *stylish* person knows;
Perfumers men of *scents* must be; some *Scilly* men are bright;
A *brown* man oft deep *read* we see, a *black* a wicked *wight*.

Most wealthy men good *manors* have, however vulgar they,
And actors still the harder slave, the oftener they *play*;
So poets can't the *baize* obtain, unless their tailors choose,
While grooms and coachmen, not in vain, each evening seek the *mews*.

***aunt*, formerly pronounced 'ant'**

The *dyer* who by *dyeing* lives, a *dire* life maintains;
The glazier, it is known, receives—his profits from his *panes*;
By gardeners *thyme* is *tied*, 'tis true, when spring is in its prime,
But *time* or *tide* won't wait for you, if you are *tied* for *time*.

Then now you see, my little dears, the way to make a pun,
A trick which you, through coming years, should sedulously shun.
The fault admits of no defence; for wheresoe'er 'tis found,
You sacrifice for *sound* the sense: the sense is never *sound*.

MARY HOWITT

1799–1888

146 *The Spider and the Fly*

'WILL you walk into my parlour?' said the Spider to the Fly,
' 'Tis the prettiest little parlour that ever you did spy;
The way into my parlour is up a winding stair,
And I have many curious things to show when you are there.'
'Oh no, no,' said the little Fly, 'to ask me is in vain,
For who goes up your winding stair can ne'er come down again.'

'I'm sure you must be weary, dear, with soaring up so high;
Will you rest upon my little bed?' said the Spider to the Fly.
'There are pretty curtains drawn around, the sheets are fine and thin;
And if you like to rest awhile, I'll snugly tuck you in!'
'Oh no, no,' said the little Fly, 'for I've often heard it said,
They never, never wake again, who sleep upon your bed!'

Said the cunning Spider to the Fly, 'Dear friend, what can I do,
To prove the warm affection I've always felt for you?
I have within my pantry good store of all that's nice;
I'm sure you're very welcome—will you please to take a slice?'
'Oh no, no,' said the little Fly, 'kind sir, that cannot be,
I've heard what's in your pantry, and I do not wish to see.'

'Sweet creature,' said the Spider, 'you're witty and you're wise;
How handsome are your gauzy wings, how brilliant are your eyes!
I have a little looking-glass upon my parlour shelf,
If you'll step in a moment, dear, you shall behold yourself.'
'I thank you, gentle sir,' she said, 'for what you're pleased to say,
And bidding you good morning now, I'll call another day.'

The Spider turned him round about, and went into his den,
For well he knew the silly Fly would soon come back again;
So he wove a subtle web, in a little corner sly,
And set his table ready, to dine upon the Fly.
Then he came out to his door again, and merrily did sing:
'Come hither, hither, pretty Fly, with the pearl and silver wing;
Your robes are green and purple—there's a crest upon your head;
Your eyes are like the diamond bright, but mine are dull as lead.'

Alas, alas! how very soon this silly little Fly,
Hearing his wily, flattering words, came slowly flitting by;
With buzzing wings she hung aloft, then near and nearer drew,
Thinking only of her brilliant eyes, and green and purple hue;
Thinking only of her crested head—poor foolish thing! At last,
Up jumped the cunning Spider, and fiercely held her fast.
He dragged her up his winding stair, into his dismal den,
Within his little parlour—but she ne'er came out again!

147 *Buttercups and Daisies*

BUTTERCUPS and daisies—
  Oh the pretty flowers,
Coming ere the springtime
  To tell of sunny hours.
While the trees are leafless,
  While the fields are bare,
Buttercups and daisies
  Spring up here and there.

Ere the snowdrop peepeth,
  Ere the crocus bold,
Ere the early primrose
  Opes its paly gold,
Somewhere on a sunny bank
  Buttercups are bright;
Somewhere 'mong the frozen grass
  Peeps the daisy white.

Little hardy flowers
  Like to children poor,
Playing in their sturdy health
  By their mother's door:
Purple with the north-wind,
  Yet alert and bold;
Fearing not and caring not,
  Though they be a-cold.

What to them is weather!
  What are stormy showers!
Buttercups and daisies
  Are these human flowers!
He who gave them hardship
  And a life of care,
Gave them likewise hardy strength,
  And patient hearts, to bear.

Welcome yellow buttercups,
  Welcome daisies white,
Ye are in my spirit
  Visioned, a delight!
Coming ere the springtime
  Of sunny hours to tell—
Speaking to our hearts of Him
  Who doeth all things well.

148

The Seagull

Oh the white seagull, the wild seagull,
  A joyful bird is he,
As he lies like a cradled thing at rest
  In the arms of a sunny sea!
The little waves rock to and fro,
  And the white gull lies asleep,
As the fisher's bark, with breeze and tide,
  Goes merrily over the deep.
The ship, with her fair sails set, goes by,
  And her people stand to note
How the seagull sits on the rocking waves
  As if in an anchored boat.

The sea is fresh, the sea is fair,
  And the sky calm overhead,
And the seagull lies on the deep, deep sea,
  Like a king in his royal bed.
Oh the white seagull, the bold seagull,
  A joyful bird is he,
Throned like a king, in calm repose
  On the breast of the heaving sea!

The waves leap up, the wild wind blows,
  And the gulls together crowd,
And wheel about, and madly scream
  To the deep sea roaring loud;
And let the sea roar ever so loud,
  And the winds pipe ever so high,
With a wilder joy the bold seagull
  Sends forth a wilder cry—

For the seagull, he is a daring bird,
  And he loves with the storm to sail;
To ride in the strength of the billowy sea,
  And to breast the driving gale.
The little boat, she is tossed about,
  Like a seaweed, to and fro;
The tall ship reels like a drunken man,
  As the gusty tempests blow.

But the seagull laughs at the fear of man,
And sails in a wild delight
On the torn-up breast of the night-black sea,
Like a foam-cloud, calm and white.
The waves may rage and the winds may roar,
But he fears not wreck nor need;
For he rides the sea, in its stormy strength,
As a strong man rides his steed.

Oh the white seagull, the bold seagull,
He makes on the shore his nest,
And he tries what the inland fields may be,
But he loveth the sea the best!
And away from land, a thousand leagues
He goes 'mid surging foam—
What matter to him is land or shore,
For the sea is his truest home!

WILLIAM HOWITT

1792–1879

149 *The Wind in a Frolic*

THE wind one morning sprung up from sleep,
Saying, 'Now for a frolic! now for a leap!
Now for a mad-cap, galloping chase!
I'll make a commotion in every place!'
So it swept with a bustle right through a great town,
Creaking the signs, and scattering down
Shutters; and whisking, with merciless squalls,
Old women's bonnets and gingerbread stalls.
There never was heard a much lustier shout,
As the apples and oranges trundled about;
And the urchins, that stand with their thievish eyes
For ever on watch, ran off each with a prize.

Then away to the field it went blustering and humming,
And the cattle all wondered whatever was coming;
It plucked by their tails the grave, matronly cows,
And tossed the colts' manes all about their brows,
Till, offended at such a familiar salute,
They all turned their backs, and stood sullenly mute.
So on it went, capering and playing its pranks:
Whistling with reeds on the broad river's banks;
Puffing the birds as they sat on the spray,
Or the traveller grave on the king's highway.
It was not too nice to hustle the bags
Of the beggar, and flutter his dirty rags:
'Twas so bold, that it feared not to play its joke
With the doctor's wig, or the gentleman's cloak.
Through the forest it roared, and cried gaily, 'Now,
You sturdy old oaks, I'll make you bow!'
And it made them bow without more ado,
Or it cracked their great branches through and through.

Then it rushed like a monster on cottage and farm,
Striking their dwellers with sudden alarm;
And they ran out like bees in a midsummer swarm.
There were dames with their 'kerchiefs tied over their caps,
To see if their poultry were free from mishaps;
The turkeys they gobbled, the geese screamed aloud,
And the hens crept to roost in a terrified crowd;
There was rearing of ladders, and logs laying on
Where the thatch from the roof threatened soon to be gone.

But the wind had passed on, and had met in a lane,
With a schoolboy, who panted and struggled in vain;
For it tossed him, and twirled him, then passed, and he stood,
With his hat in a pool, and his shoe in the mud.

There was a poor man, hoary and old,
Cutting the heath on the open wold—

The strokes of his bill were faint and few,
Ere this frolicsome wind upon him blew;
But behind him, before him, about him it came,
And the breath seemed gone from his feeble frame;
So he sat him down with a muttering tone,
Saying, 'Plague on the wind! was the like ever known?
But nowadays every wind that blows
Tells one how weak an old man grows!'

But away went the wind in its holiday glee;
And now it was far on the billowy sea,
And the lordly ships felt its staggering blow,
And the little boats darted to and fro.
But lo! it was night, and it sank to rest,
On the sea-bird's rock, in the gleaming west,
Laughing to think, in its fearful fun,
How little of mischief it had done.

bill, billhook

150 *The Migration of the Grey Squirrels*

WHEN in my youth I travelled
  Throughout each north countrie,
Many a strange thing did I hear,
  And many a strange thing see.

But nothing was there pleased me more
  Than when, in autumn brown,
I came, in the depths of the pathless woods,
  To the grey squirrels' town.

There were hundreds that in the hollow boles
  Of the old, old trees did dwell,
And laid up store, hard by their door,
  Of the sweet mast as it fell.

But soon the hungry wild swine came,
  And with thievish snouts dug up
Their buried treasure, and left them not
  So much as an acorn cup.

Then did they chatter in angry mood,
  And one and all decree,
Into the forests of rich stone-pine
  Over hill and dale to flee.

Over hill and dale, over hill and dale,
  For many a league they went,
Like a troop of undaunted travellers
  Governed by one consent.

But the hawk and eagle, and peering owl,
  Did dreadfully pursue;
And the further the grey squirrels went,
  The more their perils grew;
When lo! to cut off their pilgrimage,
  A broad stream lay in view.

But then did each wondrous creature show
  His cunning and bravery;
With a piece of the pine-bark in his mouth,
  Unto the stream came he;

And boldly his little bark he launched,
  Without the least delay;
His bushy tail was his upright sail,
  And he merrily steered away.

Never was there a lovelier sight
  Than that grey squirrels' fleet;
And with anxious eyes I watched to see
  What fortune it would meet.

Soon had they reached the rough mid-stream,
  And ever and anon
I grieved to behold some small bark wrecked,
  And its little steersman gone.

But the main fleet stoutly held across;
 I saw them leap to shore;
They entered the woods with a cry of joy,
 For their perilous march was o'er.

ANONYMOUS

c. 1830

151

Pussy

I LIKE little pussy, her coat is so warm;
And if I don't hurt her, she'll do me no harm.
So I'll not pull her tail, nor drive her away,
But pussy and I very gently will play.
She shall sit by my side, and I'll give her some food;
And she'll love me because I am gentle and good.

I'll pat pretty pussy, and then she will purr;
And thus show her thanks for my kindness to her.
But I'll not pinch her ears, nor tread on her paw,
Lest I should provoke her to use her sharp claw.
I never will vex her, nor make her displeased—
For pussy don't like to be worried and teased.

SARAH JOSEPHA HALE

1788–1879

152

Mary's Lamb

MARY had a little lamb,
 Its fleece was white as snow,
And everywhere that Mary went
 The lamb was sure to go;
He followed her to school one day—
 That was against the rule,
It made the children laugh and play
 To see a lamb at school.

And so the teacher turned him out,
  But still he lingered near,
And waited patiently about,
  Till Mary did appear.
And then he ran to her and laid
  His head upon her arm,
As if he said, 'I'm not afraid—
  You'll shield me from all harm.'

'What makes the lamb love Mary so?'
  The little children cry;
'Oh, Mary loves the lamb, you know,'
  The teacher did reply,
'And you each gentle animal
  In confidence may bind,
And make it follow at your call,
  If you are always kind.'

MARIA JANE JEWSBURY

1800–1833

153 *Partings*

I NEVER cast a flower away,
  The gift of one who cared for me,
A little flower, a faded flower,
  But it was done reluctantly.

I never looked a last adieu
  To things familiar, but my heart
Shrank with a feeling almost pain,
  E'en from their lifelessness to part.

I never spoke the word, farewell!
  But with an utterance faint and broken,
A heart-sick yearning for the time
  When it should never more be spoken.

154 To a Young Brother

On his requesting me to write him two Poems;
One on his Canary, the Other on my going to Bombay

AY, so it is in every brain—
  Extremes of thought and wish are blended;
And something which awakens pain,
  By something gay is oft attended.
The great events that chequer life,
  May be to trifles nearest neighbours;
An opera's fate—a nation's strife—
  But best to prove it, read the papers.

What is a trifle? 'Tis a thing
  We all are arrogant in chiding;
Yet each in turn, from child to king,
  Are prone to take exceeding pride in.
What is a trifle? 'Tis a word
  That in its meaning strangely varies;
Thus, what I deem a common bird,
  Frank holds the King of all Canaries!

What is a trifle? That, to one,
  Which may *my* heart and spirit rifle;
Whilst what you eager seek or shun,
  May *I*, serenely, call a trifle.
Thus recklessly we scatter forth
  Our judgement on each other's pleasure,
Forgetting that full half the worth
  Of life lies in opinion's measure.

Then let none blame thee, dearest boy,
  That in thy last request are mingled
A trial sore—a feathered toy,
  And that the last as first is singled.
A health, then, to thy pretty bird,
  And though 'tis not a first-rate singer,
Long may its merry voice be heard,
  Long may it peck both food and finger!

May never cat, with stealthy paw,
  Approach too near its wire defender;
Nor newer pet, with beak and claw,
  Prove how short-lived a favourite's splendour.
No; love him when, for glossy gold,
  Grey, ragged plumes might tempt to laughter;
If constant to your pets, I hold
  You'll faithful be in friendships after.

SARA COLERIDGE

1802–1852

155 *The Months*

JANUARY brings the snow,
Makes our feet and fingers glow.

February brings the rain,
Thaws the frozen lake again.

March brings breezes loud and shrill,
Stirs the dancing daffodil.

April brings the primrose sweet,
Scatters daisies at our feet.

May brings flocks of pretty lambs,
Skipping by their fleecy dams.

June brings tulips, lilies, roses,
Fills the children's hands with posies.

Hot July brings cooling showers,
Apricots and gillyflowers.

August brings the sheaves of corn,
Then the harvest home is borne.

Warm September brings the fruit,
Sportsmen then begin to shoot.

Fresh October brings the pheasant,
Then to gather nuts is pleasant.

Dull November brings the blast,
Then the leaves are whirling fast.

Chill December brings the sleet,
Blazing fire, and Christmas treat.

156 *Trees*

THE Oak is called the king of trees,
The Aspen quivers in the breeze,
The Poplar grows up straight and tall,
The Peach tree spreads along the wall,
The Sycamore gives pleasant shade,
The Willow droops in watery glade,
The Fir tree useful timber gives,
The Beech amid the forest lives.

WALTER SAVAGE LANDOR
1775–1864

157 *Before a Saint's Picture*

MY serious son! I see thee look
First at the picture, then the book.
I catch the wish that thou couldst paint
The yearnings of the ecstatic saint.
Give it not up, my serious son!
Wish it again, and it is done.
Seldom will any fail who tries
With patient hand and earnest eyes
And woos the arts with such pure sighs.

RICHARD MONCKTON MILNES, LORD HOUGHTON

1809–1885

158 *Lady Moon*

LADY MOON, Lady Moon, where are you roving?
　　Over the sea.
Lady Moon, Lady Moon, whom are you loving?
　　All that love me.

Are you not tired with rolling, and never
　　Resting to sleep?
Why look so pale, and so sad, as for ever
　　Wishing to weep?

Ask me not this, little child, if you love me;
　　You are too bold;
I must obey my dear Father above me,
　　And do as I'm told.

Lady Moon, Lady Moon, where are you roving?
　　Over the sea.
Lady Moon, Lady Moon, whom are you loving?
　　All that love me.

159 *Good Night and Good Morning*

A FAIR little girl sat under a tree,
Sewing as long as her eyes could see;
Then smoothed her work, and folded it right,
And said, 'Dear work, good night! good night!'

Such a number of rooks came over her head,
Crying 'Caw! caw!' on their way to bed;
She said, as she watched their curious flight,
'Little black things, good night! good night!'

The horses neighed, and the oxen lowed,
The sheep's 'bleat! bleat!' came over the road;
All seeming to say, with a quiet delight,
'Good little girl, good night! good night!'

She did not say to the sun, 'Good night!'
Though she saw him there like a ball of light,
For she knew he had God's time to keep
All over the world, and never could sleep.

The tall pink foxglove bowed his head,
The violets curtsied and went to bed;
And good little Lucy tied up her hair,
And said on her knees her favourite prayer.

And while on her pillow she softly lay,
She knew nothing more till again it was day;
And all things said to the beautiful sun,
'Good morning! good morning! our work is begun!'

WILLIAM MILLER

1810–1872

160 *Willie Winkie*

Wee Willie Winkie rins through the town,
Up stairs and doon stairs in his nicht-gown,
Tirling at the window, crying at the lock,
'Are the weans in their bed, for it's now ten o'clock?'

'Hey, Willie Winkie, are ye coming ben?
The cat's singing grey thrums to the sleeping hen,
The dog's spelder'd on the floor, and disna gie a cheep,
But here's a waukrife laddie, that winna fa' asleep.'

Tirling, tapping ***ben***, in ***spelder'd***, stretched
waukrife, wakeful

Onything but sleep, you rogue! glow'ring like the moon,
Rattling in an airn jug wi' an airn spoon,
Rumbling, tumbling round about, crawing like a cock,
Skirling like a kenna-what, wauk'ning sleeping fock.

'Hey, Willie Winkie—the wean's in a creel,
Wambling aff a bodie's knee like a very eel,
Rugging at the cat's lug, and ravelling a' her thrums—
Hey, Willie Winkie—see, there he comes!'

Wearied is the mither that has a stoorie wean,
A wee stumpie stoussie, that canna rin his lane,
That has a battle aye wi' sleep before he'll close an e'e—
But a kiss frae aff his rosy lips gies strength anew to me.

airn, iron *in a creel*, in a tizzy *rin his lane*, run alone

ROBERT BROWNING

1812–1889

161 *The Pied Piper of Hamelin*

HAMELIN TOWN's in Brunswick,
By famous Hanover city;
The river Weser, deep and wide,
Washes its wall on the southern side;
A pleasanter spot you never spied;
But, when begins my ditty,
Almost five hundred years ago,
To see the townsfolk suffer so
From vermin, was a pity.

Rats!
They fought the dogs and killed the cats,
And bit the babies in the cradles,
And ate the cheeses out of the vats,
And licked the soup from the cooks' own ladles,
Split open the kegs of salted sprats,
Made nests inside men's Sunday hats,

And even spoiled the women's chats
By drowning their speaking
With shrieking and squeaking
In fifty different sharps and flats.

At last the people in a body
To the Town Hall came flocking:
' 'Tis clear,' cried they, 'our Mayor's a noddy;
And as for our Corporation—shocking
To think we buy gowns lined with ermine
For dolts that can't or won't determine
What's best to rid us of our vermin!
You hope, because you're old and obese,
To find in the furry civic robe ease?
Rouse up, sirs! Give your brains a racking
To find the remedy we're lacking,
Or, sure as fate, we'll send you packing!'
At this the Mayor and Corporation
Quaked with a mighty consternation.

An hour they sat in council,
At length the Mayor broke silence:
'For a guilder I'd my ermine gown sell,
I wish I were a mile hence!
It's easy to bid one rack one's brain—
I'm sure my poor head aches again,
I've scratched it so, and all in vain.
Oh for a trap, a trap, a trap!'
Just as he said this, what should hap
At the chamber door but a gentle tap?
'Bless us,' cried the Mayor, 'what's that?'
(With the Corporation as he sat,
Looking little though wondrous fat;
Nor brighter was his eye, nor moister
Than a too-long-opened oyster,
Save when at noon his paunch grew mutinous
For a plate of turtle, green and glutinous)
'Only a scraping of shoes on the mat?
Anything like the sound of a rat
Makes my heart go pit-a-pat!'

'Come in!' the Mayor cried, looking bigger:
And in did come the strangest figure!
His queer long coat from heel to head
Was half of yellow and half of red,
And he himself was tall and thin,
With sharp blue eyes, each like a pin,
And light loose hair, yet swarthy skin,
No tuft on cheek nor beard on chin,
But lips where smiles went out and in;
There was no guessing his kith and kin:
And nobody could enough admire
The tall man and his quaint attire.
Quoth one: 'It's as my great-grandsire,
Starting up at the Trump of Doom's tone,
Had walked this way from his painted tombstone!'

He advanced to the council-table:
And, 'Please your honours,' said he, 'I'm able,
By means of a secret charm, to draw
  All creatures living beneath the sun,
  That creep or swim or fly or run,
After me so as you never saw!
And I chiefly use my charm
On creatures that do people harm,
The mole and toad and newt and viper;
And people call me the Pied Piper.'
(And here they noticed round his neck
  A scarf of red and yellow stripe,
To match with his coat of the self-same check;
  And at the scarf's end hung a pipe;
And his fingers, they noticed, were ever straying
As if impatient to be playing
Upon this pipe, as low it dangled
Over his vesture so old-fangled.)
'Yet,' said he, 'poor piper as I am,
In Tartary I freed the Cham,
  Last June, from his huge swarms of gnats;
I eased in Asia the Nizam
  Of a monstrous brood of vampire-bats:

And as for what your brain bewilders,
  If I can rid your town of rats
Will you give me a thousand guilders?'
'One? fifty thousand!'—was the exclamation
Of the astonished Mayor and Corporation.

Into the street the Piper stept,
  Smiling first a little smile,
As if he knew what magic slept
  In his quiet pipe the while;
Then, like a musical adept,
To blow the pipe his lips he wrinkled,
And green and blue his sharp eyes twinkled,
Like a candle-flame where salt is sprinkled;
And ere three shrill notes the pipe uttered,
You heard as if an army muttered;
And the muttering grew to a grumbling;
And the grumbling grew to a mighty rumbling;
And out of the houses the rats came tumbling.
Great rats, small rats, lean rats, brawny rats,
Brown rats, black rats, grey rats, tawny rats,
Grave old plodders, gay young friskers,
  Fathers, mothers, uncles, cousins,
Cocking tails and pricking whiskers,
  Families by tens and dozens,
Brothers, sisters, husbands, wives—
Followed the Piper for their lives.
From street to street he piped advancing,
And step for step they followed dancing,
Until they came to the river Weser,
  Wherein all plunged and perished!
—Save one who, stout as Julius Caesar,
Swam across and lived to carry
  (As he, the manuscript he cherished)
To Rat-land home his commentary:
Which was, 'At the first shrill notes of the pipe,
I heard a sound as of scraping tripe,
And putting apples, wondrous ripe,
Into a cider-press's gripe:

And a moving away of pickle-tub-boards,
And a leaving ajar of conserve-cupboards,
And a drawing the corks of train-oil-flasks,
And a breaking the hoops of butter-casks;
And it seemed as if a voice
  (Sweeter far than by harp or by psaltery
Is breathed) called out, "Oh rats, rejoice!
  The world is grown to one vast drysaltery!
So munch on, crunch on, take your nuncheon,
Breakfast, supper, dinner, luncheon!"
And just as a bulky sugar-puncheon,
All ready staved, like a great sun shone
Glorious scarce an inch before me,
Just as methought it said, "Come, bore me!"
—I found the Weser rolling o'er me.'

You should have heard the Hamelin people
Ringing the bells till they rocked the steeple.
'Go,' cried the Mayor, 'and get long poles,
Poke out the nests and block up the holes!
Consult with carpenters and builders,
And leave in our town not even a trace
Of the rats!'—when suddenly, up the face
Of the Piper perked in the market-place,
With a 'First, if you please, my thousand guilders!'

A thousand guilders! The Mayor looked blue;
So did the Corporation too.
For council dinners made rare havoc
With Claret, Moselle, Vin-de-Grave, Hock;
And half the money would replenish
Their cellar's biggest butt with Rhenish.
To pay this sum to a wandering fellow
With a gipsy coat of red and yellow!
'Beside,' quoth the Mayor with a knowing wink,
'Our business was done at the river's brink;
We saw with our eyes the vermin sink,
And what's dead can't come to life, I think.
So, friend, we're not the folks to shrink
From the duty of giving you something for drink,

And a matter of money to put in your poke;
But as for the guilders, what we spoke
Of them, as you very well know, was in joke.
Besides, our losses have made us thrifty.
A thousand guilders! Come, take fifty!'

The Piper's face fell, and he cried
'No trifling! I can't wait, beside!
I've promised to visit by dinnertime
Baghdad, and accept the prime
Of the Head-Cook's pottage, all he's rich in,
For having left, in the Caliph's kitchen,
Of a nest of scorpions no survivor:
With him I proved no bargain-driver,
With you, don't think I'll bate a stiver!
And folks who put me in a passion
May find me pipe after another fashion.'

'How?' cried the Mayor, 'd'ye think I brook
Being worse treated than a cook?
Insulted by a lazy ribald
With idle pipe and vesture piebald?
You threaten us, fellow? Do your worst,
Blow your pipe there till you burst!'

Once more he stepped into the street
  And to his lips again
  Laid his long pipe of smooth straight cane;
And ere he blew three notes (such sweet
Soft notes as yet musician's cunning
  Never gave the enraptured air)
There was a rustling that seemed like a bustling
Of merry crowds justling at pitching and hustling
Small feet were pattering, wooden shoes clattering,
Little hands clapping and little tongues chattering,
And, like fowls in a farmyard when barley is scattering,
Out came the children running.

stiver, **coin of little value**

All the little boys and girls,
With rosy cheeks and flaxen curls,
And sparkling eyes and teeth like pearls,
Tripping and skipping, ran merrily after
The wonderful music with shouting and laughter.

The Mayor was dumb, and the Council stood
As if they were changed into blocks of wood,
Unable to move a step, or cry
To the children merrily skipping by
—Could only follow with the eye
That joyous crowd at the Piper's back.
But how the Mayor was on the rack,
And the wretched Council's bosoms beat,
As the Piper turned from the High Street
To where the Weser rolled its waters
Right in the way of their sons and daughters!
However he turned from south to west,
And to Koppelberg Hill his steps addressed,
And after him the children pressed;
Great was the joy in every breast.
'He never can cross that mighty top!
He's forced to let the piping drop,
And we shall see our children stop!'
When, lo, as they reached the mountain-side,
A wondrous portal opened wide,
As if a cavern was suddenly hollowed;
And the Piper advanced and the children followed,
And when all were in to the very last,
The door in the mountain-side shut fast.
Did I say, all? No! One was lame,
  And could not dance the whole of the way;
And in after years, if you would blame
  His sadness, he was used to say—
'It's dull in our town since my playmates left!
I can't forget that I'm bereft
Of all the pleasant sights they see,
Which the Piper also promised me.
For he led us, he said, to a joyous land,
Joining the town and just at hand,

Where waters gushed and fruit trees grew
And flowers put forth a fairer hue,
And everything was strange and new;
The sparrows were brighter than peacocks here,
And their dogs outran our fallow deer,
And honey-bees had lost their stings,
And horses were born with eagles' wings:
And just as I became assured
My lame foot would be speedily cured,
The music stopped and I stood still,
And found myself outside the hill,
Left alone against my will,
To go now limping as before,
And never hear of that country more!'

Alas, alas for Hamelin!
  There came into many a burgher's pate
  A text which says that heaven's gate
  Opes to the rich at as easy rate
As the needle's eye takes a camel in!
The Mayor sent east, west, north, and south,
To offer the Piper, by word of mouth,
  Wherever it was men's lot to find him,
Silver and gold to his heart's content,
If he'd only return the way he went,
  And bring the children behind him.
But when they saw 'twas a lost endeavour,
And Piper and dancers were gone for ever,
They made a decree that lawyers never
  Should think their records dated duly
If, after the day of the month and year,
These words did not as well appear,
'And so long after what happened here
  On the Twenty-second of July,
Thirteen hundred and seventy-six':
And the better in memory to fix
The place of the children's last retreat,
They called it the Pied Piper's Street—
Where anyone playing on pipe or tabor
Was sure for the future to lose his labour.

Nor suffered they hostelry or tavern
  To shock with mirth a street so solemn;
But opposite the place of the cavern
  They wrote the story on a column;
And on the great church-window painted
The same, to make the world acquainted
How their children were stolen away,
And there it stands to this very day.
And I must not omit to say
That in Transylvania there's a tribe
Of alien people who ascribe
The outlandish ways and dress
On which their neighbours lay such stress,
To their fathers and mothers having risen
Out of some subterraneous prison
Into which they were trepanned
Long time ago in a mighty band
Out of Hamelin town in Brunswick land,
But how or why, they don't understand.

* * * *

So, Willy, let you and me be wipers
Of scores out with all men—especially pipers!
And, whether they pipe us free from rats or from mice,
If we've promised them aught, let us keep our promise!

THOMAS HOOD

1799–1845

162 *To Henrietta, on her Departure for Calais*

WHEN little people go abroad, wherever they may roam,
They will not just be treated as they used to be at home;
So take a few promiscuous hints, to warn you in advance,
Of how a little English girl will perhaps be served in France.

Of course you will be Frenchified; and first, it's my belief,
They'll dress you in their foreign style as à-la-mode as beef,
With a little row of bee-hives, as a border to your frock,
And a pair of frilly trousers, like a little bantam cock.

But first they'll seize your bundle (if you have one) in a crack,
And tie it, with a tape, by way of bustle on your back;
And make your waist so high or low, your shape will be a riddle,
For anyhow you'll never have your middle in the middle.

Your little English sandals for a while will hold together,
But woe betide you when the stones have worn away the leather;
For they'll poke your little pettitoes (and there will be a hobble!)
In such a pair of shoes as none but carpenters can cobble!

You'll have to learn a *chou* is quite another sort of thing
To that you put your foot in; that a *belle* is not to ring;
That a *corne* is not the knubble that brings trouble to your toes,
Nor *peut-être* a potato, as some Irish folks suppose.

But pray, at meals, remember this, the French are so polite,
No matter what you eat and drink, 'whatever is, is right'!
So when you're told at dinner time that some delicious stew
Is cat instead of rabbit, you must answer, '*Tant mi-eux*'!

JULIA A. CARNEY

1823–1908

163 *Little Things*

LITTLE drops of water,
  Little grains of sand,
Make the mighty ocean
  And the beauteous land.

And the little moments,
  Humble though they be,
Make the mighty ages
  Of eternity.

So our little errors
  Lead the soul away,
From the paths of virtue
  Into sin to stray.

Little deeds of kindness,
  Little words of love,
Make our earth an Eden,
  Like the heaven above.

EDWARD LEAR

1812–1888

164 *Nonsenses*

i

THERE was an Old Man with a beard,
Who said, 'It is just as I feared!—
    Two owls and a hen,
    Four larks and a wren,
Have all built their nests in my beard!'

ii

There was an Old Lady of Chertsey,
Who made a remarkable curtsey;
    She twirled round and round,
    Till she sank underground,
Which distressed all the people of Chertsey.

iii

There was an Old Man in a tree,
Who was horribly bored by a bee;
    When they said, 'Does it buzz?'
    He replied, 'Yes, it does!
It's a regular brute of a bee!'

iv

There was an Old Man who said, 'How
Shall I flee from this horrible cow?
I will sit on this stile,
And continue to smile,
Which may soften the heart of that cow.'

v

There was an Old Man who said, 'Hush!
I perceive a young bird in this bush!'
When they said, 'Is it small?'
He replied, 'Not at all!
It is four times as big as the bush!'

vi

There was an Old Person of Gretna,
Who rushed down the crater of Etna;
When they said, 'Is it hot?'
He replied, 'No, it's not!'
That mendacious Old Person of Gretna.

vii

There is a Young Lady, whose nose
Continually prospers and grows;
When it grew out of sight,
She exclaimed in a fright,
'Oh! Farewell to the end of my nose!'

viii

There was an Old Man of Dumbree,
Who taught little owls to drink tea;
For he said, 'To eat mice,
Is not proper or nice,'
That amiable Man of Dumbree.

165 *The Owl and the Pussy-cat*

THE Owl and the Pussy-cat went to sea
 In a beautiful pea-green boat,
They took some honey, and plenty of money,
 Wrapped up in a five-pound note.
The Owl looked up to the stars above,
 And sang to a small guitar,
'O lovely Pussy! O Pussy, my love,
 What a beautiful Pussy you are,
  You are,
  You are!
 What a beautiful Pussy you are!'

Pussy said to the Owl, 'You elegant fowl!
 How charmingly sweet you sing!
O let us be married! too long we have tarried:
 But what shall we do for a ring?'
They sailed away, for a year and a day,
 To the land where the Bong-tree grows,
And there in a wood a Piggy-wig stood
 With a ring at the end of his nose,
  His nose,
  His nose,
 With a ring at the end of his nose.

'Dear Pig, are you willing to sell for one shilling
 Your ring?' Said the Piggy, 'I will.'
So they took it away, and were married next day
 By the Turkey who lives on the hill.
They dined on mince, and slices of quince,
 Which they ate with a runcible spoon;
And hand in hand, on the edge of the sand,
 They danced by the light of the moon,
  The moon,
  The moon,
 They danced by the light of the moon.

166 *The Duck and the Kangaroo*

SAID the Duck to the Kangaroo,
'Good gracious! how you hop!
Over the fields and the water too,
As if you never would stop!
My life is a bore in this nasty pond,
And I long to go out in the world beyond!
I wish I could hop like you!'
Said the Duck to the Kangaroo.

'Please give me a ride on your back!'
Said the Duck to the Kangaroo.
'I would sit quite still, and say nothing but "Quack",
The whole of the long day through!
And we'd go to the Dee, and the Jelly Bo Lee,
Over the land, and over the sea;
Please take me a ride! O do!'
Said the Duck to the Kangaroo.

Said the Kangaroo to the Duck,
'This requires some little reflection;
Perhaps on the whole it might bring me luck,
And there seems but one objection,
Which is, if you'll let me speak so bold,
Your feet are unpleasantly wet and cold,
And would probably give me the roo-
Matiz!' said the Kangaroo.

Said the Duck, 'As I sate on the rocks,
I have thought over that completely,
And I bought four pairs of worsted socks
Which fit my web-feet neatly.
And to keep out the cold I've bought a cloak,
And every day a cigar I'll smoke,
All to follow my own dear true
Love of a Kangaroo!'

Said the Kangaroo, 'I'm ready!
  All in the moonlight pale;
But to balance me well, dear Duck, sit steady!
  And quite at the end of my tail!'
So away they went with a hop and a bound,
And they hopped the whole world three times round;
  And who so happy—O who,
  As the Duck and the Kangaroo?

167 *The Jumblies*

THEY went to sea in a Sieve, they did,
  In a Sieve they went to sea:
In spite of all their friends could say,
On a winter's morn, on a stormy day,
  In a Sieve they went to sea!
And when the Sieve turned round and round,
And everyone cried, 'You'll all be drowned!'
They called aloud, 'Our Sieve ain't big,
But we don't care a button! we don't care a fig!
  In a Sieve we'll go to sea!'
    Far and few, far and few,
      Are the lands where the Jumblies live;
    Their heads are green, and their hands are blue,
      And they went to sea in a Sieve.

They sailed away in a Sieve, they did,
  In a Sieve they sailed so fast,
With only a beautiful pea-green veil
Tied with a riband by way of a sail,
  To a small tobacco-pipe mast;
And everyone said, who saw them go,
'O won't they be soon upset, you know!
For the sky is dark, and the voyage is long,
And happen what may, it's extremely wrong
  In a Sieve to sail so fast!'
    Far and few, far and few,
      Are the lands where the Jumblies live;
    Their heads are green, and their hands are blue,
      And they went to sea in a Sieve.

The water it soon came in, it did,
  The water it soon came in;
So to keep them dry, they wrapped their feet
In a pinky paper all folded neat,
  And they fastened it down with a pin.
And they passed the night in a crockery-jar,
And each of them said, 'How wise we are!
Though the sky be dark, and the voyage be long,
Yet we never can think we were rash or wrong,
  While round in our Sieve we spin!'
    Far and few, far and few,
      Are the lands where the Jumblies live;
    Their heads are green, and their hands are blue,
      And they went to sea in a Sieve.

And all night long they sailed away;
  And when the sun went down,
They whistled and warbled a moony song
To the echoing sound of a coppery gong,
  In the shade of the mountains brown.
'O Timballoo! How happy we are,
When we live in a sieve and a crockery-jar,
And all night long in the moonlight pale,
We sail away with a pea-green sail,
  In the shade of the mountains brown!'
    Far and few, far and few,
      Are the lands where the Jumblies live;
    Their heads are green, and their hands are blue,
      And they went to sea in a Sieve.

They sailed to the Western Sea, they did,
  To a land all covered with trees,
And they bought an Owl, and a useful Cart,
And a pound of Rice, and a Cranberry Tart,
  And a hive of silvery Bees.
And they bought a Pig, and some green Jackdaws,
And a lovely Monkey with lollipop paws,
And forty bottles of Ring-Bo-Ree,
  And no end of Stilton Cheese.
    Far and few, far and few,
      Are the lands where the Jumblies live;
    Their heads are green, and their hands are blue,
      And they went to sea in a Sieve.

And in twenty years they all came back,
  In twenty years or more,
And everyone said, 'How tall they've grown!
For they've been to the Lakes, and the Torrible Zone,
  And the hills of the Chankly Bore;
And they drank their health, and gave them a feast
Of dumplings made of beautiful yeast;
And everyone said, 'If we only live,
We too will go to sea in a Sieve,
  To the hills of the Chankly Bore!'
    Far and few, far and few,
      Are the lands where the Jumblies live;
    Their heads are green, and their hands are blue,
      And they went to sea in a Sieve.

168 *Mr. and Mrs. Spikky Sparrow*

On a little piece of wood,
Mr. Spikky Sparrow stood;
Mrs. Sparrow sate close by,
A-making of an insect pie,
For her little children five,
In the nest and all alive,
Singing with a cheerful smile
To amuse them all the while,
Twikky wikky wikky wee,
Wikky bikky twikky tee,
Spikky bikky bee!

Mrs. Spikky Sparrow said,
'Spikky, darling! in my head
Many thoughts of trouble come,
Like to flies upon a plum!
All last night, among the trees,
I heard you cough, I heard you sneeze;
And, thought I, it's come to that
Because he does not wear a hat!
Chippy wippy sikky tee!
Bikky wikky tikky mee!
Spikky chippy wee!

'Not that you are growing old,
But the nights are growing cold.
No one stays out all night long
Without a hat: I'm sure it's wrong!'
Mr. Spikky said, 'How kind,
Dear, you are, to speak your mind!
All your life I wish you luck!
You are! you are! a lovely duck!
Witchy witchy witchy wee!
Twitchy witchy witchy bee!
Tikky tikky tee!

'I was also sad, and thinking,
When one day I saw you winking,
And I heard you sniffle-snuffle,
And I saw your feathers ruffle;
To myself I sadly said,
She's neuralgia in her head!
That dear head has nothing on it!
Ought she not to wear a bonnet?
    Witchy kitchy kitchy wee?
    Spikky wikky mikky bee?
      Chippy wippy chee?

'Let us both fly up to town!
There I'll buy you such a gown!
Which, completely in the fashion,
You shall tie a sky-blue sash on.
And a pair of slippers neat,
To fit your darling little feet,
So that you will look and feel
Quite galloobious and genteel!
    Jikky wikky bikky see,
    Chicky bikky wikky bee,
      Twicky witchy wee!'

So they both to London went,
Alighting on the Monument,
Whence they flew down swiftly—pop,
Into Moses' wholesale shop;
There they bought a hat and bonnet,
And a gown with spots upon it,
A satin sash of Cloxam blue,
And a pair of slippers too.
    Zikky wikky mikky bee,
    Witchy witchy mitchy kee,
      Sikky tikky wee.

Then when so completely drest,
Back they flew, and reached their nest.
Their children cried, 'O Ma and Pa!
How truly beautiful you are!'
Said they, 'We trust that cold or pain
We shall never feel again!
While, perched on tree, or house, or steeple,
We now shall look like other people.
Witchy witchy witchy wee,
Twikky mikky bikky bee,
Zikky sikky tee.'

169

An Alphabet

A

A WAS once an apple pie,
Pidy
Widy
Tidy
Pidy
Nice insidy
Apple Pie!

B

B was once a little bear,
Beary!
Wary!
Hairy!
Beary!
Taky cary!
Little Bear!

C

C was once a little cake,
Caky
Baky
Maky
Caky
Taky Caky,
Little Cake!

D

D was once a little doll,
Dolly
Molly
Polly
Nolly
Nursy Dolly
Little Doll!

E

E was once a little eel,
Eely
Weely
Peely
Eely
Twirly, Tweely
Little Eel!

F

F was once a little fish,
Fishy
Wishy
Squishy
Fishy
In a Dishy
Little Fish!

G

G was once a little goose,
Goosy
Moosy
Boosey
Goosey
Waddly-woosy
Little Goose!

H

H was once a little hen,
Henny
Chenny
Tenny
Henny
Eggsy-any
Little Hen?

I

I was once a bottle of ink,
Inky
Dinky
Thinky
Inky
Blacky Minky
Bottle of Ink!

J

J was once a jar of jam,
Jammy
Mammy
Clammy
Jammy
Sweety—Swammy
Jar of Jam!

K

K was once a little kite,
Kity
Whity
Flighty
Kity
Out of Sighty—
Little Kite!

L

L was once a little lark,
Larky!
Marky!
Harky!
Larky!
In the Parky,
Little Lark!

M

M was once a little mouse,
Mousey
Bousey
Sousy
Mousy
In the Housy
Little Mouse!

N

N was once a little needle,
Needly
Tweedly
Threedly
Needly
Wisky—wheedly
Little Needle!

O

O was once a little owl,
Owly
Prowly
Howly
Owly
Browny fowly
Little Owl!

P

P was once a little pump,
Pumpy
Slumpy
Flumpy
Pumpy
Dumpy, Thumpy
Little Pump!

Q

Q was once a little quail,
Quaily
Faily
Daily
Quaily
Stumpy-taily
Little Quail!

R

R was once a little rose,
Rosy
Posy
Nosy
Rosy
Blows-y—grows-y
Little Rose!

S

S was once a little shrimp,
Shrimpy
Nimpy
Flimpy
Shrimpy
Jumpy—jimpy
Little Shrimp!

T

T was once a little thrush,
Thrushy!
Hushy!
Bushy!
Thrushy!
Flitty—Flushy
Little Thrush!

U

U was once a little urn,
Urny
Burny
Turny
Urny
Bubbly—burny
Little Urn!

V

V was once a little vine,
Viny
Winy
Twiny
Viny
Twisty-twiny
Little Vine!

W

W was once a whale,
Whaly
Scaly
Shaly
Whaly
Tumbly-taily
Mighty Whale!

X

X was once a great king Xerxes,
Xerxy
Perxy
Turxy
Xerxy
Linxy Lurxy
Great King Xerxes!

Y

Y was once a little yew,
Yewdy
Fewdy
Crudy
Yewdy
Growdy, grewdy,
Little Yew!

Z

Z was once a piece of zinc,
Tinky
Winky
Blinky
Tinky
Tinkly Minky
Piece of Zinc!

170 *The Pobble who has No Toes*

THE Pobble who has no toes
Had once as many as we;
When they said, 'Some day you may lose them all'—
He replied, 'Fish fiddle de-dee!'
And his Aunt Jobiska made him drink,
Lavender water tinged with pink,
For she said, 'The World in general knows
There's nothing so good for a Pobble's toes!'

The Pobble who has no toes,
  Swam across the Bristol Channel;
But before he set out he wrapped his nose,
  In a piece of scarlet flannel.
For his Aunt Jobiska said, 'No harm
Can come to his toes if his nose is warm;
And it's perfectly known that a Pobble's toes
Are safe—provided he minds his nose.'

The Pobble swam fast and well
  And when boats or ships came near him
He tinkledy-binkledy-winkled a bell
  So that all the world could hear him.
And all the Sailors and Admirals cried,
When they saw him nearing the further side—
'He has gone to fish, for his Aunt Jobiska's
Runcible Cat with crimson whiskers!'

But before he touched the shore,
  The shore of the Bristol Channel,
A sea-green Porpoise carried away
  His wrapper of scarlet flannel.
And when he came to observe his feet
Formerly garnished with toes so neat
His face at once became forlorn
On perceiving that all his toes were gone!

And nobody ever knew
  From that dark day to the present,
Whoso had taken the Pobble's toes,
  In a manner so far from pleasant.
Whether the shrimps or crawfish grey,
Or crafty Mermaids stole them away—
Nobody knew; and nobody knows
How the Pobble was robbed of his twice five toes!

The Pobble who has no toes
  Was placed in a friendly Bark,
And they rowed him back, and carried him up,
  To his Aunt Jobiska's Park.
And she made him a feast at his earnest wish
Of eggs and buttercups fried with fish—
And she said, 'It's a fact the whole world knows,
That Pobbles are happier without their toes.'

CECIL FRANCES ALEXANDER

1818–1895

171 *All Things Bright and Beautiful*

ALL things bright and beautiful,
  All creatures great and small,
All things wise and wonderful,
  The Lord God made them all.

Each little flower that opens,
  Each little bird that sings,
He made their glowing colours,
  He made their tiny wings.

The purple-headed mountain,
  The river running by,
The sunset, and the morning,
  That brightens up the sky;

The cold wind in the winter,
  The pleasant summer sun,
The ripe fruits in the garden,
  He made them every one.

He gave us eyes to see them,
  And lips that we might tell,
How great is God Almighty,
  Who has made all things well.

172 *Once in Royal David's City*

ONCE in royal David's city
  Stood a lowly cattle shed,
Where a mother laid her baby
  In a manger for his bed:
Mary was that mother mild,
Jesus Christ her little child.

He came down to earth from heaven,
  Who is God and Lord of all,
And his shelter was a stable,
  And his cradle was a stall;
With the poor, and mean, and lowly,
Lived on earth our Saviour holy.

And through all his wondrous childhood,
  He would honour and obey,
Love and watch the lowly maiden
  In whose gentle arms he lay:
Christian children all must be
Mild, obedient, good as he.

For he is our childhood's pattern,
  Day by day like us he grew,
He was little, weak, and helpless,
  Tears and smiles like us he knew,
And he feeleth for our sadness,
And he shareth in our gladness.

And our eyes at last shall see him,
  Through his own redeeming love,
For that child so dear and gentle
  Is our Lord in heaven above;
And he leads his children on
To the place where he is gone.

Not in that poor lowly stable,
With the oxen standing by,
We shall see him; but in heaven,
Set at God's right hand on high;
When like stars his children crowned,
All in white shall wait around.

173 *There is a Green Hill*

THERE is a green hill far away,
Without a city wall,
Where the dear Lord was crucified,
Who died to save us all.

We may not know, we cannot tell
What pains he had to bear;
But we believe it was for us,
He hung and suffered there.

He died that we might be forgiven,
He died to make us good,
That we might go at last to heaven,
Saved by his precious blood.

There was no other good enough
To pay the price of sin,
He only could unlock the gate
Of heaven, and let us in.

O dearly, dearly has he loved,
And we must love him too,
And trust in his redeeming blood,
And try his works to do.

174

The Beggar Boy

WHEN the wind blows loud and fearful,
  And the rain is pouring fast,
And the cottage matron careful
  Shuts her door against the blast;

When lone mothers as they hearken,
  Think of sailor sons at sea,
And the eve begins to darken,
  While the clocks are striking three;

When the pavement echoes only
  Now and then to passing feet;
Still the beggar boy goes lonely,
  Up and down the empty street.

On his brow the wet hair bristles,
  And his feet are blue with cold,
And the wind at pleasure whistles
  Through his garments torn and old.

You can hear the plaint he utters,
  Standing dripping at your door,
Through the splashing in the gutters,
  When the wind has lulled its roar.

Little children playing gladly,
  In the parlour bright and warm,
Look out kindly, look out sadly
  On the beggar in the storm.

Speak ye softly to each other,
  Standing by the window pane;
'Had he father, had he mother,
  Would they leave him in the rain?

'In our home is peace and pleasure,
  We are loved and cared about,
We must give from our full measure,
  To the wanderer without.'

175 *The Fieldmouse*

WHERE the acorn tumbles down,
  Where the ash tree sheds its berry,
With your fur so soft and brown,
  With your eye so round and merry,
Scarcely moving the long grass,
Fieldmouse, I can see you pass.

Little thing, in what dark den,
  Lie you all the winter sleeping?
Till warm weather comes again,
  Then once more I see you peeping
Round about the tall tree roots,
Nibbling at their fallen fruits.

Fieldmouse, fieldmouse, do not go,
  Where the farmer stacks his treasure,
Find the nut that falls below,
  Eat the acorn at your pleasure,
But you must not steal the grain
He has stacked with so much pain.

Make your hole where mosses spring,
  Underneath the tall oak's shadow,
Pretty, quiet, harmless thing,
  Play about the sunny meadow.
Keep away from corn and house,
None will harm you, little mouse.

HEINRICH HOFFMANN

1809–1894

176 *The Story of Augustus who would Not have any Soup*

AUGUSTUS was a chubby lad;
Fat ruddy cheeks Augustus had:
And everybody saw with joy
The plump and hearty, healthy boy.
He ate and drank as he was told,
And never let his soup get cold.
But one day, one cold winter's day,
He screamed out 'Take the soup away!
O take the nasty soup away!
I won't have any soup today.'

Next day, now look, the picture shows
How lank and lean Augustus grows!
Yet, though he feels so weak and ill,
The naughty fellow cries out still
'Not any soup for me, I say:
O take the nasty soup away!
I *won't* have any soup today.'

The third day comes: Oh what a sin!
To make himself so pale and thin.
Yet, when the soup is put on table,
He screams, as loud as he is able,
'Not any soup for me, I say:
O take the nasty soup away!
I WON'T have any soup today.'

Look at him, now the fourth day's come!
He scarcely weighs a sugar-plum;
He's like a little bit of thread,
And, on the fifth day, he was—dead!

177 *The Story of Johnny Head-in-Air*

As he trudged along to school,
It was always Johnny's rule
To be looking at the sky
And the clouds that floated by;
But what just before him lay,
In his way,
Johnny never thought about;
So that everyone cried out
'Look at little Johnny there,
Little Johnny Head-in-Air!'

Running just in Johnny's way
Came a little dog one day;
Johnny's eyes were still astray
Up on high,
In the sky;
And he never heard them cry
'Johnny, mind, the dog is nigh!'
Bump!
Dump!
Down they fell, with such a thump,
Dog and Johnny in a lump!

Once, with head as high as ever,
Johnny walked beside the river.
Johnny watched the swallows trying
Which was cleverest at flying.
Oh! what fun!
Johnny watched the bright round sun
Going in and coming out;
This was all he thought about.
So he strode on, only think!
To the river's very brink,
Where the bank was high and steep,
And the water very deep;
And the fishes, in a row,
Stared to see him coming so.

One step more! oh! sad to tell!
Headlong in poor Johnny fell.
And the fishes, in dismay,
Wagged their tails and swam away.

There lay Johnny on his face,
With his nice red writing-case;
But, as they were passing by,
Two strong men had heard him cry;
And, with sticks, these two strong men
Hooked poor Johnny out again.

Oh! you should have seen him shiver
When they pulled him from the river.
He was in a sorry plight,
Dripping wet, and such a fright!
Wet all over, everywhere,
Clothes, and arms, and face, and hair:
Johnny never will forget
What it is to be so wet.

And the fishes, one, two, three,
Are come back again, you see;
Up they came the moment after,
To enjoy the fun and laughter.
Each popped out his little head,
And, to tease poor Johnny, said
'Silly little Johnny, look,
You have lost your writing-book!'

178 *The Story of Fidgety Philip*

'LET me see if Philip can
Be a little gentleman;
Let me see if he is able
To sit still for once at table':
Thus Papa bade Phil behave;
And Mamma looked very grave.
But fidgety Phil,
He won't sit still;
He wriggles,
And giggles,
And then, I declare,
Swings backwards and forwards,
And tilts up his chair,
Just like any rocking-horse—
'Philip! I am getting cross!'

See the naughty, restless child
Growing still more rude and wild,
Till his chair falls over quite.
Philip screams with all his might,
Catches at the cloth, but then
That makes matters worse again.
Down upon the ground they fall,
Glasses, plates, knives, forks, and all.
How Mamma did fret and frown,
When she saw them tumbling down!
And Papa made such a face!
Philip is in sad disgrace.

Where is Philip, where is he?
Fairly covered up you see!
Cloth and all are lying on him;
He has pulled down all upon him.

What a terrible to-do!
Dishes, glasses, snapped in two!
Here a knife, and there a fork!
Philip, this is cruel work.
Table all so bare, and ah!
Poor Papa, and poor Mamma
Look quite cross, and wonder how
They shall have their dinner now.

ELIZA COOK

1818–1889

179 *The Mouse and the Cake*

A MOUSE found a beautiful piece of plum cake,
The richest and sweetest that mortal could make;
'Twas heavy with citron and fragrant with spice,
And covered with sugar all sparkling as ice.

'My stars!' cried the mouse, while his eye beamed with glee,
'Here's a treasure I've found: what a feast it will be;
But, hark! there's a noise, 'tis my brothers at play;
So I'll hide with the cake, lest they wander this way.

'Not a bit shall they have, for I know I can eat
Every morsel myself, and I'll have such a treat.'
So off went the mouse as he held the cake fast;
While his hungry young brothers went scampering past.

He nibbled, and nibbled, and panted, but still
He kept gulping it down till he made himself ill;
Yet he swallowed it all, and 'tis easy to guess,
He was soon so unwell that he groaned with distress.

His family heard him, and as he grew worse,
They sent for the doctor, who made him rehearse
How he'd eaten the cake to the very last crumb,
Without giving his playmates and relatives some.

'Ah me!' cried the doctor, 'advice is too late;
You must die before long, so prepare for your fate.
If you had but divided the cake with your brothers,
'Twould have done you no harm, and been good for the others.

'Had you shared it, the treat had been wholesome enough;
But eaten by *one*, it was dangerous stuff;
So prepare for the worst—' and the word had scarce fled,
When the doctor turned round, and the patient was dead.

Now all little people the lesson may take,
And *some* large ones may learn from the mouse and the cake;
Not to be over-selfish with what we may gain,
Or the best of our pleasures may turn into pain.

THOMAS MILLER

1807–1874

180

Evening

(In words of one syllable)

THE day is past, the sun is set,
  And the white stars are in the sky;
While the long grass with dew is wet,
  And through the air the bats now fly.

The lambs have now lain down to sleep,
  The birds have long since sought their nests;
The air is still; and dark, and deep
  On the hill side the old wood rests.

Yet of the dark I have no fear,
  But feel as safe as when 'tis light;
For I know God is with me there,
  And He will guard me through the night.

For God is by me when I pray,
  And when I close mine eyes in sleep,
I know that He will with me stay,
  And will all night watch by me keep.

For He who rules the stars and sea,
  Who makes the grass and trees to grow,
Will look on a poor child like me,
  When on my knees I to Him bow.

He holds all things in His right hand,
  The rich, the poor, the great, the small;
When we sleep, or sit, or stand,
  Is with us, for He loves us all.

181 *The Watercress Seller*

Now all aloud the wind and rain
Beat sharp upon the window pane,
    And though 'tis hardly light,
I hear that little girl go by,
Who does 'Fine watercresses' cry,
    Morning, and noon, and night.

I saw her pass by yesterday,
The snow upon the pavement lay,
    Her hair was white with sleet;
She shook with cold, as she did cry,
'Fine watercresses, come and buy,'
    And naked were her feet.

And with one hand, so red and cold,
She did her tattered bonnet hold,
    The other held her shawl,
Which was too thin to keep her warm,
But naked left each little arm,
    It was so very small.

Her watercresses froze together,
Yet she, through the cold, bitter weather,
    Went on from street to street:
And thus she goes out every day,
For she can earn no other way
    The bread which she doth eat.

LORD TENNYSON

1809–1892

182 *Sweet and Low*

SWEET and low, sweet and low,
  Wind of the western sea,
Low, low, breathe and blow,
  Wind of the western sea!
Over the rolling waters go,
Come from the dying moon, and blow,
  Blow him again to me;
While my little one, while my pretty one, sleeps.

Sleep and rest, sleep and rest,
  Father will come to thee soon;
Rest, rest, on mother's breast,
  Father will come to thee soon;
Father will come to his babe in the nest,
Silver sails all out of the west
  Under the silver moon:
Sleep, my little one, sleep, my pretty one, sleep.

183 *Cradle Song*

WHAT does little birdie say
In her nest at peep of day?
Let me fly, says little birdie,
Mother, let me fly away.
Birdie, rest a little longer,
Till the little wings are stronger;
So she rests a little longer,
Then she flies away.

What does little baby say,
In her bed at peep of day?
Baby says, like little birdie,
Let me rise and fly away.
Baby, sleep a little longer,
Till the little limbs are stronger;
If she sleeps a little longer,
Baby too shall fly away.

184 *The City Child*

DAINTY little maiden, whither would you wander?
  Whither from this pretty home, the home where mother dwells?
'Far and far away,' said the dainty little maiden,
'All among the gardens, auriculas, anemones,
  Roses and lilies and Canterbury-bells.'

Dainty little maiden, whither would you wander?
  Whither from this pretty house, this city house of ours?
'Far and far away,' said the dainty little maiden,
'All among the meadows, the clover and the clematis,
  Daisies and kingcups and honeysuckle-flowers.'

185 *Minnie and Winnie*

MINNIE and Winnie
  Slept in a shell.
Sleep, little ladies!
  And they slept well.

Pink was the shell within,
  Silver without;
Sounds of the great sea
  Wandered about.

Sleep, little ladies,
  Wake not soon!
Echo on echo
  Dies to the moon.

Two bright stars
  Peeped into the shell.
'What are they dreaming of?
  Who can tell?'

Started a green linnet
  Out of the croft;
Wake, little ladies,
  The sun is aloft!

WILLIAM ALLINGHAM

1824–1889

186 *The Fairies*

UP the airy mountain,
  Down the rushy glen,
We daren't go a-hunting
  For fear of little men;
Wee folk, good folk,
  Trooping all together;
Green jacket, red cap,
  And white owl's feather!

Down along the rocky shore
  Some make their home,
They live on crispy pancakes
  Of yellow tide-foam;
Some in the reeds
  Of the black mountain-lake,
With frogs for their watchdogs,
  All night awake.

High on the hill-top
  The old King sits;
He is now so old and grey
  He's nigh lost his wits.
With a bridge of white mist
  Columbkill he crosses,
On his stately journeys
  From Slieveleague to Rosses;
Or going up with music
  On cold starry nights,
To sup with the Queen
  Of the gay Northern Lights.

They stole little Bridget
  For seven years long;
When she came down again
  Her friends were all gone.
They took her lightly back,
  Between the night and morrow,
They thought that she was fast asleep,
  But she was dead with sorrow.
They have kept her ever since
  Deep within the lake,
On a bed of flag-leaves,
  Watching till she wake.

By the craggy hillside,
  Through the mosses bare,
They have planted thorn trees
  For pleasure, here and there.
Is any man so daring
  As dig them up in spite,
He shall find their sharpest thorns
  In his bed at night.

Up the airy mountain,
  Down the rushy glen,
We daren't go a-hunting
  For fear of little men;
Wee folk, good folk,
  Trooping all together;
Green jacket, red cap,
  And white owl's feather!

187

Riding

His lordship's steed
Of a noble breed
Is trotting fleetly, fleetly,
Her ladyship's pony,
Sleek and bonny,
Cantering neatly, neatly.

How shall they pass
The turf-cadger's ass,
Creels and all, creels and all?
Man on him bumping,
Shouting and thumping,
Heels and all, heels and all!

Lane is not wide,
A hedge on each side,
The ass is beginning to bray;
'Now,' says my lord,
With an angry word,
'Fellow, get out of the way!'

'Ha!' says the cadger,
As bold as a badger,
'This way is *my* way too!'
Says the lady mild,
And sweetly smiled,
'My friend, that's perfectly true.'

The cadger looked round,
Then jumped to the ground,
And into the hedge pulled Neddy.
'O thank you!' says she,
'Ax pardon!' says he,
And touched his old hat to the lady.

His lordship's steed
Of a noble breed
Went trotting it fleetly, fleetly,
Her ladyship's pony,
Sleek and bonny
Cantering neatly, neatly.

***turf-cadger*, seller of turf and peat** ***creels*, large wicker baskets**

The cadger he rode
As well as he could,
Heels and all, heels and all,
Jolting and bumping,
Shouting and thumping,
Creels and all, creels and all.

188 *Wishing*

RING—TING! I wish I were a primrose,
A bright yellow primrose, blowing in the spring!
The stooping boughs above me,
The wandering bee to love me,
The fern and moss to creep across,
And the elm tree for our king!

Nay—stay! I wish I were an elm tree,
A great lofty elm tree, with green leaves gay!
The winds would set them dancing,
The sun and moonshine glance in,
The birds would house among the boughs,
And sweetly sing!

O—no! I wish I were a robin,
A robin or a little wren, everywhere to go;
Through forest, field, or garden,
And ask no leave or pardon,
Till winter comes with icy thumbs
To ruffle up our wing!

Well—tell! Where should I fly to,
Where go to sleep in the dark wood or dell?
Before a day was over,
Home comes the rover,
For mother's kiss, sweeter this
Than any other thing!

189 *Robin Redbreast*

GOODBYE, goodbye to summer!
  For summer's nearly done;
The garden smiling faintly,
  Cool breezes in the sun;
Our thrushes now are silent,
  Our swallows flown away—
But Robin's here, in coat of brown,
  With ruddy breast-knot gay.
Robin, Robin Redbreast,
  O Robin dear!
Robin singing sweetly
  In the falling of the year.

Bright yellow, red, and orange,
  The leaves come down in hosts;
The trees are Indian princes,
  But soon they'll turn to ghosts;
The leathery pears and apples
  Hang russet on the bough,
It's autumn, autumn, autumn late,
  'Twill soon be winter now.
Robin, Robin Redbreast,
  O Robin dear!
And what will this poor Robin do?
  For pinching days are near.

The fireside for the cricket,
  The wheatstack for the mouse,
When trembling night-winds whistle
  And moan all round the house;
The frosty ways like iron,
  The branches plumed with snow—
Alas! in winter, dead and dark,
  Where can poor Robin go?
Robin, Robin Redbreast,
  O Robin dear!
And a crumb of bread for Robin,
  His little heart to cheer.

NINETEENTH CENTURY
SECOND HALF

WILLIAM MAKEPEACE THACKERAY

1811–1863

190 *At the Zoo*

FIRST I saw the white bear, then I saw the black;
Then I saw the camel with a hump upon his back;
Then I saw the grey wolf, with mutton in his maw;
Then I saw the wombat waddle in the straw;
Then I saw the elephant a-waving of his trunk;
Then I saw the monkeys—mercy, how unpleasantly they—smelt!

AUNT EFFIE (JANE EUPHEMIA BROWNE)

1811–1898

191 *The Rooks*

THE rooks are building on the trees;
  They build there every spring:
'Caw, caw,' is all they say,
  For none of them can sing.

They're up before the break of day,
  And up till late at night;
For they must labour busily
  As long as it is light.

And many a crooked stick they bring,
  And many a slender twig,
And many a tuft of moss, until
  Their nests are round and big.

'Caw, caw.' Oh, what a noise
  They make in rainy weather!
Good children always speak by turns,
  But rooks all talk together.

AUNT EFFIE (JANE EUPHEMIA BROWNE)

192 *Little Raindrops*

OH, where do you come from,
  You little drops of rain,
Pitter patter, pitter patter,
  Down the window pane?

They won't let me walk,
  And they won't let me play,
And they won't let me go
  Out of doors at all today.

They put away my playthings
  Because I broke them all,
And then they locked up all my bricks,
  And took away my ball.

Tell me, little raindrops,
  Is that the way you play,
Pitter patter, pitter patter,
  All the rainy day?

They say I'm very naughty,
  But I've nothing else to do
But sit here at the window;
  I should like to play with you.

The little raindrops cannot speak,
  But 'pitter patter pat'
Means, 'We can play on *this* side,
  Why can't you play on *that*?'

193 *The Great Brown Owl*

THE brown owl sits in the ivy bush,
  And she looketh wondrous wise,
With a horny beak beneath her cowl,
  And a pair of large round eyes.

She sat all day on the selfsame spray,
  From sunrise till sunset;
And the dim, grey light it was all too bright
  For the owl to see in yet.

'Jenny Owlet, Jenny Owlet,' said a merry little bird,
  'They say you're wondrous wise;
But I don't think you see, though you're looking at *me*
  With your large, round, shining eyes.'

But night came soon, and the pale white moon
  Rolled high up in the skies;
And the great brown owl flew away in her cowl,
  With her large, round, shining eyes.

194 *Pleasant Changes*

SUMMER'S sun is warm and bright,
Winter's snow is cold and white,
Autumn brings the sheaves of grain,
Spring will scatter flowers again;
    Pleasant changes
    God arranges
      All throughout the year!

First there's darkness then there's light,
First we've day and then we've night,
First we're hot and then we're cold,
First we're young and then we're old;
    Are we knowing
    Where we're going,
      What we're doing here?

HENRY WADSWORTH LONGFELLOW?

1807–1882

195 *There Was a Little Girl*

There was a little girl
Who had a little curl
Right in the middle of her forehead.
When she was good
She was very, very good,
But when she was bad she was horrid.

ANONYMOUS

c. 1858

196 *Table Rules for Little Folks*

In silence I must take my seat,
And give God thanks before I eat;
Must for my food in patience wait,
Till I am asked to hand my plate;
I must not scold, nor whine, nor pout,
Nor move my chair nor plate about;
With knife, or fork, or napkin ring,
I must not play, nor must I sing.
I must not speak a useless word,
For children should be seen, not heard;
I must not talk about my food,
Nor fret if I don't think it good;
I must not say, 'The bread is old,'
'The tea is hot,' 'The coffee's cold';
My mouth with food I must not crowd,
Nor while I'm eating speak aloud;
Must turn my head to cough or sneeze,
And when I ask, say 'If you please';
The tablecloth I must not spoil,
Nor with my food my fingers soil;
Must keep my seat when I have done,
Nor round the table sport or run;

When told to rise, then I must put
My chair away with noiseless foot;
And lift my heart to God above,
In praise for all his wondrous love.

CHARLES KINGSLEY

1819–1875

197 *A Farewell*

My fairest child, I have no song to give you;
No lark could pipe to skies so dull and grey:
Yet, ere we part, one lesson I can leave you
For every day.

Be good, sweet maid, and let who will be clever;
Do noble things, not dream them, all day long:
And so make life, death, and that vast forever
One grand, sweet song.

198 *The Tide River*

Clear and cool, clear and cool,
By laughing shallow, and dreaming pool;
Cool and clear, cool and clear,
By shining shingle, and foaming weir;
Under the crag where the ouzel sings,
And the ivied wall where the church-bell rings,
Undefiled, for the undefiled;
Play by me, bathe in me, mother and child.

Dank and foul, dank and foul,
By the smoky town in its murky cowl;
Foul and dank, foul and dank,
By wharf and sewer and slimy bank;
Darker and darker the further I go,
Baser and baser the richer I grow;
Who dare sport with the sin-defiled?
Shrink from me, turn from me, mother and child.

Strong and free, strong and free,
The floodgates are open, away to the sea.
Free and strong, free and strong,
Cleansing my streams as I hurry along,
To the golden sands, and the leaping bar,
And the taintless tide that awaits me afar,
As I lose myself in the infinite main,
Like a soul that has sinned and is pardoned again.
Undefiled, for the undefiled;
Play by me, bathe in me, mother and child.

199

Young and Old

WHEN all the world is young, lad,
And all the trees are green;
And every goose a swan, lad,
And every lass a queen;
Then hey for boot and horse, lad,
And round the world away;
Young blood must have its course, lad,
And every dog his day.

When all the world is old, lad,
And all the trees are brown;
When all the sport is stale, lad,
And all the wheels run down;
Creep home, and take your place there,
The spent and maimed among:
God grant you find one face there,
You loved when all was young.

200

The Little Doll

I ONCE had a sweet little doll, dears,
The prettiest doll in the world;
Her cheeks were so red and so white, dears,
And her hair was so charmingly curled.

But I lost my poor little doll, dears,
As I played in the heath one day;
And I cried for her more than a week, dears;
But I never could find where she lay.

I found my poor little doll, dears,
As I played in the heath one day:
Folks say she is terribly changed, dears,
For her paint is all washed away,
And her arm trodden off by the cows, dears,
And her hair not the least bit curled:
Yet for old sakes' sake she is still, dears,
The prettiest doll in the world.

ALBERT MIDLANE

1825–1909

201 *Above the Bright Blue Sky*

THERE'S a Friend for little children
Above the bright blue sky,
A Friend who never changes,
Whose love will never die;
Our earthly friends may fail us,
And change with changing years,
This Friend is always worthy
Of that dear name he bears.

There's a home for little children
Above the bright blue sky,
Where Jesus reigns in glory,
A home of peace and joy;
No home on earth is like it,
Nor can with it compare;
And everyone is happy,
Nor could be happier there.

WILLIAM E. HICKSON

1803–1870

202 *Walking Song*

We waited for an omnibus,
In which there was no room for us,
But Right foot first, then Left, his brother,
Tried which could overtake the other;
And that's the way,
With nought to pay,
To do without an omnibus,
In which there is no room for us.

ROBERT TENNANT

1830–1879

203 *Wee Davie Daylicht*

Wee Davie Daylicht keeks owre the sea,
Early in the mornin', wi' a clear e'e;
Waukens a' the birdies that are sleepin' soun',
Wee Davie Daylicht is nae lazy loon.

Wee Davie Daylicht glow'rs owre the hill,
Glints through the greenwood, dances on the rill;
Smiles on the wee cot, shines on the ha';
Wee Davie Daylicht cheers the hearts o' a'.

Come, bonnie bairnie, come awa' to me;
Cuddle in my bosie, sleep upon my knee.
Wee Davie Daylicht noo has closed his e'e.
In amang the rosy clouds, far ayont the sea.

CHARLES HENRY ROSS

c. 1842–1897

204 *John, Tom, and James*

JOHN was a bad boy, and beat a poor cat;
Tom put a stone in a blind man's hat;
James was the boy who neglected his prayers;
They've all grown up ugly, and nobody cares.

205 *An Old Woman*

THERE was an old woman as ugly as sin,
Who lived upon Lucifer-matches and gin;
But she was so greedy, and ate such a many,
You could not have kept her a week on a penny.

206 *Jack*

THAT'S Jack;
Lay a stick on his back!
What's he done? I cannot say.
We'll find out tomorrow,
And beat him today.

D'ARCY WENTWORTH THOMPSON

1829–1902

207 *That Little Black Cat*

WHO'S that ringing at our door-bell?
'I'm a little black cat, and I'm not very well.'
'Then rub your little nose with a little mutton-fat,
And that's the best cure for a little pussy cat.'

208 *A Very Odd Fish*

GRANNY and I with dear Dadu,
Went rambling on the shore;
With pebbles smooth and cockleshells
We filled his pinafore.

Beneath the stones and in the pool
We found, to our delight,
Shrimps, periwinkles, and a most
Voracious appetite.

WILLIAM BRIGHTY RANDS

1823–1882

209 *Topsyturvey-World*

IF the butterfly courted the bee,
  And the owl the porcupine;
If churches were built in the sea,
  And three times one was nine;
If the pony rode his master,
  If the buttercups ate the cows,
If the cat had the dire disaster
  To be worried, sir, by the mouse;
If mamma, sir, sold the baby
  To a gipsy for half-a-crown;
If a gentleman, sir, was a lady—
  The world would be Upside-Down!
If any or all of these wonders
  Should ever come about,
I should not consider them blunders,
  For I should be Inside-Out!

Chorus

Ba-ba, black wool,
  Have you any sheep?
Yes, sir, a pack-full,
  Creep, mouse, creep!
Four-and-twenty little maids
  Hanging out the pie,
Out jumped the honey-pot,
  Guy Fawkes, Guy!
Cross-latch, cross-latch,
  Sit and spin the fire,
When the pie was opened,
  The bird was on the brier!

210 *The Pedlar's Caravan*

I WISH I lived in a caravan,
With a horse to drive, like the pedlar-man!
Where he comes from nobody knows,
Or where he goes to, but on he goes!

His caravan has windows two,
And a chimney of tin, that the smoke comes through;
He has a wife, with a baby brown,
And they go riding from town to town.

Chairs to mend, and delf to sell!
He clashes the basins like a bell;
Tea-trays, baskets ranged in order,
Plates with the alphabet round the border!

The roads are brown, and the sea is green,
But his house is just like a bathing-machine;
The world is round, and he can ride,
Rumble and splash, to the other side!

***delf*, glazed earthenware made at Delft, or Delf, in Holland**

With the pedlar-man I should like to roam,
And write a book when I came home;
All the people would read my book,
Just like the Travels of Captain Cook.

211 *A Shooting Song*

To shoot, to shoot, would be my delight,
To shoot the cats that howl in the night;
To shoot the lion, the wolf, the bear,
To shoot the mad dogs out in the square.

I learnt to shoot with a pop-gun good,
Made out of a branch of elder-wood;
It was round, and long, full half a yard,
The plug was strong, the pellets were hard.

I should like to shoot with a bow of yew,
As the English at Agincourt used to do;
The strings of a thousand bows went twang,
And a thousand arrows whizzed and sang.

On Hounslow Heath I should like to ride,
With a great horse-pistol at my side:
It is dark—hark! A robber, I know!
Click! crick-crack! and away we go!

I will shoot with a double-barrelled gun,
Two bullets are better than only one;
I will shoot some rooks to put in a pie;
I will shoot an eagle up in the sky.

I once shot a bandit in a dream,
In a mountain pass I heard a scream;
I rescued the lady, and set her free,
'Do not fear, madam, lean on me!'

With a boomerang I could not aim;
A poison blow-pipe would be the same;
A double-barrelled is my desire,
Get out of the way—one, two, three, fire!

212 *The Dream of a Boy who lived at Nine Elms*

NINE grenadiers, with bayonets in their guns;
Nine bakers' baskets, with hot-cross buns;
Nine brown elephants, standing in a row;
Nine new velocipedes, good ones to go;
Nine knickerbocker suits, with buttons all complete;
Nine pair of skates with straps for the feet;
Nine clever conjurors eating hot coals;
Nine sturdy mountaineers leaping on their poles;
Nine little drummer-boys beating on their drums;
Nine fat aldermen sitting on their thumbs;
Nine new knockers to our front door;
Nine new neighbours that I never saw before;
Nine times running I dreamt it all plain;
With bread and cheese for supper I could dream it all again!

velocipedes, early bicycles

213 *The Dream of a Girl who lived at Sevenoaks*

SEVEN sweet singing birds up in a tree;
Seven swift sailing-ships white upon the sea;
Seven bright weathercocks shining in the sun;
Seven slim racehorses ready for a run;
Seven gold butterflies, flitting overhead;
Seven red roses blowing in a garden bed;
Seven white lilies, with honey bees inside them;
Seven round rainbows with clouds to divide them;
Seven pretty little girls with sugar on their lips;
Seven witty little boys, whom everybody tips;
Seven nice fathers, to call little maids 'joys';
Seven nice mothers, to kiss the little boys;
Seven nights running I dreamt it all plain;
With bread and jam for supper I could dream it all again!

214 *The World*

Great, wide, beautiful, wonderful World,
With the wonderful water round you curled,
And the wonderful grass upon your breast—
World, you are beautifully drest.

The wonderful air is over me,
And the wonderful wind is shaking the tree,
It walks on the water, and whirls the mills,
And talks to itself on the tops of the hills.

You friendly Earth, how far do you go,
With the wheatfields that nod and the rivers that flow,
With cities and gardens, and cliffs, and isles,
And people upon you for thousands of miles?

Ah, you are so great, and I am so small,
I tremble to think of you, World, at all;
And yet, when I said my prayers today,
A whisper inside me seemed to say,
'You are more than the Earth, though you are such a dot:
You can love and think, and the Earth cannot.'

215 *The Cat of Cats*

I am the cat of cats. I am
  The everlasting cat!
Cunning, and old, and sleek as jam,
  The everlasting cat!
I hunt the vermin in the night—
  The everlasting cat!
For I see best without the light—
  The everlasting cat!

216 *Winifred Waters*

WINIFRED WATERS sat and sighed
  Under a weeping willow;
When she went to bed she cried,
  Wetting all her pillow;

Kept on crying night and day,
  Till her friends lost patience;
'What shall we do to stop her, pray?'
  So said her relations.

Send her to the sandy plains
  In the zone called torrid.
Send her where it never rains,
  Where the heat is horrid.

Mind that she has only flour
  For her daily feeding;
Let her have a page an hour
  Of the driest reading—

Navigation, logarithm,
  All that kind of knowledge—
Ancient pedigrees go with 'em
  From the Herald's College.

When the poor girl has endured
  Six months of this drying,
Winifred will come back cured,
  Let us hope, of crying.

SABINE BARING-GOULD

1834–1924

217 *Now the Day is Over*

Now the day is over,
  Night is drawing nigh,
Shadows of the evening
  Steal across the sky.

Now the darkness gathers,
  Stars begin to peep,
Birds and beasts and flowers
  Soon will be asleep.

Jesu, give the weary
  Calm and sweet repose;
With thy tenderest blessing
  May our eyelids close.

Grant to little children
  Visions bright of thee;
Guard the sailors tossing
  On the deep blue sea.

Comfort every sufferer
  Watching late in pain;
Those who plan some evil
  From their sin restrain.

Through the long night-watches
  May thine angels spread
Their white wings above me,
  Watching round my bed.

When the morning wakens,
  Then may I arise
Pure and fresh and sinless
  In thy holy eyes.

Glory to the Father,
  Glory to the Son,
And to thee, blest Spirit,
  Whilst all ages run.

LEWIS CARROLL (CHARLES LUTWIDGE DODGSON)

1832–1898

218 *You are old, Father William*

'You are old, Father William,' the young man said,
  'And your hair has become very white;
And yet you incessantly stand on your head—
  Do you think, at your age, it is right?'

'In my youth,' Father William replied to his son,
  'I feared it might injure the brain;
But, now that I'm perfectly sure I have none,
  Why, I do it again and again.'

'You are old,' said the youth, 'as I mentioned before,
  And have grown most uncommonly fat;
Yet you turned a back-somersault in at the door—
  Pray, what is the reason of that?'

'In my youth,' said the sage, as he shook his grey locks,
  'I kept all my limbs very supple
By the use of this ointment—one shilling the box—
  Allow me to sell you a couple?'

'You are old,' said the youth, 'and your jaws are too weak
  For anything tougher than suet;
Yet you finished the goose, with the bones and the beak—
  Pray, how did you manage to do it?'

'In my youth,' said his father, 'I took to the law,
And argued each case with my wife;
And the muscular strength, which it gave to my jaw,
Has lasted the rest of my life.'

'You are old,' said the youth, 'one would hardly suppose
That your eye was as steady as ever;
Yet you balanced an eel on the end of your nose—
What made you so awfully clever?'

'I have answered three questions, and that is enough,'
Said his father. 'Don't give yourself airs!
Do you think I can listen all day to such stuff?
Be off, or I'll kick you downstairs!'

219 *The Lobster Quadrille*

'WILL you walk a little faster?' said a whiting to a snail.
'There's a porpoise close behind us, and he's treading on my tail.
See how eagerly the lobsters and the turtles all advance!
They are waiting on the shingle—will you come and join the dance?
Will you, won't you, will you, won't you, will you join the dance?
Will you, won't you, will you, won't you, won't you join the dance?

'You can really have no notion how delightful it will be,
When they take us up and throw us, with the lobsters, out to sea!'
But the snail replied 'Too far, too far!' and gave a look askance—
Said he thanked the whiting kindly, but he would not join the dance.
Would not, could not, would not, could not, would not join the dance.
Would not, could not, would not, could not, could not join the dance.

'What matters it how far we go?' his scaly friend replied.
'There is another shore, you know, upon the other side.
The further off from England the nearer is to France—
Then turn not pale, beloved snail, but come and join the dance.
Will you, won't you, will you, won't you, will you join the dance?
Will you, won't you, will you, won't you, won't you join the dance?'

220 *The Lobster*

'TIS the voice of the Lobster: I heard him declare,
'You have baked me too brown, I must sugar my hair.'
As a duck with its eyelids, so he with his nose
Trims his belt and his buttons, and turns out his toes.

I passed by his garden, and marked, with one eye,
How the Owl and the Oyster were sharing a pie;
While the Duck and the Dodo, the Lizard and Cat,
Were swimming in milk round the brim of a hat.

221 *Jabberwocky*

'TWAS brillig, and the slithy toves
Did gyre and gimble in the wabe:
All mimsy were the borogoves,
And the mome raths outgrabe.

'Beware the Jabberwock, my son!
The jaws that bite, the claws that catch!
Beware the Jubjub bird, and shun
The frumious Bandersnatch!'

He took his vorpal sword in hand:
Long time the manxome foe he sought—
So rested he by the Tumtum tree,
And stood awhile in thought.

And as in uffish thought he stood,
The Jabberwock, with eyes of flame,
Came whiffling through the tulgey wood,
And burbled as it came!

One, two! One, two! And through and through
The vorpal blade went snicker-snack!
He left it dead, and with its head
He went galumphing back.

'And hast thou slain the Jabberwock?
Come to my arms, my beamish boy!
O frabjous day! Callooh! Callay!'
He chortled in his joy.

'Twas brillig, and the slithy toves
Did gyre and gimble in the wabe:
All mimsy were the borogoves,
And the mome raths outgrabe.

222 *The Walrus and the Carpenter*

THE sun was shining on the sea,
Shining with all his might:
He did his very best to make
The billows smooth and bright—
And this was odd, because it was
The middle of the night.

The moon was shining sulkily,
Because she thought the sun
Had got no business to be there
After the day was done—
'It's very rude of him,' she said,
'To come and spoil the fun!'

The sea was wet as wet could be,
  The sands were dry as dry.
You could not see a cloud, because
  No cloud was in the sky:
No birds were flying overhead—
  There were no birds to fly.

The Walrus and the Carpenter
  Were walking close at hand;
They wept like anything to see
  Such quantities of sand:
'If this were only cleared away,'
  They said, 'it *would* be grand!'

'If seven maids with seven mops
  Swept it for half a year,
Do you suppose,' the Walrus said,
  'That they could get it clear?'
'I doubt it,' said the Carpenter,
  And shed a bitter tear.

'O Oysters, come and walk with us!'
  The Walrus did beseech.
'A pleasant walk, a pleasant talk,
  Along the briny beach:
We cannot do with more than four,
  To give a hand to each.'

The eldest Oyster looked at him,
  But never a word he said:
The eldest Oyster winked his eye,
  And shook his heavy head—
Meaning to say he did not choose
  To leave the oyster-bed.

But four young Oysters hurried up,
  All eager for the treat:
Their coats were brushed, their faces washed,
  Their shoes were clean and neat—
And this was odd, because, you know,
  They hadn't any feet.

Four other Oysters followed them,
  And yet another four;
And thick and fast they came at last,
  And more, and more, and more—
All hopping through the frothy waves,
  And scrambling to the shore.

The Walrus and the Carpenter
  Walked on a mile or so,
And then they rested on a rock
  Conveniently low:
And all the little Oysters stood
  And waited in a row.

'The time has come,' the Walrus said,
  'To talk of many things:
Of shoes—and ships—and sealing-wax—
  Of cabbages—and kings—
And why the sea is boiling hot—
  And whether pigs have wings.'

'But wait a bit,' the Oysters cried,
  'Before we have our chat;
For some of us are out of breath,
  And all of us are fat!'
'No hurry!' said the Carpenter.
  They thanked him much for that.

'A loaf of bread,' the Walrus said,
  'Is what we chiefly need:
Pepper and vinegar besides
  Are very good indeed—
Now if you're ready, Oysters dear,
  We can begin to feed.'

'But not on us!' the Oysters cried,
  Turning a little blue.
'After such kindness, that would be
  A dismal thing to do!'
'The night is fine,' the Walrus said,
  'Do you admire the view?

'It was so kind of you to come!
  And you are very nice!'
The Carpenter said nothing but
  'Cut us another slice:
I wish you were not quite so deaf—
  I've had to ask you twice!'

'It seems a shame,' the Walrus said,
  'To play them such a trick,
After we've brought them out so far,
  And made them trot so quick!'
The Carpenter said nothing but
  'The butter's spread too thick!'

'I weep for you,' the Walrus said:
  'I deeply sympathize.'
With sobs and tears he sorted out
  Those of the largest size,
Holding his pocket-handkerchief
  Before his streaming eyes.

'O Oysters,' said the Carpenter,
  'You've had a pleasant run!
Shall we be trotting home again?'
  But answer came there none—
And this was scarcely odd, because
  They'd eaten every one.

223 *Humpty Dumpty's Song*

IN winter, when the fields are white,
I sing this song for your delight.

In spring, when woods are getting green,
I'll try and tell you what I mean.

In summer, when the days are long,
Perhaps you'll understand the song.

In autumn, when the leaves are brown,
Take pen and ink, and write it down.

I sent a message to the fish:
I told them 'This is what I wish.'

The little fishes of the sea,
They sent an answer back to me.

The little fishes' answer was
'We cannot do it, Sir, because—'

I sent to them again to say
'It will be better to obey.'

The fishes answered, with a grin,
'Why, what a temper you are in!'

I told them once, I told them twice:
They would not listen to advice.

I took a kettle large and new,
Fit for the deed I had to do.

My heart went hop, my heart went thump:
I filled the kettle at the pump.

Then someone came to me and said
'The little fishes are in bed.'

I said to him, I said it plain,
'Then you must wake them up again.'

I said it very loud and clear:
I went and shouted in his ear.

But he was very stiff and proud:
He said 'You needn't shout so loud!'

And he was very proud and stiff:
He said 'I'd go and wake them, if—'

I took a corkscrew from the shelf:
I went to wake them up myself.

And when I found the door was locked,
I pulled and pushed and kicked and knocked.

And when I found the door was shut,
I tried to turn the handle, but—

224 *The Aged Aged Man*

I'LL tell thee everything I can:
  There's little to relate.
I saw an aged aged man,
  A-sitting on a gate.
'Who are you, aged man?' I said.
  'And how is it you live?'
And his answer trickled through my head
  Like water through a sieve.

He said 'I look for butterflies
  That sleep among the wheat:
I make them into mutton pies,
  And sell them in the street.
I sell them unto men,' he said,
  'Who sail on stormy seas;
And that's the way I get my bread—
  A trifle, if you please.'

But I was thinking of a plan
  To dye one's whiskers green,
And always use so large a fan
  That they could not be seen.
So, having no reply to give
  To what the old man said,
I cried 'Come, tell me how you live!'
  And thumped him on the head.

His accents mild took up the tale:
 He said 'I go my ways,
And when I find a mountain-rill,
 I set it in a blaze;
And thence they make a stuff they call
 Rowland's Macassar Oil—
Yet twopence-halfpenny is all
 They give me for my toil.'

But I was thinking of a way
 To feed oneself on batter,
And so go on from day to day
 Getting a little fatter.
I shook him well from side to side,
 Until his face was blue:
'Come, tell me how you live,' I cried,
 'And what it is you do!'

He said 'I hunt for haddocks' eyes
 Among the heather bright,
And work them into waistcoat-buttons
 In the silent night.
And these I do not sell for gold
 Or coin of silvery shine,
But for a copper halfpenny,
 And that will purchase nine.

'I sometimes dig for buttered rolls,
 Or set limed twigs for crabs;
I sometimes search the grassy knolls
 For wheels of Hansom-cabs.
And that's the way' (he gave a wink)
 'By which I get my wealth—
And very gladly will I drink
 Your Honour's noble health.'

I heard him then, for I had just
  Completed my design
To keep the Menai bridge from rust
  By boiling it in wine.
I thanked him much for telling me
  The way he got his wealth,
But chiefly for his wish that he
  Might drink my noble health.

And now, if e'er by chance I put
  My fingers into glue,
Or madly squeeze a right-hand foot
  Into a left-hand shoe,
Or if I drop upon my toe
  A very heavy weight,
I weep, for it reminds me so
Of that old man I used to know—
Whose look was mild, whose speech was slow,
Whose hair was whiter than the snow,
Whose face was very like a crow,
With eyes, like cinders, all aglow,
Who seemed distracted with his woe,
Who rocked his body to and fro,
And muttered mumblingly and low,
As if his mouth were full of dough,
Who snorted like a buffalo—
That summer evening long ago,
  A-sitting on a gate.

225 *The Mad Gardener's Song*

He thought he saw an Elephant,
  That practised on a fife:
He looked again, and found it was
  A letter from his wife.
'At length I realise,' he said,
  'The bitterness of Life!'

He thought he saw a Buffalo
  Upon the chimney-piece:
He looked again, and found it was
  His Sister's Husband's Niece.
'Unless you leave this house,' he said,
  'I'll send for the Police!'

He thought he saw a Rattlesnake
  That questioned him in Greek:
He looked again, and found it was
  The Middle of Next Week.
'The one thing I regret,' he said,
  'Is that it cannot speak!'

He thought he saw a Banker's Clerk
  Descending from the bus:
He looked again, and found it was
  A Hippopotamus:
'If this should stay to dine,' he said,
  'There won't be much for us!'

He thought he saw a Kangaroo
  That worked a coffee-mill:
He looked again, and found it was
  A Vegetable-Pill.
'Were I to swallow this,' he said,
  'I should be very ill!'

He thought he saw a Coach-and-Four
  That stood beside his bed:
He looked again, and found it was
  A Bear without a Head.
'Poor thing,' he said, 'poor silly thing!
  It's waiting to be fed!'

He thought he saw an Albatross
  That fluttered round the lamp:
He looked again, and found it was
  A Penny-Postage-Stamp.
'You'd best be getting home,' he said:
  'The nights are very damp!'

He thought he saw a Garden-Door
  That opened with a key:
He looked again, and found it was
  A Double Rule of Three:
'And all its mystery,' he said,
  'Is clear as day to me!'

He thought he saw an Argument
  That proved he was the Pope:
He looked again, and found it was
  A Bar of Mottled Soap.
'A fact so dread,' he faintly said,
  'Extinguishes all hope!'

MENELLA BUTE SMEDLEY

1820–1877

226 *A North Pole Story*

Up where the world grows cold,
  Under the sharp North star,
The wrinkled ice is very old,
  And the life of man is far;
None to see when the fog falls white,
  And none to shiver and hear
How wild the bears are in the night,
  Which lasts for half a year.

The wind may blow as it will,
  But it cannot shake a tree,
Nor stir the waves which lie so still—
  It is the corpse of a sea!
The sun comes out over flowerless strands
  Where only ice-tears flow,
When the pale North weeps for sweet woodlands
  Which she must never know.

Earth speaks with awful lips:
  'No place for man is here!
Between my bergs I'll crush your ships,
  If you will come too near;
You shall be slain by bitter wind,
  Or starved on barren shore,
My cruel snow shall strike you blind;
  Go—trouble me no more!'

But British men are fain
  To venture on and through,
And when you tell them to refrain,
  They set themselves to do;
Into the secrets of the snow
  They hurry and they press,
And answer Nature's coldest 'No'
  With a great shout of 'Yes'.

It was a little band
  Went on that dangerous track,
To take a message from our land
  And to bring an answer back;
The frost had bound their good ship tight,
  And years were come and gone,
When a few brave hearts, as best they might,
  Went over the shores alone.

And as one strode so bold,
  He saw a sight of fear—
Nine white wolves came over the wold,
  And they were watching a deer;
By three and by two and by one
  A cunning half-moon they made,
They glanced at each other and did not run,
  But crept like creatures afraid.

They knew what they were about,
  And the poor thing knew it too,
It turned its head like a child in doubt,
  And shrank, and backward drew;
But whether it looked to left or right
  It met a savage eye,
And the man stood still and saw the sight,
  And felt that it must die.

Backward, trembling and fast,
  And onward, crafty and slow,
And over the cliff's sheer edge at last,
  And crash on the ice below;
But then with a whirl and a plunge and a whoop,
  The wolves are down the hill;
They break their ranks, that wild white troop,
  When it is time to kill.

And days and nights went past,
  And the men grew weary and pale,
Scanty food and freezing blast,
  And hearts beginning to fail.
The wanderer knew his steps were slow,
  And his eyes were languid and dim,
When nine white wolves came over the snow,
  And they were watching—him.

He saw them gather and glance,
  And he remembered the deer.
He saw them frame their cunning advance,
  And he felt a little fear.
But never a hair's breadth did he swerve,
  Nor lower his looks a whit,
He faced the cruel scimitar-curve,
  And then walked up to it!

There is never a beast so strong
  As to bear a brave man's eye.
They crouched; they looked as if nothing was wrong;
  And then they turned to fly.
The man stood still and drew his breath,
  When he saw the scattering ranks;
He had been face to face with death:
  I hope he uttered thanks.

There's a fireside far away,
  A little anxious now,
Where a man shall sit one joyful day,
  And tell of the world of snow;
And tell of the wolves who sup so grim,
  And leave no bone behind;
And how they meant to sup on him,
  But looked, and changed their mind!

JULIANA HORATIA EWING

1841–1885

227 *The Burial of the Linnet*

FOUND in the garden—dead in his beauty.
  Ah, that a linnet should die in the spring!
Bury him, comrades, in pitiful duty,
  Muffle the dinner bell, solemnly ring.

Bury him kindly—up in the corner;
  Bird, beast, and goldfish are sepulchred there.
Bid the black kitten march as chief mourner,
  Waving her tail like a plume in the air.

Bury him nobly—next to the donkey;
  Fetch the old banner, and wave it about.
Bury him deeply—think of the monkey,
  Shallow his grave, and the dogs got him out.

Bury him softly—white wool around him,
  Kiss his poor feathers—the first kiss and last;
Tell his poor widow kind friends have found him:
  Plant his poor grave with whatever grows fast.

Farewell, sweet singer! dead in thy beauty,
  Silent through summer, though other birds sing.
Bury him, comrades, in pitiful duty,
  Muffle the dinner bell, mournfully ring.

228 *The Willow-Man*

THERE once was a Willow, and he was very old,
And all his leaves fell off from him, and left him in the cold;
But ere the rude winter could buffet him with snow,
There grew upon his hoary head a crop of mistletoe.

All wrinkled and furrowed was this old Willow's skin,
His taper fingers trembled, and his arms were very thin;
Two round eyes and hollow, that stared but did not see,
And sprawling feet that never walked, had this most ancient tree

A dame who dwelt near was the only one who knew
That every year upon his head the Christmas berries grew;
And when the dame cut them, she said—it was her whim—
'A merry Christmas to you, sir!' *and left a bit for him.*

'Oh, Granny dear, tell us,' the children cried, 'where we
May find the shining mistletoe that grows upon the tree?'
At length the dame told them, but cautioned them to mind
To greet the Willow civilly, *and leave a bit behind.*

'Who cares,' said the children, 'for this old Willow-man?
We'll take the mistletoe, and he may catch us if he can.'
With rage the ancient Willow shakes in every limb,
For they have taken all, and *have not left a bit for him*!

Then bright gleamed the holly, the Christmas berries shone,
But in the wintry wind without the Willow-man did moan:
'Ungrateful, and wasteful! the mystic mistletoe
A hundred years hath grown on me, but never more shall grow.'

A year soon passed by, and the children came once more,
But not a spring of mistletoe the aged Willow bore.
Each slender spray pointed; he mocked them in his glee,
And chuckled in his wooden heart, that ancient Willow tree.

229 *A Friend in the Garden*

HE is not John the gardener,
And yet the whole day long
Employs himself most usefully,
The flower beds among.

He is not Tom the pussy cat,
And yet the other day,
With stealthy stride and glistening eye,
He crept upon his prey.

He is not Dash the dear old dog,
And yet, perhaps, if you
Took pains with him and petted him,
You'd come to love him too.

He's not a blackbird, though he chirps,
And though he once was black;
And now he wears a loose grey coat,
All wrinkled on the back.

He's got a very dirty face,
And very shining eyes;
He sometimes comes and sits indoors;
He looks—and p'r'aps is—wise.

But in a sunny flower bed
He has a fixed abode;
He eats the things that eat my plants—
He is a friendly TOAD.

230 *The Dolls' Wash*

SALLY is the laundress, and every Saturday
She sends our clean clothes up from the wash, and Nurse puts them away.
Sometimes Sally is very kind, but sometimes she's as cross as a Turk;
When she's good-humoured we like to go and watch her at work.
She has tubs and a copper in the wash-house, and a great big fire and plenty of soap;
And outside is the drying-ground with tall posts, and pegs bought from the gipsies, and long lines of rope.
The laundry is indoors with another big fire, and long tables, and a lot of irons, and a crimping-machine;
And horses (not live ones with tails, but *clothes*-horses), and the same starch that is used by the Queen.
Sally wears pattens in the wash-house, and turns up her sleeves, and splashes, and rubs,
And makes beautiful white lather which foams over the tops of the tubs.
Like waves at the seaside dashing against the rocks, only not so strong.
If I were Sally I should sit and blow soap-bubbles all the day long.
Sally is angry sometimes because of the way we dirty our frocks,
Making mud pies, and rolling down the lawn, and climbing trees, and scrambling over the rocks.
She says we do it on purpose, and never try to take care;
But if things have got to go to the wash what can it matter how dirty they are?
Last week Mary and I got a lot of kingcups from the bog, and I carried them home in my skirt;
It was the end of the week, and our frocks were done, so we didn't mind about the dirt.
But Sally was as cross as two sticks, and won't wash our dolls' clothes any more—so she said—

pattens, **wooden soles with iron heighteners, strapped to the shoes to raise them out of the wet**

But never mind, for we'll ask Mamma if we may have a real
Dolls' Wash of our own instead.

Mamma says we may on one condition, to which we agree,
We're to *really* wash the dolls' clothes, and make them just what
clean clothes should be.
She says we must wash them thoroughly, which of course we
intend to do;
We mean to rub, wring, dry, mangle, starch, iron, and air them
too.
A regular wash must be splendid fun, and everybody knows
That anyone in the world can wash out a few dirty clothes.

Well, we've had the Dolls' Wash, but it's only pretty good fun.
We're glad we've had it, you know, but we're gladder still that
it's done.
As we wanted to have as big a wash as we could, we collected
everything we could muster,
From the dolls' bed dimity hangings to Victoria's dress, which
I'd used as a duster.
It was going to the wash, and Mary and I were housemaids—
fancy housemaids I mean—
And I took it to dust the bookshelf, for I knew it would come
back clean.
Well, we washed in the wash-hand basin, which holds a good
deal, as the things are small;
We made a glorious lather, and splashed half over the floor; but
the clothes weren't white after all.
However, we hung them out in our drying-ground in the garden,
which we made with dahlia-sticks and long strings,
And then Dash went and knocked over one of the posts, and
down in the dirt went our things!
So we washed them again and hung them on the towel-horse, and
most of them came all right,
But Victoria's muslin dress—though I rinsed it three times—
will never dry white!
And the grease spots on Mary's doll's dress don't seem to come
out, and we can't think how they got there;

Unless it was when we bought that Macassar oil, because she has real hair.
I knew mine was going to the wash, but I'm sorry I used it as a duster before it went;
We think dirty clothes perhaps shouldn't be *too* dirty before they are sent.
We had sad work in trying to make the starch—I wonder what the Queen does with hers?
I stirred mine up with a candle, like Sally, but it only made it worse.
So we had to ask Mamma's leave to have ours made by Nurse.
Nurse makes beautiful starch—like water-arrowroot when you're ill—in a minute or two.
It's a very odd thing that what looks so easy should be so difficult to do!
Then Mary put the iron down to heat, but as soon as she'd turned her back
A jet of gas came spluttering out of the coals and smoked it black.
We dared not ask Sally for another, for we knew she'd refuse it,
So we had to clean this one with sand and brown paper before we could use it.
It was very hard work, but I rubbed till I made it shine;
Yet as soon as it got on a damped 'fine thing' it left a brown line.
I rubbed for a long, long time before it would iron without a mark,
But it did at last, and we finished our Dolls' Wash just before dark.

Sally's very kind, for she praised our wash, and she's taken away
Victoria's dress to do it again; and I really must say
She was right when she said, 'You see, young ladies, a week's wash isn't all play.'
Our backs ache, our faces are red, our hands are all wrinkled, and we've rubbed our fingers quite sore;
We feel very sorry for Sally every week, and we don't mean to dirty our dresses so much any more.

231 *Garden Lore*

EVERY child who has gardening tools,
Should learn by heart these gardening rules:

He who owns a gardening spade,
Should be able to dig the depth of its blade.

He who owns a gardening rake,
Should know what to leave and what to take.

He who owns a gardening hoe,
Must be sure how he means his strokes to go.

But he who owns a gardening fork,
May make it do all the other tools' work

Though to shift, or to pot, or annex what you can,
A trowel's the tool for child, woman, or man.

'Twas the bird that sits in the medlar-tree,
Who sang these gardening saws to me.

JOHN TOWNSEND TROWBRIDGE

1827–1916

232 *Darius Green and his Flying-Machine*

IF ever there lived a Yankee lad,
Wise or otherwise, good or bad,
Who, seeing the birds fly, didn't jump
With flapping arms from stake or stump,
        Or, spreading the tail
        Of his coat for a sail,
Take a soaring leap from post or rail,
        And wonder why
        He couldn't fly,
And flap and flutter and wish and try—

If ever you knew a country dunce
Who didn't try that as often as once,
All I can say is, that's a sign
He never would do for a hero of mine.

An aspiring genius was D. Green:
The son of a farmer, age fourteen;
His body was long and lank and lean,
Just right for flying, as will be seen;
He had two eyes each bright as a bean,
And a freckled nose that grew between,
A little awry—for I must mention
That he had riveted his attention
Upon his wonderful invention,
Twisting his tongue as he twisted the strings,
And working his face as he worked the wings,
And with every turn of gimlet and screw
Turning and screwing his mouth round too,
        Till his nose seemed bent
        To catch the scent,
Around some corner, of new-baked pies,
And his wrinkled cheeks and his squinting eyes
Grew puckered into a queer grimace,
That made him look very droll in the face,
        And also very wise.

And wise he must have been, to do more
Than ever a genius did before,
Excepting Daedalus of yore
And his son Icarus, who wore
        Upon their backs
        Those wings of wax
He had read of in the old almanacs.
Darius was clearly of the opinion
That the air is also man's dominion,
And that, with paddle or fin or pinion,
        We soon or late
        Shall navigate

The azure as now we sail the sea.
The thing looks simple enough to me;
        And if you doubt it,
Hear how Darius reasoned about it.

        'Birds can fly,
        An' why can't I?
        Must we give in,'
        Says he with a grin,
        'That the bluebird an' phoebe
        Are smarter 'n we be?
Jest fold our hands an' see the swaller
An' blackbird an' catbird beat us holler?
Doos the little chatterin', sassy wren,
No bigger 'n my thumb, know more than men?
        Jest show me that!
        Er prove 't the bat
Hez got more brains than's in my hat,
An' I'll back down, an' not till then!'

He argued further: 'Ner I can't see
What's th' use o' wings to a bumble-bee,
Fer to git a livin' with, more 'n to me:
        Ain't my business
        Important 's his'n is?

        'That Icarus
        Made a perty muss,
Him an' his daddy Daedalus.
They might a knowed wings made o' wax
Wouldn't stand sun-heat an' hard whacks.
        I'll make mine o' luther,
        Er suthin' er other.'

And he said to himself, as he tinkered and planned:
'But I ain't goin' to show my hand
To nummies that never can understand
The fust idee that's big an' grand.
They'd a laft an' made fun
O' Creation itself afore't was done!'

catbird, black-capped thrush   *nummies*, numskulls

So he kept his secret from all the rest,
Safely buttoned within his vest;
And in the loft above the shed
Himself he locks, with thimble and thread
And wax and hammer and buckles and screws,
And all such things as geniuses use;
Two bats for patterns, curious fellows!
A charcoal-pot and a pair of bellows;
An old hoop-skirt or two, as well as
Some wire, and several old umbrellas;
A carriage-cover, for tail and wings;
A piece of harness; and straps and strings;
        And a big strong box,
        In which he locks
These and a hundred other things.

His grinning brothers, Reuben and Burke
And Nathan and Jotham and Solomon, lurk
Around the corner to see him work,
Sitting cross-legged, like a Turk,
Drawing the waxed end through with a jerk,
And boring the holes with a comical quirk
Of his wise old head, and a knowing smirk.
But vainly they mounted each other's backs,
And poked through knot-holes and pried through cracks;
With wood from the pile and straw from the stacks
He plugged the knot-holes and caulked the cracks;
And a bucket of water, which one would think
He had brought up into the loft to drink
        When he chanced to be dry,
        Stood always nigh,
        For Darius was sly!
And whenever at work he happened to spy
At chink or crevice a blinking eye,
He let a dipper of water fly.
'Take that! an' ef ever ye git a peep,
Guess ye'll ketch a weasel asleep!'
        And he sings as he locks
        His big strong box:

Song

'The weasel's head is small an' trim,
An' he is little an' long an' slim,
An' quick of motion an' nimble of limb,
An' ef you'll be
Advised by me,
Keep wide awake when ye're ketchin' him!'

So day after day
He stitched and tinkered and hammered away,
Till at last 'twas done—
The greatest invention under the sun!
'An' now,' says Darius, 'hooray fer some fun!'

'Twas the Fourth of July,
And the weather was dry,
And not a cloud was on all the sky,
Save a few light fleeces, which here and there,
Half mist, half air,
Like foam on the ocean went floating by:
Just as lovely a morning as ever was seen
For a nice little trip in a flying-machine.

Thought cunning Darius: 'Now I shan't go
Along with the fellers to see the show.
I'll say I've got sich a terrible cough!
An' then, when the folks 'ave all gone off,
I'll hev full swing
Fer to try the thing,
An' practise a little on the wing.'

'Ain't goin' to see the celebration?'
Says brother Nate. 'No, botheration!
I've got sich a cold—a toothache—I—
My gracious!—feel's though I should fly!'
Said Jotham, ''Sho!
Guess ye better go.'
But Darius said, 'No!

Shouldn't wonder ef you might see me, though,
'Long 'bout noon, ef I git red
O' this jumpin', thumpin' pain in my head.'
For all the while to himself he said:

'I tell ye what!
I'll fly a few times around the lot,
To see how't seems, then soon's I've got
The hang o' the thing, ez likely's not,
I'll astonish the nation,
An' all creation,
By flyin' over the celebration!
Over their heads I'll sail like an eagle;
I'll balance myself on my wings like a seagull;
I'll dance on the chimbleys; I'll stand on the steeple;
I'll flop up to winders an' scare the people!
I'll light on the liberty-pole, an' crow;
An' I'll say to the gawpin' fools below,
"What world's this 'ere
That I've come near?"
Fer I'll make 'em believe I'm a chap from the moon;
An' I'll try a race with their ol' balloon!'

He crept from his bed;
And, seeing the others were gone, he said,
'I'm a gittin' over the cold in my head.'
And away he sped,
To open the wonderful box in the shed.

His brothers had walked but a little way
When Jotham to Nathan chanced to say,
'What is the feller up to, hey?'
'Don'no—there's suthin' er other to pay,
Er he wouldn't a stayed to hum today.'
Says Burke, 'His toothache's all in his eye!
He never'd miss a Fo'th-o'-July,
Ef he hedn't got some machine to try.'

to hum, at home

Then Sol, the little one, spoke: 'By darn!
Let's hurry back an' hide in the barn,
An' pay him fer tellin' us that yarn!'
'Agreed!' Through the orchard they creep back,
Along by the fences, behind the stack,
And one by one, through a hole in the wall,
In under the dusty barn they crawl,
Dressed in their Sunday garments all;
And a very astonishing sight was that,
When each in his cobwebbed coat and hat
Came up through the floor like an ancient rat.
        And there they hid;
        And Reuben slid
The fastenings back, and the door undid.
        'Keep dark!' said he,
'While I squint an' see what there is to see.'

As knights of old put on their mail—
        From head to foot
        An iron suit,
Iron jacket and iron boot,
Iron breeches, and on the head
No hat, but an iron pot instead,
        And under the chin the bail
(I believe they called the thing a helm),
Then sallied forth to overwhelm
The dragons and pagans that plagued the realm—
        So this modern knight
        Prepared for flight,
Put on his wings and strapped them tight,
Jointed and jaunty, strong and light;
Buckled them fast to shoulder and hip—
Ten feet they measured from tip to tip!
And a helm had he, but that he wore,
Not on his head like those of yore,
        But more like the helm of a ship.

bail, handle

'Hush!' Reuben said,
'He's up in the shed!
He's opened the winder—I see his head!
He stretches it out,
An' pokes it about,
Lookin' to see ef the coast is clear,
An' nobody near—
Guess he don'no who's hid in here!—
He's riggin' a spring-board over the sill!
Stop laffin', Solomon! Burke, keep still!
He's a climbin' out now—Of all the things!
What's he got on? I van, it's wings!
An' that t'other thing? I vum, it's a tail!
An' there he sets like a hawk on a rail!
Steppin' careful, he travels the length
Of his spring-board, and teeters to try its strength.
Now he stretches his wings, like a monstrous bat;
Peeks over his shoulder, this way an' that,
Fer to see ef there's anyone passin' by;
But there's on'y a calf an' a goslin' nigh.
They turn up at him a wonderin' eye,
To see—The dragon! he's goin' to fly!
Away he goes! Jimminy! what a jump!
Flop—flop—an' plump
To the ground with a thump!
Flutt'rin' an' flound'rin', all in a lump!'

As a demon is hurled by an angel's spear,
Heels over head, to his proper sphere—
Heels over head, and head over heels,
Dizzily down the abyss he wheels—
So fell Darius. Upon his crown,
In the midst of the barnyard, he came down,
In a wonderful whirl of tangled strings,
Broken braces and broken springs,
Broken tail and broken wings,
Shooting-stars, and various things!

Away with a bellow fled the calf,
And what was that? Did the gosling laugh?
'Tis a merry roar
From the old barn-door,
And he hears the voice of Jotham crying,
'Say, D'rius! how de you like flyin'?'

Slowly, ruefully, where he lay,
Darius just turned and looked that way,
As he staunched his sorrowful nose with his cuff.
'Wal, I like flyin' well enough,'
He said, 'but there ain't sich a thunderin' sight
O' fun in it when ye come to light.'

Moral

I just have room for the moral here,
And this is the moral: Stick to your sphere.
Or if you insist, as you have the right,
On spreading your wings for a loftier flight,
The moral is—Take care how you light.

ELIZABETH ANNA HART

1822–1888?

233 *Mother Tabbyskins*

SITTING at a window
In her cloak and hat,
I saw Mother Tabbyskins,
The *real* old cat!
Very old, very old,
Crumplety and lame;
Teaching kittens how to scold—
Is it not a shame?

Kittens in the garden
Looking in her face,
Learning how to spit and swear—
Oh, what a disgrace!
Very wrong, very wrong,
Very wrong and bad;
Such a subject for our song,
Makes us all too sad.

Old Mother Tabbyskins,
Sticking out her head,
Gave a howl, and then a yowl,
Hobbled off to bed.
Very sick, very sick,
Very savage, too;
Pray send for a doctor quick—
Any one will do!

Doctor Mouse came creeping,
Creeping to her bed;
Lanced her gums and felt her pulse,
Whispered she was dead.
Very sly, very sly,
The *real* old cat
Open kept her weather eye—
Mouse! beware of that!

Old Mother Tabbyskins,
Saying 'Serves him right',
Gobbled up the doctor, with
Infinite delight.
Very fast, very fast,
Very pleasant, too—
'What a pity it can't last!
Bring another, do!'

Doctor Dog comes running,
Just to see her begs;
Round his neck a comforter,
Trousers on his legs.
Very grand, very grand—
Golden-headed cane
Swinging gaily from his hand,
Mischief in his brain!

'Dear Mother Tabbyskins,
And how are you now?
Let me feel your pulse—so, so;
Show your tongue—bow, wow!
Very ill, very ill,
Please attempt to purr;
Will you take a draught or pill?
Which do you prefer?'

Ah, Mother Tabbyskins,
Who is now afraid?
Of poor little Doctor Mouse
You a mouthful made.
Very nice, very nice
Little doctor he;
But for Doctor Dog's advice
You must pay the fee.

Doctor Dog comes nearer,
Says she must be bled;
I heard Mother Tabbyskins
Screaming in her bed.
Very near, very near,
Scuffling out and in;
Doctor Dog looks full and queer—
Where is Tabbyskin?

I will tell the Moral
Without any fuss:
Those who lead the young astray
Always suffer thus.
Very nice, very nice,
Let our conduct be;
For all doctors are not mice,
Some are dogs, you see!

JEAN INGELOW

1820–1897

234 *One Morning, Oh, so Early!*

ONE morning, oh, so early! my belovèd, my belovèd,
All the birds were singing blithely, as if they would never cease;
'Twas a thrush sang in my garden, 'Hear the story, hear the story!'
And the lark sang, 'Give us glory!'
And the dove said, 'Give us peace!'

Then I listened, oh, so early! my belovèd, my belovèd,
To that murmur from the woodland of the dove, my dear, the dove;
When the nightingale came after, 'Give us fame to sweeten duty!'
When the wren sang, 'Give us beauty!'
She made answer, 'Give us love!'

Sweet is spring, and sweet the morning, my belovèd, my belovèd;
Now for us doth spring, doth morning, wait upon the year's increase,
And my prayer goes up, 'Oh, give us, crowned in youth with marriage glory,
Give for all our life's dear story,
Give us love, and give us peace!'

JOHN GREENLEAF WHITTIER

1807–1892

235 *In School-Days*

STILL sits the school-house by the road,
  A ragged beggar sleeping;
Around it still the sumachs grow,
  And blackberry vines are creeping.

Within, the master's desk is seen,
  Deep scarred by raps official;
The warping floor, the battered seats,
  The jack-knife's carved initial;

The charcoal frescoes on its wall;
  Its door's worn sill, betraying
The feet that, creeping slow to school,
  Went storming out to playing!

Long years ago a winter sun
  Shone over it at setting;
Lit up its western window-panes,
  And low eaves' icy fretting.

It touched the tangled golden curls,
  And brown eyes full of grieving,
Of one who still her steps delayed
  When all the school were leaving.

For near her stood the little boy
  Her childish favour singled:
His cap pulled low upon a face
  Where pride and shame were mingled.

Pushing with restless feet the snow
  To right and left, he lingered—
As restlessly her tiny hands
  The blue-checked apron fingered.

***sumach*, a species of small tree**

He saw her lift her eyes; he felt
  The soft hand's light caressing,
And heard the tremble of her voice,
  As if a fault confessing.

'I'm sorry that I spelt the word:
  I hate to go above you,
Because'—the brown eyes lower fell—
  'Because, you see, I love you!'

Still memory to a grey-haired man
  That sweet child-face is showing.
Dear girl! the grasses on her grave
  Have forty years been growing.

He lives to learn, in life's hard school,
  How few who pass above him
Lament their triumph and his loss,
  Like her,—because they love him.

GEORGE MACDONALD

1824–1905

236 *Where did you come from, baby dear?*

WHERE did you come from, baby dear?
Out of the everywhere into here.

Where did you get your eyes so blue?
Out of the sky as I came through.

What makes the light in them sparkle and spin?
Some of the starry spikes left in.

Where did you get that little tear?
I found it waiting when I got here.

What makes your forehead so smooth and high?
A soft hand stroked it as I went by.

What makes your cheek like a warm white rose?
I saw something better than anyone knows.

Whence that three-cornered smile of bliss?
Three angels gave me at once a kiss.

Where did you get this pearly ear?
God spoke, and it came out to hear.

Where did you get those arms and hands?
Love made itself into hooks and bands.

Feet, whence did you come, you darling things?
From the same box as the cherubs' wings.

How did they all just come to be you?
God thought about me, and so I grew.

But how did you come to us, you dear?
God thought about you, and so I am here.

237

A Baby-Sermon

THE lightning and thunder
They go and they come;
But the stars and the stillness
Are always at home.

ALFRED SCOTT GATTY

1847–1918

238

The Three Little Pigs

A JOLLY old sow once lived in a sty,
And three little piggies had she,
And she waddled about saying 'Umph! umph! umph!'
While the little ones said 'Wee! wee!'

'My dear little brothers,' said one of the brats,
  'My dear little piggies,' said he;
'Let us all for the future say Umph! umph! umph!
  'Tis so childish to say Wee! wee!'

Then these little pigs grew skinny and lean,
  And lean they might very well be;
For somehow they *couldn't* say 'Umph! umph! umph!'
  And they *wouldn't* say 'Wee! wee! wee!'

So after a time these little pigs died,
  They all died of *felo de se*;
From trying too hard to say 'Umph! umph! umph!'
  When they only could say 'Wee! wee!'

Moral

A moral there is to this little song,
  A moral that's easy to see;
Don't try when you're young to say 'Umph! umph! umph!'
  For you only can say 'Wee! wee!'

felo de se, self-murder

JAMES FERGUSON

1842–*c.* 1910

239 *Auld Daddy Darkness*

AULD DADDY DARKNESS creeps frae his hole,
Black as a blackamoor, blin' as a mole;
Stir the fire till it lowes, let the bairnie sit,
Auld Daddy Darkness is no' wantit yet.

See him in the corners hidin' frae the licht,
See him at the window gloomin' at the nicht;
Turn up the gas licht, close the shutters a',
An' Auld Daddy Darkness will flee far awa'.

Awa' to hide the birdie within its cosy nest,
Awa' to hap the wee flooers on their mither's breast,
Awa' to loosen Gaffer Toil frae his daily ca',
For Auld Daddy Darkness is kindly to a'.

He comes when we're weary to wean's frae oor waes,
He comes when the bairnies are gettin' aff their claes,
To cover them sae cosy, an' bring bonnie dreams,
So Auld Daddy Darkness is better than he seems.

Shut yer een, my wee tot, ye'll see Daddy then;
He's in below the bed claes, to cuddle ye he's fain.
Noo nestle in his bosie, sleep an' dream yer fill,
Till Wee Davie Daylicht comes keekin' owre the hill.

CHRISTINA ROSSETTI

1830–1894

240 *A Crown of Windflowers*

'TWIST me a crown of windflowers
That I may fly away
To hear the singers at their song,
And players at their play.'

'Put on your crown of windflowers;
But whither would you go?'
'Beyond the surging of the sea
And the storms that blow.'

'Alas! your crown of windflowers
Can never make you fly;
I twist them in a crown today,
And tonight they die.'

241 *Comparisons*

HOPE is like a harebell trembling from its birth,
Love is like a rose the joy of all the earth;
Faith is like a lily lifted high and white,
Love is like a lovely rose the world's delight;
Harebells and sweet lilies show a thornless growth,
But the rose with all its thorns excels them both.

242 *Ferry me across the Water*

'FERRY me across the water,
Do, boatman, do.'
'If you've a penny in your purse
I'll ferry you.'

'I have a penny in my purse,
And my eyes are blue;
So ferry me across the water,
Do, boatman, do.'

'Step into my ferry-boat,
Be they black or blue,
And for the penny in your purse
I'll ferry you.'

243 *Flint*

AN emerald is as green as grass,
A ruby red as blood;
A sapphire shines as blue as heaven;
A flint lies in the mud.

A diamond is a brilliant stone,
To catch the world's desire;
An opal holds a fiery spark;
But a flint holds fire.

244 *Lady Moon*

O LADY MOON, your horns point toward the east:
Shine, be increased.
O Lady Moon, your horns point toward the west:
Wane, be at rest.

245 *The Wind*

WHO has seen the wind?
   Neither I nor you;
But when the leaves hang trembling
   The wind is passing through.

Who has seen the wind?
   Neither you nor I;
But when the trees bow down their heads
   The wind is passing by.

246 *What are Heavy?*

WHAT are heavy? Sea-sand and sorrow;
What are brief? Today and tomorrow;
What are frail? Spring blossoms and youth;
What are deep? The ocean and truth.

247 *The Rainbow*

BOATS sail on the rivers,
   And ships sail on the seas;
But clouds that sail across the sky
   Are prettier far than these.

There are bridges on the rivers,
   As pretty as you please;
But the bow that bridges heaven,
   And overtops the trees,
And builds a road from earth to sky,
   Is prettier far than these.

248

What does the Bee do?

WHAT does the bee do?
  Bring home honey.
And what does Father do?
  Bring home money.
And what does Mother do?
  Lay out the money.
And what does baby do?
  Eat up the honey.

249

A Riddle

THERE is one that has a head without an eye,
  And there's one that has an eye without a head.
You may find the answer if you try;
    And when all is said,
  Half the answer hangs upon a thread.

250

Caterpillar

BROWN and furry
Caterpillar in a hurry,
Take your walk
To the shady leaf, or stalk,
Or what not,
Which may be the chosen spot.
No toad spy you,
Hovering bird of prey pass by you;
Spin and die,
To live again a butterfly.

251 *Hope and Joy*

IF hope grew on a bush,
And joy grew on a tree,
What a nosegay for the plucking
There would be!
But oh, in windy autumn
When frail flowers wither,
What should we do for hope and joy,
Fading together?

252 *Last Rites*

DEAD in the cold, a song-singing thrush,
Dead at the foot of a snowberry bush—
Weave him a coffin of rush,
Dig him a grave where the soft mosses grow,
Raise him a tombstone of snow.

253 *What is Pink?*

WHAT is pink? A rose is pink
By the fountain's brink.
What is red? A poppy's red
In its barley bed.
What is blue? The sky is blue
Where the clouds float through.
What is white? A swan is white
Sailing in the light.
What is yellow? Pears are yellow,
Rich and ripe and mellow.
What is green? The grass is green,
With small flowers between.
What is violet? Clouds are violet
In the summer twilight.
What is orange? Why, an orange,
Just an orange!

CELIA THAXTER

1835–1894

254

The Sandpiper

ACROSS the lonely beach we flit,
   One little sandpiper and I;
And fast I gather, bit by bit,
   The scattered driftwood, bleached and dry.
The wild waves reach their hands for it,
   The wild wind raves, the tide runs high,
As up and down the beach we flit—
   One little sandpiper and I.

Above our heads the sullen clouds
   Scud black and swift across the sky;
Like silent ghosts in misty shrouds
   Stand out the white lighthouses high.
Almost as far as eye can reach
   I see the close-reefed vessels fly,
As fast we flit along the beach—
   One little sandpiper and I.

I watch him as he skims along
   Uttering his sweet and mournful cry;
He starts not at my fitful song
   Or flash of fluttering drapery.
He has no thought of any wrong,
   He scans me with a fearless eye;
Staunch friends are we, well-tried and strong,
   The little sandpiper and I.

Comrade, where wilt thou be tonight
   When the loosed storm breaks furiously?
My driftwood fire will burn so bright!
   To what warm shelter canst thou fly?
I do not fear for thee, though wroth
   The tempest rushes through the sky:
For are we not God's children both,
   Thou, little sandpiper, and I?

SUSAN COOLIDGE (SARAH CHAUNCEY WOOLSEY)

1835–1905

255

Measles in the Ark

THE night it was horribly dark,
The measles broke out in the Ark;
Little Japheth, and Shem, and all the young Hams,
Were screaming at once for potatoes and clams.
And 'What shall I do,' said poor Mrs. Noah,
'All alone by myself in this terrible shower?
I know what I'll do: I'll step down in the hold,
And wake up a lioness grim and old,
And tie her close to the children's door,
And give her a ginger-cake to roar
At the top of her voice for an hour or more;
And I'll tell the children to cease their din,
Or I'll let that grim old party in,
To stop their squeazles and likewise their measles.'
She practised this with the greatest success:
She was everyone's grandmother, I guess.

JAMES RUSSELL LOWELL

1819–1891

256

Birthday Verses
Written in a Child's Album

'TWAS sung of old in hut and hall
How once a king in evil hour
Hung musing o'er his castle wall,
And, lost in idle dreams, let fall
Into the sea his ring of power.

Then, let him sorrow as he might,
And pledge his daughter and his throne
To who restored the jewel bright,
The broken spell would ne'er unite;
The grim old ocean held his own.

Those awful powers on man that wait,
On man, the beggar or the king,
To hovel bare or hall of state
A magic ring that masters fate
With each succeeding birthday bring.

Therein are set four jewels rare:
Pearl winter, summer's ruby blaze,
Spring's emerald, and, than all more fair,
Fall's pensive opal, doomed to bear
A heart of fire bedreamed with haze.

To him the simple spell who knows
The spirits of the ring to sway,
Fresh power with every sunrise flows,
And royal pursuivants are those
That fly his mandates to obey.

But he that with a slackened will
Dreams of things past or things to be,
From him the charm is slipping still,
And drops, ere he suspect the ill,
Into the inexorable sea.

ELIZABETH T. CORBETT

fl. 1878

257 *Three Wise Old Women*

THREE wise old women were they, were they,
Who went to walk on a winter day:
One carried a basket to hold some berries,
One carried a ladder to climb for cherries,
The third, and she was the wisest one,
Carried a fan to keep off the sun.

But they went so far, and they went so fast,
They quite forgot their way at last,
So one of the wise women cried in a fright,
'Suppose we should meet a bear tonight!
Suppose he should eat me!' 'And me!!' 'And me!!!'
'What is to be done?' cried all the three.

'Dear, dear!' said one, 'we'll climb a tree,
There out of the way of the bears we'll be.'
But there wasn't a tree for miles around;
They were too frightened to stay on the ground,
So they climbed their ladder up to the top,
And sat there screaming 'We'll drop! We'll drop!'

But the wind was strong as wind could be,
And blew their ladder right out to sea;
So the three wise women were all afloat
In a leaky ladder instead of a boat,
And every time the waves rolled in,
Of course the poor things were wet to the skin.

Then they took their basket, the water to bale,
They put up their fan instead of a sail:
But what became of the wise women then,
Whether they ever sailed home again,
Whether they saw any bears, or no,
You must find out, for I don't know.

ANONYMOUS

c. 1879

258

Two Little Kittens

TWO little kittens, one stormy night,
Began to quarrel, and then to fight;
One had a mouse, the other had none,
And that's the way the quarrel begun.

'I'll have that mouse,' said the biggest cat;
'You'll have that mouse? We'll see about that!'
'I *will* have that mouse,' said the eldest son;
'You *shan't* have the mouse,' said the little one.

I told you before 'twas a stormy night
When these two little kittens began to fight;
The old woman seized her sweeping broom,
And swept the two kittens right out of the room.

The ground was covered with frost and snow,
And the two little kittens had nowhere to go;
So they laid them down on the mat at the door,
While the old woman finished sweeping the floor.

Then they crept in, as quiet as mice,
All wet with the snow, and as cold as ice,
For they found it was better, that stormy night,
To lie down and sleep than to quarrel and fight.

SYDNEY DAYRE (MRS. COCHRAN)

fl. 1881

259 *A Lesson for Mamma*

DEAR Mamma, if you just could be
A tiny little girl like me,
And I your mamma, you would see
  How nice I'd be to you.
I'd always let you have your way;
I'd never frown at you and say,
  'You are behaving ill today,
  Such conduct will not do.'

I'd always give you jelly-cake
For breakfast, and I'd never shake
My head, and say, 'You must not take
  So very large a slice.'
I'd never say, 'My dear, I trust
You will not make me say you *must*
Eat up your oatmeal'; or 'The crust
  You'll find, is very nice.'

I'd buy you candy every day;
I'd go down town with you, and say,
'What would my darling like? You may
  Have anything you see.'
I'd never say, 'My pet, you know
'Tis bad for health and teeth, and so
I cannot let you have it. No—
  It would be wrong in me.'

And every day I'd let you wear
Your nicest dress, and never care
If it should get a great big tear;
  I'd only say to you,

'My precious treasure, never mind,
For little clothes *will* tear, I find.'
Now, Mamma, wouldn't that be kind?
That's just what *I* should do.

I'd never say, 'Well, just a *few*!'
I'd let you stop your lessons too;
I'd say, 'They are too hard for you,
Poor child, to understand.'
I'd put the books and slates away;
You shouldn't do a thing but play,
And have a party every day.
Ah-h-h! wouldn't that be grand!

But, Mamma dear, you cannot grow
Into a little girl, you know,
And I can't be your mamma; so
The only thing to do,
Is just for you to try and see
How very, very nice 'twould be
For *you* to do all this for *me*,
Now, Mamma, *couldn't* you?

260 *Morning Compliments*

A LIGHT little zephyr came flitting,
Just breaking the morning repose.
The rose made a bow to the lily,
The lily she bowed to the rose.

And then, in a soft little whisper,
As faint as a perfume that blows:
'You are brighter than I,' said the lily;
'You are fairer than I,' said the rose.

LAURA E. RICHARDS

1850–1943

261 *Mrs. Snipkin and Mrs. Wobblechin*

SKINNY Mrs. Snipkin,
With her little pipkin,
Sat by the fireside a-warming of her toes.
Fat Mrs. Wobblechin,
With her little doublechin,
Sat by the window a-cooling of her nose.

Says this one to that one,
'Oh! you silly fat one,
Will you shut the window down? You're freezing me to death!'
Says that one to t'other one,
'Good gracious, how you bother one!
There isn't air enough for me to draw my precious breath!'

Skinny Mrs. Snipkin,
Took her little pipkin,
Threw it straight across the room as hard as she could throw;
Hit Mrs. Wobblechin
On her little doublechin,
And out of the window a-tumble she did go.

262 *My Uncle Jehoshaphat*

MY Uncle Jehoshaphat had a pig,
A pig of high degree;
And he always wore a brown scratch wig,
Most beautiful for to see.

My Uncle Jehoshaphat loved this pig,
And the piggywig he loved him;
And they both jumped into the lake one day,
To see which best could swim.

My Uncle Jehoshaphat he swam up,
  And the piggywig he swam down;
And so they both did win the prize,
  Which same was a velvet gown.

My Uncle Jehoshaphat wore one half,
  And piggywig wore the other;
And they both rode to town on the brindled calf,
  To carry it home to its mother.

263 *Eletelephony*

ONCE there was an elephant,
Who tried to use the telephant—
No! No! I mean an elephone
Who tried to use the telephone—
(Dear me! I am not certain quite
That even now I've got it right.)

Howe'er it was, he got his trunk
Entangled in the telephunk;
The more he tried to get it free,
The louder buzzed the telephee—
(I fear I'd better drop the song
Of elephop and telephong!)

ANONYMOUS

c. 1880

264 *What Became of Them?*

HE was a rat, and she was a rat,
  And down in one hole they did dwell;
And both were as black as a witch's cat,
  And they loved one another well.

He had a tail, and she had a tail,
  Both long and curling and fine;
And each said, 'Yours is the finest tail
  In the world, excepting mine.'

He smelt the cheese, and she smelt the cheese,
  And they both pronounced it good;
And both remarked it would greatly add
  To the charms of their daily food.

So he ventured out, and she ventured out,
  And I saw them go with pain;
But what befell them I never can tell,
  For they never came back again.

WILLIAM CORY
1823–1892

265 *A Ballad for a Boy*

WHEN George the Third was reigning a hundred years ago,
He ordered Captain Farmer to chase the foreign foe.
'You're not afraid of shot,' said he, 'you're not afraid of wreck,
So cruise about the west of France in the frigate called *Quebec*.

'Quebec was once a Frenchman's town, but twenty years ago
King George the Second sent a man called General Wolfe, you know,
To clamber up a precipice and look into Quebec,
As you'd look down a hatchway when standing on the deck.

'If Wolfe could beat the Frenchmen then so you can beat them now.
Before he got inside the town he died, I must allow.
But since the town was won for us it is a lucky name,
And you'll remember Wolfe's good work, and you shall do the same.'

Then Farmer said, 'I'll try, sir,' and Farmer bowed so low
That George could see his pigtail tied in a velvet bow.
George gave him his commission, and that it might be safer,
Signed 'King of Britain, King of France,' and sealed it with a wafer.

Then proud was Captain Farmer in a frigate of his own,
And grander on his quarter-deck than George upon his throne.
He'd two guns in his cabin, and on the spar-deck ten,
And twenty on the gun-deck, and more than ten score men.

And as a huntsman scours the brakes with sixteen brace of dogs,
With two-and-thirty cannon the ship explored the fogs.
From Cape la Hogue to Ushant, from Rochefort to Belleisle,
She hunted game till reef and mud were rubbing on her keel.

The fogs are dried, the frigate's side is bright with melting tar,
The lad up in the foretop sees square white sails afar;
The east wind drives three square-sailed masts from out the
  Breton bay,
And 'Clear for action!' Farmer shouts, and reefers yell 'Hooray!'

The Frenchmen's captain had a name I wish I could pronounce;
A Breton gentleman was he, and wholly free from bounce,
One like those famous fellows who died by guillotine
For honour and the fleurs-de-lys, and Antoinette the Queen.

The Catholic for Louis, the Protestant for George,
Each captain drew as bright a sword as saintly smiths could
  forge;
And both were simple seamen, but both could understand
How each was bound to win or die for flag and native land.

The French ship was *La Surveillante*, which means the watchful
  maid;
She folded up her head-dress and began to cannonade.
Her hull was clean, and ours was foul; we had to spread more
  sail.
On canvas, stays, and topsail yards her bullets came like hail.

Sore smitten were both captains, and many lads beside,
And still to cut our rigging the foreign gunners tried.
A sail-clad spar came flapping down athwart a blazing gun;
We could not quench the rushing flames, and so the Frenchman
  won.

Our quarter-deck was crowded, the waist was all aglow;
Men hung upon the taffrail, half scorched but loath to go;
Our captain sat where once he stood, and would not quit his chair.
He bade his comrades leap for life, and leave him bleeding there.

The guns were hushed on either side, the Frenchmen lowered boats,
They flung us planks and hencoops, and everything that floats.
They risked their lives, good fellows! to bring their rivals aid.
'Twas by the conflagration the peace was strangely made.

La Surveillante was like a sieve; the victors had no rest.
They had to dodge the east wind to reach the port of Brest;
And where the waves leapt lower and the riddled ship went slower,
In triumph, yet in funeral guise, came fisher-boats to tow her.

They dealt with us as brethren, they mourned for Farmer dead;
And as the wounded captives passed each Breton bowed the head.
Then spoke the French Lieutenant, ''Twas fire that won, not we
You never struck your flag to us; you'll go to England free.'

'Twas the sixth day of October, seventeen hundred seventy-nine,
A year when nations ventured against us to combine,
Quebec was burnt and Farmer slain, by us remembered not;
But thanks be to the French book wherein they're not forgot.

Now you, if you've to fight the French, my youngster, bear in mind
Those seamen of King Louis so chivalrous and kind;
Think of the Breton gentlemen who took our lads to Brest,
And treat some rescued Breton as a comrade and a guest.

ROBERT LOUIS STEVENSON

1850–1894

266 *Bed in Summer*

IN winter I get up at night
And dress by yellow candle-light.
In summer, quite the other way,
I have to go to bed by day.

I have to go to bed and see
The birds still hopping on the tree,
Or hear the grown-up people's feet
Still going past me in the street.

And does it not seem hard to you,
When all the sky is clear and blue,
And I should like so much to play,
To have to go to bed by day?

267 *At the Seaside*

WHEN I was down beside the sea
A wooden spade they gave to me
  To dig the sandy shore.
My holes were empty like a cup,
In every hole the sea came up,
  Till it could come no more.

268 *Whole Duty of Children*

A CHILD should always say what's true,
And speak when he is spoken to,
And behave mannerly at table:
At least as far as he is able.

269 *Windy Nights*

WHENEVER the moon and stars are set,
  Whenever the wind is high,
All night long in the dark and wet,
  A man goes riding by.
Late in the night when the fires are out,
Why does he gallop and gallop about?

Whenever the trees are crying aloud,
  And ships are tossed at sea,
By, on the highway, low and loud,
  By at the gallop goes he.
By at the gallop he goes, and then
By he comes back at the gallop again.

270 *Looking Forward*

WHEN I am grown to man's estate
I shall be very proud and great,
And tell the other girls and boys
Not to meddle with my toys.

271 *Where Go the Boats?*

DARK brown is the river,
  Golden is the sand.
It flows along for ever,
  With trees on either hand.

Green leaves a-floating,
  Castles of the foam,
Boats of mine a-boating—
  Where will all come home?

On goes the river,
  And out past the mill,
Away down the valley,
  Away down the hill.

Away down the river,
    A hundred miles or more,
Other little children
    Shall bring my boats ashore.

272 *The Land of Counterpane*

WHEN I was sick and lay a-bed,
I had two pillows at my head,
And all my toys beside me lay
To keep me happy all the day.

And sometimes for an hour or so
I watched my leaden soldiers go,
With different uniforms and drills,
Among the bedclothes, through the hills;

And sometimes sent my ships in fleets
All up and down among the sheets;
Or brought my trees and houses out,
And planted cities all about.

I was the giant great and still
That sits upon the pillow-hill,
And sees before him, dale and plain,
The pleasant land of counterpane.

273 *My Shadow*

I HAVE a little shadow that goes in and out with me,
And what can be the use of him is more than I can see.
He is very, very like me from the heels up to the head;
And I see him jump before me, when I jump into my bed.

The funniest thing about him is the way he likes to grow—
Not at all like proper children, which is always very slow;
For he sometimes shoots up taller like an indiarubber ball,
And he sometimes gets so little that there's none of him at all.

He hasn't got a notion of how children ought to play,
And can only make a fool of me in every sort of way.
He stays so close beside me, he's a coward you can see;
I'd think shame to stick to nursie as that shadow sticks to me!

One morning, very early, before the sun was up,
I rose and found the shining dew on every buttercup;
But my lazy little shadow, like an arrant sleepy-head,
Had stayed at home behind me and was fast asleep in bed.

274

The Cow

THE friendly cow, all red and white,
  I love with all my heart:
She gives me cream with all her might,
  To eat with apple tart.

She wanders lowing here and there,
  And yet she cannot stray,
All in the pleasant open air,
  The pleasant light of day;

And blown by all the winds that pass
  And wet with all the showers,
She walks among the meadow grass
  And eats the meadow flowers.

275

Happy Thought

THE world is so full of a number of things,
I'm sure we should all be as happy as kings.

276

Good and Bad Children

CHILDREN, you are very little,
And your bones are very brittle;
If you would grow great and stately,
You must try to walk sedately.

You must still be bright and quiet,
And content with simple diet;
And remain, through all bewild'ring,
Innocent and honest children.

Happy hearts and happy faces,
Happy play in grassy places—
That was how, in ancient ages,
Children grew to kings and sages.

But the unkind and the unruly,
And the sort who eat unduly,
They must never hope for glory—
Theirs is quite a different story!

Cruel children, crying babies,
All grow up as geese and gabies,
Hated, as their age increases,
By their nephews and their nieces.

277 *The Lamplighter*

My tea is nearly ready and the sun has left the sky;
It's time to take the window to see Leerie going by;
For every night at teatime and before you take your seat,
With lantern and with ladder he comes posting up the street.

Now Tom would be a driver and Maria go to sea,
And my papa's a banker and as rich as he can be;
But I, when I am stronger and can choose what I'm to do,
O Leerie, I'll go round at night and light the lamps with you!

For we are very lucky, with a lamp before the door,
And Leerie stops to light it as he lights so many more;
And O! before you hurry by with ladder and with light,
O Leerie, see a little child and nod to him tonight!

278 *Time to Rise*

A BIRDIE with a yellow bill
Hopped upon the window sill,
Cocked his shining eye and said:
'Ain't you 'shamed, you sleepy-head?'

279 *From a Railway Carriage*

FASTER than fairies, faster than witches,
Bridges and houses, hedges and ditches;
And charging along like troops in a battle,
All through the meadows the horses and cattle:
All of the sights of the hill and the plain
Fly as thick as driving rain;
And ever again, in the wink of an eye,
Painted stations whistle by.

Here is a child who clambers and scrambles,
All by himself and gathering brambles;
Here is a tramp who stands and gazes;
And there is the green for stringing the daisies!
Here is a cart run away in the road
Lumping along with man and load;
And here is a mill, and there is a river:
Each a glimpse and gone for ever!

280 *Winter Time*

LATE lies the wintry sun a-bed,
A frosty, fiery sleepy-head;
Blinks but an hour or two; and then,
A blood-red orange, sets again.

Before the stars have left the skies,
At morning in the dark I rise;
And shivering in my nakedness,
By the cold candle, bathe and dress.

Close by the jolly fire I sit
To warm my frozen bones a bit;
Or with a reindeer-sled, explore
The colder countries round the door.

When to go out, my nurse doth wrap
Me in my comforter and cap,
The cold wind burns my face, and blows
Its frosty pepper up my nose.

Black are my steps on silver sod;
Thick blows my frosty breath abroad;
And tree and house, and hill and lake,
Are frosted like a wedding-cake.

281 *The Dumb Soldier*

When the grass was closely mown,
Walking on the lawn alone,
In the turf a hole I found
And hid a soldier underground.

Spring and daisies came apace;
Grasses hid my hiding-place;
Grasses run like a green sea
O'er the lawn up to my knee.

Under grass alone he lies,
Looking up with leaden eyes,
Scarlet coat and pointed gun,
To the stars and to the sun.

When the grass is ripe like grain,
When the scythe is stoned again,
When the lawn is shaven clear,
Then my hole shall reappear.

I shall find him, never fear,
I shall find my grenadier;
But, for all that's gone and come,
I shall find my soldier dumb.

He has lived, a little thing,
In the grassy woods of spring;
Done, if he could tell me true,
Just as I should like to do.

He has seen the starry hours
And the springing of the flowers;
And the fairy things that pass
In the forests of the grass.

In the silence he has heard
Talking bee and ladybird,
And the butterfly has flown
O'er him as he lay alone.

Not a word will he disclose,
Not a word of all he knows.
I must lay him on the shelf,
And make up the tale myself.

JAMES WHITCOMB RILEY

1849–1916

282 *Little Orphant Annie*

LITTLE ORPHANT ANNIE's come to our house to stay,
An' wash the cups an' saucers up, an' brush the crumbs away,
An' shoo the chickens off the porch, an' dust the hearth, an' sweep,
An' make the fire, an' bake the bread, an' earn her board-an'-keep;
An' all us other childern, when the supper things is done,
We set around the kitchen fire an' has the mostest fun
A-list'nin' to the witch-tales 'at Annie tells about,
An' the Gobble-uns 'at gits you
Ef you
Don't
Watch
Out!

Onc't they was a little boy wouldn't say his prayers,—
So when he went to bed at night, away up stairs,
His Mammy heerd him holler, an' his Daddy heerd him bawl,
An' when they turn't the kivvers down, he wasn't there at all!
An' they seeked him in the rafter-room, an' cubby-hole, an' press,
An' seeked him up the chimbly-flue, an' ever'wheres, I guess;
But all they ever found was thist his pants an' roundabout—
An' the Gobble-uns'll git you
Ef you
Don't
Watch
Out!

An' one time a little girl 'ud allus laugh an' grin,
An' make fun of ever'one, an' all her blood an' kin;
An' onc't, when they was 'company', an' ole folks was there,
She mocked 'em an' shocked 'em, an' said she didn't care!
An' thist as she kicked her heels, an' turn't to run an' hide,
They was two great big Black Things a-standin' by her side,
An' they snatched her through the ceilin' 'fore she knowed what she's about!
An' the Gobble-uns'll git you
Ef you
Don't
Watch
Out!

An' little Orphant Annie says when the blaze is blue,
An' the lamp-wick sputters, an' the wind goes *woo-oo*!
An' you hear the crickets quit, an' the moon is gray,
An' the lightnin'-bugs in dew is all squenched away,—
You better mind yer parents, an' yer teachers fond an' dear,
An' churish them 'at loves you, an' dry the orphant's tear,
An' he'p the pore an' needy ones 'at clusters all about,
Er the Gobble-uns'll git you
Ef you
Don't
Watch
Out!

kivvers, covers, i.e. bedclothes ***roundabout***, short jacket

283 *The Raggedy Man*

O THE Raggedy Man! He works fer Pa;
An' he's the goodest man ever you saw!
He comes to our house every day,
An' waters the horses, an' feeds 'em hay;
An' he opens the shed—an' we all ist laugh
When he drives out our little old wobble-ly calf;
An' nen—ef our hired girl says he can—
He milks the cow fer 'Lizabuth Ann.
  Ain't he a' awful good Raggedy Man?
    Raggedy! Raggedy! Raggedy Man!

W'y, the Raggedy Man—he's ist so good
He splits the kindlin' an' chops the wood;
An' nen he spades in our garden, too,
An' does most things 'at *boys* can't do!
He clumbed clean up in our big tree
An' shooked a' apple down fer me—
An' nother'n', too, fer 'Lizabuth Ann—
An' nother'n, too, fer the Raggedy Man.
  Ain't he a' awful kind Raggedy Man?
    Raggedy! Raggedy! Raggedy Man!

An' the Raggedy Man, he knows most rhymes
An' tells 'em, ef I be good, sometimes:
Knows 'bout Giunts, an' Griffuns, an' Elves,
An' the Squidgicum-Squees 'at swallers therselves!
An', right by the pump in our pasture-lot,
He showed me the hole 'at the Wunks is got,
'At lives 'way deep in the ground, an' can
Turn into me, er 'Lizabuth Ann!
  Ain't he a funny old Raggedy Man?
    Raggedy! Raggedy! Raggedy Man!

The Raggedy Man—one time when he
Wuz makin' a little bow-'n'-orry fer me,
Says 'When *you're* big like your Pa is,
Air you go' to keep a fine store like his—
An' be a rich merchunt—an' wear fine clothes?
Er what *air* you go' to be, goodness knows!'
An' nen he laughed at 'Lizabuth Ann,
An' I says ' 'M go' to be a Raggedy Man!—
  I'm ist go' to be a nice Raggedy Man!'
    Raggedy! Raggedy! Raggedy Man!

EUGENE FIELD

1850–1895

284 ### *Wynken, Blynken, and Nod*

WYNKEN, Blynken, and Nod one night
  Sailed off in a wooden shoe—
Sailed on a river of crystal light,
  Into a sea of dew.
  'Where are you going, and what do you wish?'
  The old moon asked the three.
  'We have come to fish for the herring fish
  That live in this beautiful sea;
  Nets of silver and gold have we!'
        Said Wynken,
        Blynken,
        And Nod.

The old moon laughed and sang a song,
  As they rocked in the wooden shoe,
And the wind that sped them all night long
  Ruffled the waves of dew.
The little stars were the herring fish
  That lived in that beautiful sea—
  'Now cast your nets wherever you wish—
  Never afeard are we';
  So cried the stars to the fishermen three:
        Wynken,
        Blynken,
        And Nod.

All night long their nets they threw
  To the stars in the twinkling foam—
Then down from the skies came the wooden shoe,
  Bringing the fishermen home;
'Twas all so pretty a sail it seemed
  As if it could not be,
And some folks thought 'twas a dream they'd dreamed
  Of sailing that beautiful sea—
  But I shall name you the fishermen three:
      Wynken,
      Blynken,
      And Nod.

Wynken and Blynken are two little eyes,
  And Nod is a little head,
And the wooden shoe that sailed the skies
  Is the wee one's trundle-bed.
So shut your eyes while mother sings
  Of wonderful sights that be,
And you shall see the beautiful things
  As you rock in the misty sea,
  Where the old shoe rocked the fishermen three:
      Wynken,
      Blynken,
      And Nod.

285 *The Sugar-Plum Tree*

HAVE you ever heard of the Sugar-Plum Tree?
  'Tis a marvel of great renown!
It blooms on the shore of the Lollipop sea
  In the garden of Shut-Eye Town;
The fruit that it bears is so wondrously sweet
  (As those who have tasted it say)
That good little children have only to eat
  Of that fruit to be happy next day.

When you've got to the tree, you would have a hard time
To capture the fruit which I sing;
The tree is so tall that no person could climb
To the boughs where the sugar-plums swing.
But up in that tree sits a chocolate cat,
And a gingerbread dog prowls below—
And this is the way you contrive to get at
Those sugar-plums tempting you so:

You say but the word to that gingerbread dog
And he barks with such terrible zest
That the chocolate cat is at once all agog,
As her swelling proportions attest.
And the chocolate cat goes cavorting around
From this leafy limb unto that,
And the sugar-plums tumble, of course, to the ground—
Hurrah for that chocolate cat!

There are marshmallows, gumdrops, and peppermint canes,
With stripings of scarlet or gold,
And you carry away of the treasure that rains
As much as your apron can hold!
So come, little child, cuddle closer to me
In your dainty white nightcap and gown,
And I'll rock you away to that Sugar-Plum Tree
In the garden of Shut-Eye Town.

CHARLES E. CARRYL

1841–1920

286 *The Camel's Complaint*

CANARY-BIRDS feed on sugar and seed,
Parrots have crackers to crunch;
And as for the poodles, they tell me the noodles
Have chicken and cream for their lunch.
But there's never a question
About *my* digestion—
Anything does for me.

Cats, you're aware, can repose in a chair,
Chickens can roost upon rails;
Puppies are able to sleep in a stable,
And oysters can slumber in pails.
But no one supposes
A poor camel dozes—
Any place does for me.

Lambs are enclosed where it's never exposed,
Coops are constructed for hens;
Kittens are treated to houses well heated,
And pigs are protected by pens.
But a camel comes handy
Wherever it's sandy—
Anywhere does for me.

People would laugh if you rode a giraffe,
Or mounted the back of an ox;
It's nobody's habit to ride on a rabbit,
Or try to bestraddle a fox.
But as for a camel, he's
Ridden by families—
Any load does for me.

A snake is as round as a hole in the ground,
And weasels are wavy and sleek;
And no alligator could ever be straighter
Than lizards that live in a creek.
But a camel's all lumpy
And bumpy and humpy—
Any shape does for me.

FRANCIS THOMPSON

1859–1907

287 *Ex Ore Infantium*

LITTLE Jesus, wast Thou shy
Once, and just so small as I?
And what did it feel like to be
Out of Heaven, and just like me?
Didst Thou sometimes think of *there*,
And ask where all the angels were?
I should think that I would cry
For my house all made of sky;
I would look about the air,
And wonder where my angels were;
And at waking 'twould distress me—
Not an angel there to dress me!

Hadst Thou ever any toys,
Like us little girls and boys?
And didst Thou play in Heaven with all
The angels, that were not too tall,
With stars for marbles? Did the things
Play 'Can you see me?' through their wings?

Didst Thou kneel at night to pray,
And didst Thou join Thy hands, this way?
And did they tire sometimes, being young,
And make the prayer seem very long?
And dost Thou like it best, that we
Should join our hands to pray to Thee?
I used to think, before I knew,
The prayer not said unless we do.
And did Thy Mother at the night
Kiss Thee, and fold the clothes in right?
And didst Thou feel quite good in bed,
Kissed, and sweet, and Thy prayers said?

Thou canst not have forgotten all
That it feels like to be small:
And Thou know'st I cannot pray
To Thee in my father's way—
When Thou wast so little, say,
Couldst Thou talk Thy Father's way?—

So, a little Child, come down
And hear a child's tongue like Thy own;
Take me by the hand and walk,
And listen to my baby-talk.
To Thy Father show my prayer
(He will look, Thou art so fair),
And say: 'O Father, I, Thy Son,
Bring the prayer of a little one.'

And He will smile, that children's tongue
Has not changed since Thou wast young!

E. NESBIT

1858–1924

288 *Child's Song in Spring*

THE silver birch is a dainty lady,
  She wears a satin gown;
The elm tree makes the old churchyard shady,
  She will not live in town.

The English oak is a sturdy fellow,
  He gets his green coat late;
The willow is smart in a suit of yellow,
  While brown the beech trees wait.

Such a gay green gown God gives the larches—
  As green as He is good!
The hazels hold up their arms for arches
  When Spring rides through the wood.

The chestnut's proud and the lilac's pretty,
  The poplar's gentle and tall,
But the plane tree's kind to the poor dull city—
  I love him best of all!

EDWARD ABBOTT PARRY

1863–1943

289 *Pater's Bathe*

YOU can take a tub with a rub and a scrub in a two-foot tank of tin,
You can stand and look at the whirling brook and think about jumping in,
You can chatter and shake in the cold black lake, but the kind of bath for me,
Is to take a dip from the side of a ship, in the trough of the rolling sea.

You may lie and dream in the bed of a stream when an August day is dawning,
Or believe 'tis nice to break the ice on your tub of a winter morning,
You may sit and shiver beside the river, but the kind of bath for me
Is to take a dip from the side of a ship, in the trough of the rolling sea.

290 *I would like you for a Comrade*

I WOULD like you for a comrade,
  For I love you, that I do,
I never met a little girl
  As amiable as you;
I would teach you how to dance and sing,
  And how to talk and laugh,
If I were not a little girl
  And you were not a calf.

I would like you for a comrade,
  You should share my barley meal,
And butt me with your little horns
  Just hard enough to feel;
We would lie beneath the chestnut trees
  And watch the leaves uncurl,
If I were not a clumsy calf
  And you a little girl.

291 *The Jam Fish*

A JAM FISH sat on a hard-bake rock,
  His head in his left hand fin,
He was knitting his wife a sky-blue sock
  With a second-hand rolling pin.
His wife was watching her old Aunt Brill
  Sew acid drops on to his shirt,
While his grandmother fitted a caramel frill
  To a Butterscotch tartan skirt.

His cousin Jelly Fish gently swam
  In a pool of parsley sauce,
While the Jam Fish sighed, 'I am only Jam,
  And must wait for the second course.
When the rice mould quivers on the dish,
  And shakes at the children's sneers,
Till the scented voice of the old Jam Fish
  Shall melt their scorn to tears.'

HILAIRE BELLOC
1870–1953

292 *The Yak*

As a friend to the children commend me the Yak.
  You will find it exactly the thing:
It will carry and fetch, you can ride on its back,
  Or lead it about with a string.

The Tartar who dwells on the plains of Tibet
  (A desolate region of snow)
Has for centuries made it a nursery pet,
  And surely the Tartar should know!

Then tell your papa where the Yak can be got,
  And if he is awfully rich
He will buy you the creature—or else he will *not*.
  (I cannot be positive which.)

293

The Frog

BE kind and tender to the Frog,
  And do not call him names,
As 'Slimy skin', or 'Polly-wog',
  Or likewise 'Ugly James',
Or 'Gape-a-grin', or 'Toad-gone-wrong',
  Or 'Billy Bandy-knees':
The Frog is justly sensitive
  To epithets like these.
No animal will more repay
  A treatment kind and fair;
At least so lonely people say
Who keep a frog (and, by the way,
  They are extremely rare).

294

The Python

A PYTHON I should not advise,—
It needs a doctor for its eyes,
And has the measles yearly.
However, if you feel inclined
To get one (to improve your mind,
And not from fashion merely),
Allow no music near its cage;
And when it flies into a rage
Chastise it, most severely.

I had an Aunt in Yucatan
Who bought a Python from a man
And kept it for a pet.
She died, because she never knew
These simple little rules and few;—
The snake is living yet.

295

The Vulture

The Vulture eats between his meals
And that's the reason why
He very, very rarely feels
As well as you and I.

His eye is dull, his head is bald,
His neck is growing thinner.
Oh! what a lesson for us all
To only eat at dinner!

296

Jim
Who ran away from his Nurse, and was eaten by a Lion

There was a boy whose name was Jim;
His friends were very good to him.
They gave him tea, and cakes, and jam,
And slices of delicious ham,
And chocolate with pink inside,
And little tricycles to ride,
And read him stories through and through,
And even took him to the Zoo—
But there it was the dreadful fate
Befell him, which I now relate.

You know—at least you *ought* to know,
For I have often told you so—
That children never are allowed
To leave their nurses in a crowd;
Now this was Jim's especial foible,
He ran away when he was able,
And on this inauspicious day
He slipped his hand and ran away!
He hadn't gone a yard when—Bang!
With open jaws, a lion sprang,
And hungrily began to eat
The boy: beginning at his feet.

Now, just imagine how it feels
When first your toes and then your heels,
And then by gradual degrees,
Your shins and ankles, calves and knees,
Are slowly eaten, bit by bit.
No wonder Jim detested it!
No wonder that he shouted 'Hi!'
The honest keeper heard his cry,
Though very fat he almost ran
To help the little gentleman.
'Ponto!' he ordered as he came
(For Ponto was the lion's name),
'Ponto!' he cried, with angry frown.
'Let go, Sir! Down, Sir! Put it down!'

The lion made a sudden stop,
He let the dainty morsel drop,
And slunk reluctant to his cage,
Snarling with disappointed rage.
But when he bent him over Jim,
The honest keeper's eyes were dim.
The lion having reached his head,
The miserable boy was dead!

When Nurse informed his parents, they
Were more concerned than I can say:—
His Mother, as she dried her eyes,
Said, 'Well—it gives me no surprise,
He would not do as he was told!'
His Father, who was self-controlled,
Bade all the children round attend
To James's miserable end,
And always keep a-hold of Nurse
For fear of finding something worse.

297

Matilda
Who told Lies, and was Burned to Death

MATILDA told such dreadful lies,
It made one gasp and stretch one's eyes;
Her Aunt, who, from her earliest youth,
Had kept a strict regard for truth,
Attempted to believe Matilda:
The effort very nearly killed her,
And would have done so, had not she
Discovered this infirmity.
For once, towards the close of day,
Matilda, growing tired of play,
And finding she was left alone,
Went tiptoe to the telephone
And summoned the immediate aid
Of London's noble fire-brigade.
Within an hour the gallant band
Were pouring in on every hand,
From Putney, Hackney Downs, and Bow
With courage high and hearts a-glow
They galloped, roaring through the town,
'Matilda's house is burning down!'
Inspired by British cheers and loud
Proceeding from the frenzied crowd,
They ran their ladders through a score
Of windows on the ballroom floor;

And took peculiar pains to souse
The pictures up and down the house,
Until Matilda's Aunt succeeded
In showing them they were not needed;
And even then she had to pay
To get the men to go away!

It happened that a few weeks later
Her Aunt was off to the theatre
To see that interesting play
The Second Mrs. Tanqueray,
She had refused to take her niece
To hear this entertaining piece:
A deprivation just and wise
To punish her for telling lies.
That night a fire *did* break out—
You should have heard Matilda shout!
You should have heard her scream and bawl,
And throw the window up and call
To people passing in the street—
(The rapidly increasing heat
Encouraging her to obtain
Their confidence)—but all in vain!
For every time she shouted 'Fire!'
They only answered 'Little liar!'
And therefore when her Aunt returned,
Matilda, and the house, were burned.

LAURENCE ALMA-TADEMA

c. 1865–1940

298 *If No One Ever Marries Me*

IF no one ever marries me—
  And I don't see why they should,
For nurse says I'm not pretty
  And I'm seldom very good—

If no one ever marries me
  I shan't mind very much;
I shall buy a squirrel in a cage,
  And a little rabbit hutch.

I shall have a cottage near a wood,
  And a pony all my own,
And a little lamb, quite clean and tame,
  That I can take to town.

And when I'm getting really old,
  At twenty eight or nine,
I shall buy a little orphan girl
  And bring her up as mine.

TWENTIETH CENTURY

RUDYARD KIPLING

1865–1936

299 *The Hump*

THE Camel's hump is an ugly lump
  Which well you may see at the Zoo;
But uglier yet is the hump we get
  From having too little to do.

Kiddies and grown-ups too-oo-oo,
If we haven't enough to do-oo-oo,
        We get the hump—
        Cameelious hump—
The hump that is black and blue!

We climb out of bed with a frouzly head,
  And a snarly-yarly voice.
We shiver and scowl and we grunt and we growl
  At our bath and our boots and our toys;

And there ought to be a corner for me
(And I know there is one for you)
        When we get the hump—
        Cameelious hump—
The hump that is black and blue!

The cure for this ill is not to sit still,
  Or frowst with a book by the fire;
But to take a large hoe and a shovel also,
  And dig till you gently perspire;

And then you will find that the sun and the wind,
And the Djinn of the Garden too,
        Have lifted the hump—
        The horrible hump—
The hump that is black and blue!

I get it as well as you-oo-oo—
If I haven't enough to do-oo-oo!
We all get hump—
Cameelious hump—
Kiddies and grown-ups too!

300 *Puck's Song*

SEE you the ferny ride that steals
Into the oak-woods far?
O that was whence they hewed the keels
That rolled to Trafalgar.

And mark you where the ivy clings
To Bayham's mouldering walls?
O there we cast the stout railings
That stand around St. Paul's.

See you the dimpled track that runs
All hollow through the wheat?
O that was where they hauled the guns
That smote King Philip's fleet.

(Out of the Weald, the secret Weald,
Men sent in ancient years,
The horseshoes red at Flodden Field,
The arrows at Poitiers!)

See you the little mill that clacks,
So busy by the brook?
She has ground her corn and paid her tax
Ever since Domesday Book.

See you our stilly woods of oak,
And the dread ditch beside?
O that was where the Saxons broke
On the day that Harold died.

See you the windy levels spread
About the gates of Rye?
O that was where the Northmen fled,
When Alfred's ships came by.

See you our pastures wide and lone,
Where the red oxen browse?
O there was a City thronged and known,
Ere London boasted a house.

And see you, after rain, the trace
Of mound and ditch and wall?
O that was a Legion's camping-place,
When Caesar sailed from Gaul.

And see you marks that show and fade,
Like shadows on the Downs?
O they are the lines the Flint Men made,
To guard their wondrous towns.

Trackway and Camp and City lost,
Salt Marsh where now is corn—
Old Wars, old Peace, old Arts that cease,
And so was England born!

She is not any common Earth,
Water or wood or air,
But Merlin's Isle of Gramarye,
Where you and I will fare!

301 *A Smuggler's Song*

If you wake at midnight, and hear a horse's feet,
Don't go drawing back the blind, or looking in the street,
Them that asks no questions isn't told a lie.
Watch the wall, my darling, while the Gentlemen go by!
Five and twenty ponies
Trotting through the dark—
Brandy for the Parson,
'Baccy for the Clerk;
Laces for a lady, letters for a spy,
And watch the wall, my darling, while the Gentlemen go by!

Running round the woodlump if you chance to find
Little barrels, roped and tarred, all full of brandy-wine,
Don't you shout to come and look, nor use 'em for your play.
Put the brishwood back again—and they'll be gone next day!

If you see the stable-door setting open wide;
If you see a tired horse lying down inside;
If your mother mends a coat cut about and tore;
If the lining's wet and warm—don't you ask no more!

If you meet King George's men, dressed in blue and red,
You be careful what you say, and mindful what is said.
If they call you 'pretty maid', and chuck you 'neath the chin,
Don't you tell where no one is, nor yet where no one's been!

Knocks and footsteps round the house—whistles after dark—
You've no call for running out till the house-dogs bark.
Trusty's here, and *Pincher*'s here, and see how dumb they lie—
They don't fret to follow when the Gentlemen go by!

If you do as you've been told, 'likely there's a chance,
You'll be give a dainty doll, all the way from France,
With a cap of Valenciennes, and a velvet hood—
A present from the Gentlemen, along o' being good!

Five and twenty ponies,
Trotting through the dark—
Brandy for the Parson,
'Baccy for the Clerk.
Them that asks no questions isn't told a lie—
Watch the wall, my darling, while the Gentlemen go by!

302 *The Way through the Woods*

THEY shut the road through the woods
Seventy years ago.
Weather and rain have undone it again,
And now you would never know
There was once a road through the woods
Before they planted the trees.
It is underneath the coppice and heath,
And the thin anemones.
Only the keeper sees
That, where the ring-dove broods,
And the badgers roll at ease,
There was once a road through the woods.

Yet, if you enter the woods
Of a summer evening late,
When the night-air cools on the trout-ringed pools
Where the otter whistles his mate,
(They fear not men in the woods,
Because they see so few.)
You will hear the beat of a horse's feet,
And the swish of a skirt in the dew,
Steadily cantering through
The misty solitudes,
As though they perfectly knew
The old lost road through the woods . . .
But there is no road through the woods.

303 *If—*

IF you can keep your head when all about you
  Are losing theirs and blaming it on you,
If you can trust yourself when all men doubt you,
  But make allowance for their doubting too;
If you can wait and not be tired by waiting,
  Or being lied about, don't deal in lies,
Or being hated don't give way to hating,
  And yet don't look too good, nor talk too wise:

If you can dream—and not make dreams your master;
  If you can think—and not make thoughts your aim:
If you can meet with Triumph and Disaster
  And treat those two impostors just the same;
If you can bear to hear the truth you've spoken
  Twisted by knaves to make a trap for fools,
Or watch the things you gave your life to, broken,
  And stoop and build 'em up with worn-out tools:

If you can make one heap of all your winnings
  And risk it on one turn of pitch-and-toss,
And lose, and start again at your beginnings
  And never breathe a word about your loss;
If you can force your heart and nerve and sinew
  To serve your turn long after they are gone,
And so hold on when there is nothing in you
  Except the Will which says to them: 'Hold on!'

If you can talk with crowds and keep your virtue,
  Or walk with Kings—nor lose the common touch,
If neither foes nor loving friends can hurt you,
  If all men count with you, but none too much;
If you can fill the unforgiving minute
  With sixty seconds' worth of distance run,
Yours is the Earth and everything that's in it,
  And—which is more—you'll be a Man, my son!

WALTER DE LA MARE

1873–1956

304 *Tartary*

If I were Lord of Tartary,
  Myself, and me alone,
My bed should be of ivory,
  Of beaten gold my throne;
And in my court should peacocks flaunt,
And in my forests tigers haunt,
And in my pools great fishes slant
    Their fins athwart the sun.

If I were Lord of Tartary,
  Trumpeters every day
To all my meals should summon me,
  And in my courtyards bray;
And in the evening lamps should shine,
Yellow as honey, red as wine,
While harp, and flute, and mandoline
    Made music sweet and gay.

If I were Lord of Tartary,
  I'd wear a robe of beads,
White, and gold, and green they'd be—
  And small and thick as seeds;
And ere should wane the morning star,
I'd don my robe and scimitar,
And zebras seven should draw my car
    Through Tartary's dark glades.

Lord of the fruits of Tartary,
  Her rivers silver-pale!
Lord of the hills of Tartary,
  Glen, thicket, wood, and dale!
Her flashing stars, her scented breeze,
Her trembling lakes, like foamless seas,
Her bird-delighting citron-trees,
    In every purple vale!

305 *John Mouldy*

I SPIED John Mouldy in his cellar,
Deep down twenty steps of stone;
In the dusk he sat a-smiling,
Smiling there alone.

He read no book, he snuffed no candle;
The rats ran in, the rats ran out;
And far and near, the drip of water
Went whisp'ring about.

The dusk was still, with dew a-falling,
I saw the Dog-star bleak and grim,
I saw a slim brown rat of Norway
Creep over him.

I spied John Mouldy in his cellar,
Deep down twenty steps of stone;
In the dusk he sat a-smiling,
Smiling there alone.

306 *Bunches of Grapes*

'BUNCHES of grapes,' says Timothy;
'Pomegranates pink,' says Elaine;
'A junket of cream and a cranberry tart
For me,' says Jane.

'Love-in-a-mist,' says Timothy;
'Primroses pale,' says Elaine;
'A nosegay of pinks and mignonette
For me,' says Jane.

'Chariots of gold,' says Timothy;
'Silvery wings,' says Elaine;
'A bumpity ride in a wagon of hay
For me,' says Jane.

307 *Alas, Alack!*

ANN, Ann!
  Come! quick as you can!
There's a fish that *talks*
  In the frying-pan.
Out of the fat,
  As clear as glass,
He put up his mouth
  And moaned 'Alas!'
Oh, most mournful,
  'Alas, alack!'
Then turned to his sizzling,
  And sank him back.

308 *Old Shellover*

'COME!' said Old Shellover.
'What?' says Creep.
'The horny old Gardener's fast asleep;
The fat cock Thrush
To his nest has gone;
And the dew shines bright
In the rising Moon;
Old Sallie Worm from her hole doth peep:
Come!' said Old Shellover.
'Ay!' said Creep.

309 *The Song of the Mad Prince*

WHO said, 'Peacock Pie'?
  The old King to the sparrow:
Who said, 'Crops are ripe'?
  Rust to the harrow:
Who said, 'Where sleeps she now?
  Where rests she now her head,
Bathed in eve's loveliness'?—
  That's what I said.

Who said, 'Ay, mum's the word'?
  Sexton to willow:
Who said, 'Green dusk for dreams,
  Moss for a pillow'?
Who said, 'All Time's delight
  Hath she for narrow bed;
Life's troubled bubble broken'?—
  That's what I said.

ANONYMOUS

1907?

310 *Greedy Jane*

'PUDDING *and* pie,'
Said Jane; 'O my!'
'Which would you rather?'
Said her father.
'Both,' cried Jane,
Quite bold and plain.

KENNETH GRAHAME

1859–1932

311 *Ducks' Ditty*

ALL along the backwater,
Through the rushes tall,
Ducks are a-dabbling,
Up tails all!

Ducks' tails, drakes' tails,
Yellow feet a-quiver,
Yellow bills all out of sight
Busy in the river!

Slushy green undergrowth
Where the roach swim—
Here we keep our larder,
Cool and full and dim.

Every one for what he likes!
We like to be
Heads down, tails up,
Dabbling free!

High in the blue above
Swifts whirl and call—
We are down a-dabbling
Up tails all!

EDWARD THOMAS

1878–1917

312 *If I Should Ever by Chance*

If I should ever by chance grow rich
I'll buy Codham, Cockridden, and Childerditch,
Roses, Pyrgo, and Lapwater,
And let them all to my elder daughter.
The rent I shall ask of her will be only
Each year's first violets, white and lonely,
The first primroses and orchises—
She must find them before I do, that is.
But if she finds a blossom on furze
Without rent they shall all for ever be hers,
Whenever I am sufficiently rich:
Codham, Cockridden, and Childerditch,
Roses, Pyrgo, and Lapwater—
I shall give them all to my elder daughter.

313 *What Shall I Give?*

WHAT shall I give my daughter the younger
More than will keep her from cold and hunger?
I shall not give her anything.
If she shared South Weald and Havering,
Their acres, the two brooks running between,
Paine's Brook and Weald Brook,
With pewit, woodpecker, swan, and rook,
She would be no richer than the queen
Who once on a time sat in Havering Bower
Alone, with the shadows, pleasure and power.
She could do no more with Samarcand,
Or the mountains of a mountain land
And its far white house above cottages
Like Venus above the Pleiades.
Her small hands I would not cumber
With so many acres and their lumber,
But leave her Steep and her own world
And her spectacled self with hair uncurled,
Wanting a thousand little things
That time without contentment brings.

ELEANOR FARJEON

1881–1965

314 *Blackfriars*

SEVEN Black Friars sitting back to back
Fished from the bridge for a pike or a jack.
The first caught a tiddler, the second caught a crab,
The third caught a winkle, the fourth caught a dab,
The fifth caught a tadpole, the sixth caught an eel,
And the seventh one caught an old cart-wheel.

315 *The Night will Never Stay*

THE night will never stay,
The night will still go by,
Though with a million stars
You pin it to the sky;
Though you bind it with the blowing wind
And buckle it with the moon,
The night will slip away
Like sorrow or a tune.

316 *Lewis Carroll*

'YOU are wise, Mr. Dodgson,' the young child said,
'And your forehead is getting a wrinkle;
And yet you've so twinkling an eye in your head—
I'm wondering what makes it twinkle?'

'In my youth,' Mr. Dodgson replied to the child,
'I acquired mathematical habits
To keep my odd thoughts from becoming as wild
As March Hares, and as frequent as Rabbits.'

'You are wise, Lewis Carroll,' the child said again,
'And the College you live in is hoary;
But if you've such numbers of thoughts in your brain—
Do you think you could tell me a story?'

'In my youth, if you must know the truth,' whispered he,
'I kept those same thoughts very supple
By letting my stories run quite fancy-free—
Allow me to tell you a couple!'

317 *Tailor*

I SAW a little tailor sitting stitch, stitch, stitching
Cross-legged on the floor of his kitch, kitch, kitchen.
His thumbs and his fingers were so nim, nim, nimble
With his wax and his scissors and his thim, thim, thimble.

His silk and his cotton he was thread, thread, threading
For a gown and a coat for a wed, wed, wedding,
His needle flew as swift as a swal, swal, swallow,
And his spools and his reels had to fol, fol, follow.

He hummed as he worked a merry dit, dit, ditty:
'The bride is as plump as she's pret, pret, pretty,
I wouldn't have her taller or short, short, shorter,
She can laugh like the falling of wat, wat, water.

'She can put a cherry-pie togeth, geth, gether,
She can dance as light as a feath, feath, feather,
She can sing as sweet as a fid, fid, fiddle,
And she's only twenty inches round the mid, mid, middle.'

The happy little tailor went on stitch, stitch, stitching
The black and the white in his kitch, kitch, kitchen.
He will wear the black one, she will wear the white one,
And the knot the parson ties will be a tight, tight, tight one.

318 *Mrs. Malone*

Mrs. Malone
Lived hard by a wood
All on her lonesome
As nobody should.
With her crust on a plate
And her pot on the coal
And none but herself
To converse with, poor soul.
In a shawl and a hood
She got sticks out-o'-door,
On a bit of old sacking
She slept on the floor,
And nobody, nobody
Asked how she fared
Or knew how she managed,
For nobody cared.
  Why make a pother
  About an old crone?
  What for should they bother
  With Mrs. Malone?

One Monday in winter
With snow on the ground
So thick that a footstep
Fell without sound,
She heard a faint frostbitten
Peck on the pane
And went to the window
To listen again.
There sat a cock-sparrow
Bedraggled and weak,
With half-open eyelid
And ice on his beak.
She threw up the sash
And she took the bird in,
And mumbled and fumbled it
Under her chin.
  'Ye're all of a smother,
  Ye're fair overblown!
  I've room fer another,'
  Said Mrs. Malone.

Come Tuesday while eating
Her dry morning slice
With the sparrow a-picking
('Ain't company nice!')
She heard on her doorpost
A curious scratch,
And there was a cat
With its claw on the latch.
It was hungry and thirsty
And thin as a lath,
It mewed and it mowed
On the slithery path.
She threw the door open
And warmed up some pap,
And huddled and cuddled it
In her old lap.
  'There, there, little brother,
  Ye poor skin-an'-bone,
  There's room fer another,'
  Said Mrs. Malone.

Come Wednesday while all of them
Crouched on the mat
With a crumb for the sparrow,
A sip for the cat,
There was wailing and whining
Outside in the wood,
And there sat a vixen
With six of her brood.
She was haggard and ragged
And worn to a shred,
And her half-dozen babies
Were only half-fed,
But Mrs. Malone, crying
'My! ain't they sweet!'
Happed them and lapped them
And gave them to eat.
 'You warm yerself, mother,
 Ye're cold as a stone!
 There's room fer another,'
 Said Mrs. Malone.

Come Thursday a donkey
Stepped in off the road
With sores on his withers
From bearing a load.
Come Friday when icicles
Pierced the white air
Down from the mountainside
Lumbered a bear.
For each she had something,
If little, to give—
'Lord knows, the poor critters
Must all of 'em live.'
She gave them her sacking,
Her hood and her shawl,
Her loaf and her teapot—
She gave them her all.
 'What with one thing and t'other
 Me fambily's grown,
 And there's room fer another,'
 Said Mrs. Malone.

Come Saturday evening
When time was to sup
Mrs. Malone
Had forgot to sit up.
The cat said *meeow*,
And the sparrow said *peep*,
The vixen, *she's sleeping*,
The bear, *let her sleep*.
On the back of the donkey
They bore her away,
Through trees and up mountains
Beyond night and day,
Till come Sunday morning
They brought her in state
Through the last cloudbank
As far as the Gate.
  'Who is it,' asked Peter,
  'You have with you there?'
  And donkey and sparrow,
  Cat, vixen, and bear

Exclaimed, 'Do you tell us
Up here she's unknown?
It's our mother, God bless us!
It's Mrs. Malone
Whose havings were few
And whose holding was small
And whose heart was so big
It had room for us all.'
Then Mrs. Malone
Of a sudden awoke,
She rubbed her two eyeballs
And anxiously spoke:
'Where am I, to goodness,
And what do I see?
My dears, let's turn back,
This ain't no place fer me!'
  But Peter said, 'Mother
  Go in to the Throne.
  There's room for another
  One, Mrs. Malone.'

ROSE FYLEMAN

1877–1957

319 *Fairies*

THERE are fairies at the bottom of our garden!
It's not so very, very far away;
You pass the gardener's shed and you just keep straight ahead—
I do so hope they've really come to stay.
There's a little wood, with moss in it and beetles,
And a little stream that quietly runs through;
You wouldn't think they'd dare to come merry-making there—
Well, they do.

There are fairies at the bottom of our garden!
They often have a dance on summer nights;
The butterflies and bees make a lovely little breeze,
And the rabbits stand about and hold the lights.
Did you know that they could sit upon the moonbeams
And pick a little star to make a fan,
And dance away up there in the middle of the air?
Well, they can.

There are fairies at the bottom of our garden!
You cannot think how beautiful they are;
They all stand up and sing when the Fairy Queen and King
Come gently floating down upon their car.
The King is very proud and *very* handsome;
The Queen—now can you guess who that could be
(She's a little girl all day, but at night she steals away)?
Well—it's ME!

320 *A Fairy Went A-Marketing*

A FAIRY went a-marketing—
She bought a little fish;
She put it in a crystal bowl
Upon a golden dish.
An hour she sat in wonderment
And watched its silver gleam,
And then she gently took it up
And slipped it in a stream.

A fairy went a-marketing—
She bought a coloured bird;
It sang the sweetest, shrillest song
That ever she had heard.
She sat beside its painted cage
And listened half the day,
And then she opened wide the door
And let it fly away.

A fairy went a-marketing—
She bought a winter gown
All stitched about with gossamer
And lined with thistledown.
She wore it all the afternoon
With prancing and delight,
Then gave it to a little frog
To keep him warm at night.

A fairy went a-marketing—
She bought a gentle mouse
To take her tiny messages,
To keep her tiny house.
All day she kept its busy feet
Pit-patting to and fro,
And then she kissed its silken ears,
Thanked it, and let it go.

321 *The Fairies Have Never a Penny to Spend*

THE fairies have never a penny to spend,
They haven't a thing put by,
But theirs is the dower of bird and of flower
And theirs are the earth and the sky.
And though you should live in a palace of gold
Or sleep in a dried-up ditch,
You could never be poor as the fairies are,
And never as rich.

Since ever and ever the world began
They have danced like a ribbon of flame,
They have sung their song through the centuries long
And yet it is never the same.
And though you be foolish or though you be wise,
With hair of silver or gold,
You could never be young as the fairies are,
And never as old.

322 *I Don't Like Beetles*

I DON'T like beetles, tho' I'm sure they're very good,
I don't like porridge, tho' my Nanna says I should;
I don't like the cistern in the attic where I play,
And the funny noise the bath makes when the water runs away.

I don't like the feeling when my gloves are made of silk,
And that dreadful slimy skinny stuff on top of hot milk;
I don't like tigers, not even in a book,
And, I know it's very naughty, but I *don't like Cook*!

323 *Mrs. Brown*

As soon as I'm in bed at night
And snugly settled down,
The little girl I am by day
Goes very suddenly away,
And then I'm Mrs. Brown.

I have a family of six,
And all of them have names,
The girls are Joyce and Nancy Maud,
The boys are Marmaduke and Claude
And Percival and James.

We have a house with twenty rooms
A mile away from town;
I think it's good for girls and boys
To be allowed to make a noise—
And so does Mr. Brown.

We do the most exciting things,
Enough to make you creep;
And on and on and on we go—
I sometimes wonder if I know
When I have gone to sleep.

324 *Temper*

'BLOW out the light,' they said, they said
(She'd got to the very last page);
'Blow out the light,' they said, they said,
'It's dreadfully wicked to read in bed';
Her eyes grew black and her face grew red
And she blew in a terrible rage.

She put out the moon, she did, she did,
So frightfully hard she blew,
She put out the moon, she did, she did;
Over the sky the darkness slid,
The stars all scuttled away and hid—
(A very wise thing to do).

But please don't whisper the tale about,
She'd get into trouble, she would;
Please don't whisper the tale about,
If anyone else should ever find out
She'd get into trouble without a doubt,
And now she's *ever* so good.

A. A. MILNE

1882–1956

325 *Buckingham Palace*

THEY'RE changing guard at Buckingham Palace—
Christopher Robin went down with Alice.
Alice is marrying one of the guard.
'A soldier's life is terrible hard,'
Says Alice.

They're changing guard at Buckingham Palace—
Christopher Robin went down with Alice.
We saw a guard in a sentry-box.
'One of the sergeants looks after their socks,'
Says Alice.

They're changing guard at Buckingham Palace—
Christopher Robin went down with Alice.
We looked for the King, but he never came.
'Well, God take care of him, all the same,'
Says Alice.

They're changing guard at Buckingham Palace—
Christopher Robin went down with Alice.
They've great big parties inside the grounds.
'I wouldn't be King for a hundred pounds,'
Says Alice.

They're changing guard at Buckingham Palace—
Christopher Robin went down with Alice.
A face looked out, but it wasn't the King's.
'He's much too busy a-signing things,'
Says Alice.

They're changing guard at Buckingham Palace—
Christopher Robin went down with Alice.
'Do you think the King knows all about *me*?'
'Sure to, dear, but it's time for tea,'
Says Alice.

326 *The Three Foxes*

ONCE upon a time there were three little foxes
Who didn't wear stockings, and they didn't wear sockses,
But they all had handkerchiefs to blow their noses,
And they kept their handkerchiefs in cardboard boxes.

They lived in the forest in three little houses,
And they didn't wear coats, and they didn't wear trousies.
They ran through the woods on their little bare tootsies,
And they played 'Touch last' with a family of mouses.

They didn't go shopping in the High Street shopses,
But caught what they wanted in the woods and copses.
They all went fishing, and they caught three wormses,
They went out hunting, and they caught three wopses.

They went to a Fair, and they all won prizes—
Three plum-puddingses and three mince-pieses.
They rode on elephants and swang on swingses,
And hit three coco-nuts at coco-nut shieses.

That's all that I know of the three little foxes
Who kept their handkerchiefs in cardboard boxes.
They lived in the forest in three little houses,
But they didn't wear coats and they didn't wear trousies,
And they didn't wear stockings and they didn't wear sockses.

327 *The King's Breakfast*

THE King asked
The Queen, and
The Queen asked
The Dairymaid:
'Could we have some butter for
The Royal slice of bread?'
The Queen asked
The Dairymaid,

The Dairymaid
Said, 'Certainly,
I'll go and tell
The cow
Now
Before she goes to bed.'

The Dairymaid
She curtsied,
And went and told
The Alderney:
'Don't forget the butter for
The Royal slice of bread.'
The Alderney
Said sleepily:
'You'd better tell
His Majesty
That many people nowadays
Like marmalade
Instead.'

The Dairymaid
Said, 'Fancy!'
And went to
Her Majesty.
She curtsied to the Queen, and
She turned a little red:
'Excuse me,
Your Majesty,
For taking of
The liberty,
But marmalade is tasty, if
It's very
Thickly
Spread.'

The Queen said
'Oh!'
And went to
His Majesty:

'Talking of the butter for
The Royal slice of bread,
Many people
Think that
Marmalade
Is nicer.
Would you like to try a little
Marmalade
Instead?'

The King said,
'Bother!'
And then he said,
'Oh, deary me!'
The King sobbed, 'Oh, deary me!'
And went back to bed.
'Nobody,'
He whimpered,
'Could call me
A fussy man;
I *only* want
A little bit
Of butter for
My bread!'

The Queen said,
'There, there!'
And went to
The Dairymaid.
The Dairymaid
Said, 'There, there!'
And went to the shed.
The cow said,
'There, there!
I didn't really
Mean it;
Here's milk for his porringer
And butter for his bread.'

The Queen took
The butter
And brought it to
His Majesty;
The King said,
'Butter, eh?'
And bounced out of bed.
'Nobody,' he said,
As he kissed her
Tenderly,
'Nobody,' he said,
As he slid down
The banisters,
'Nobody,
My darling,
Could call me
A fussy man—
BUT
I do like a little bit of butter to my bread!'

328 *Vespers*

LITTLE Boy kneels at the foot of the bed,
Droops on the little hands little gold head.
Hush! Hush! Whisper who dares!
Christopher Robin is saying his prayers.

God bless Mummy. I know that's right.
Wasn't it fun in the bath tonight?
The cold's so cold, and the hot's so hot.
Oh! *God bless Daddy*—I quite forgot.

If I open my fingers a little bit more,
I can see Nanny's dressing-gown on the door.
It's a beautiful blue, but it hasn't a hood.
Oh! *God bless Nanny and make her good.*

Mine has a hood, and I lie in bed,
And pull the hood right over my head,
And I shut my eyes, and I curl up small,
And nobody knows that I'm there at all.

Oh! *Thank you, God, for a lovely day.*
And what was the other I had to say?
I said 'Bless Daddy,' so what can it be?
Oh! Now I remember it. *God bless Me.*

Little Boy kneels at the foot of the bed,
Droops on the little hands little gold head.
Hush! Hush! Whisper who dares!
Christopher Robin is saying his prayers.

329 *Us Two*

WHEREVER I am, there's always Pooh,
There's always Pooh and Me.
Whatever I do, he wants to do,
'Where are you going today?' says Pooh:
'Well, that's very odd 'cos I was too.
Let's go together,' says Pooh, says he.
'Let's go together,' says Pooh.

'What's twice eleven?' I said to Pooh.
('Twice what?' said Pooh to Me.)
'I *think* it ought to be twenty-two.'
'Just what I think myself,' said Pooh.
'It wasn't an easy sum to do,
But that's what it is,' said Pooh, said he.
'That's what it is,' said Pooh.

'Let's look for dragons,' I said to Pooh.
'Yes, let's,' said Pooh to Me.
We crossed the river and found a few—
'Yes, those are dragons all right,' said Pooh.
'As soon as I saw their beaks I knew.
That's what they are,' said Pooh, said he.
'That's what they are,' said Pooh.

'Let's frighten the dragons,' I said to Pooh.
'That's right,' said Pooh to Me.
'*I'm* not afraid,' I said to Pooh,
And I held his paw and I shouted 'Shoo!
Silly old dragons!'—and off they flew.
'I wasn't afraid,' said Pooh, said he,
'I'm *never* afraid with you.'

So wherever I am, there's always Pooh,
There's always Pooh and Me.
'What would I do,' I said to Pooh,
'If it wasn't for you,' and Pooh said: 'True,
It isn't much fun for One, but Two
Can stick together,' says Pooh, says he.
'That's how it is,' says Pooh.

T. S. ELIOT

1888–1965

330 *Macavity: The Mystery Cat*

MACAVITY'S a Mystery Cat: he's called the Hidden Paw—
For he's the master criminal who can defy the Law.
He's the bafflement of Scotland Yard, the Flying Squad's despair:
For when they reach the scene of crime—*Macavity's not there!*

Macavity, Macavity, there's no one like Macavity,
He's broken every human law, he breaks the law of gravity.
His powers of levitation would make a fakir stare,
And when you reach the scene of crime—*Macavity's not there!*
You may seek him in the basement, you may look up in the air—
But I tell you once and once again, *Macavity's not there!*

Macavity's a ginger cat, he's very tall and thin;
You would know him if you saw him, for his eyes are sunken in.
His brow is deeply lined with thought, his head is highly domed;
His coat is dusty from neglect, his whiskers are uncombed.
He sways his head from side to side, with movements like a snake;
And when you think he's half asleep, he's always wide awake.

Macavity, Macavity, there's no one like Macavity,
For he's a fiend in feline shape, a monster of depravity.
You may meet him in a by-street, you may see him in the square—
But when a crime's discovered, then *Macavity's not there!*

He's outwardly respectable. (They say he cheats at cards.)
And his footprints are not found in any file of Scotland Yard's.
And when the larder's looted, or the jewel-case is rifled,
Or when the milk is missing, or another Peke's been stifled,
Or the greenhouse glass is broken, and the trellis past repair—
Ay, there's the wonder of the thing! *Macavity's not there!*

And when the Foreign Office find a Treaty's gone astray,
Or the Admiralty lose some plans and drawings by the way,
There may be a scrap of paper in the hall or on the stair—
But it's useless to investigate—*Macavity's not there!*
And when the loss has been disclosed, the Secret Service say:
'It *must* have been Macavity!'—but he's a mile away.
You'll be sure to find him resting, or a-licking of his thumbs,
Or engaged in doing complicated long division sums.

Macavity, Macavity, there's no one like Macavity,
There never was a Cat of such deceitfulness and suavity.
He always has an alibi, and one or two to spare:
At whatever time the deed took place—MACAVITY WASN'T THERE!
And they say that all the Cats whose wicked deeds are widely known
(I might mention Mungojerrie, I might mention Griddlebone)
Are nothing more than agents for the Cat who all the time
Just controls their operations: the Napoleon of Crime!

331 *The Song of the Jellicles*

JELLICLE Cats come out tonight
Jellicle Cats come one come all:
The Jellicle Moon is shining bright—
Jellicles come to the Jellicle Ball.

Jellicle Cats are black and white,
Jellicle Cats are rather small;
Jellicle Cats are merry and bright,
And pleasant to hear when they caterwaul.
Jellicle Cats have cheerful faces,
Jellicle Cats have bright black eyes;
They like to practise their airs and graces
And wait for the Jellicle Moon to rise.

Jellicle Cats develop slowly,
Jellicle Cats are not too big;
Jellicle Cats are roly-poly,
They know how to dance a gavotte and a jig.
Until the Jellicle Moon appears
They make their toilette and take their repose:
Jellicles wash behind their ears,
Jellicles dry between their toes.

Jellicle Cats are white and black,
Jellicle Cats are of moderate size;
Jellicles jump like a jumping-jack,
Jellicle Cats have moonlit eyes.
They're quiet enough in the morning hours,
They're quiet enough in the afternoon,
Reserving their terpsichorean powers
To dance by the light of the Jellicle Moon.

Jellicle Cats are black and white,
Jellicle Cats (as I said) are small;
If it happens to be a stormy night
They will practise a caper or two in the hall.
If it happens the sun is shining bright
You would say they had nothing to do at all:
They are resting and saving themselves to be right
For the Jellicle Moon and the Jellicle Ball.

OGDEN NASH

1902–1971

332

Morning Prayer

Now another day is breaking,
Sleep was sweet and so is waking.
Dear Lord, I promised you last night
Never again to sulk or fight.
Such vows are easier to keep
When a child is sound asleep.
Today, O Lord, for your dear sake,
I'll try to keep them when awake.

AUTHORS AND SOURCES

AUTHORS AND SOURCES

c.	*circa*, about	MS.	manuscript
e.g.	*exempli gratia*, for example	q.v.	*quod vide*, which see
fl.	flourished	qq.v.	*quae vide*, which see (more than one)

AIKIN, JOHN (1747–1822), brother of Mrs. Barbauld and father of Lucy Aikin (qq.v.), was born at Kibworth in Leicestershire, of Scottish descent. He was a man of many parts, practising doctor, scholar, scientist, outspoken dissenter, and active friend of John Howard the prison reformer, as well as writer for the young. His *Evenings at Home; or, The Juvenile Budget Opened*, six volumes, 1792–6, in the third volume of which appeared 'Tit for Tat', was a favourite work in the first half of the nineteenth century. Mrs. Molesworth was scarcely exaggerating when she remarked of the cultured class in 1870: 'I should think *everybody's* grandfathers and grandmothers had an *Evenings at Home* among their few, dearly-prized children's books.'

AIKIN, LUCY (1781–1864), gifted member of a gifted family (see John Aikin above), learnt French, Italian, and Latin; and began contributing to magazines when she was seventeen, eventually making her name as a historian. She was twenty, and living in Stoke Newington, when she compiled *Poetry for Children: Consisting of Short Pieces to be Committed to Memory*, choosing with 'much thought' verses on subjects likely to interest children; and supplementing them with poems of her own, among them 'The Beggar Man' and 'The Swallow'. The collection was published in 1801, and went into five editions in its first seven years.

ALEXANDER, CECIL FRANCES (1818–1895), was born in County Wicklow, the daughter of a Royal Marine officer, Major John Humphreys, and she lived in Ireland all her life. In 1850 she married the Revd. William Alexander, who was to become Archbishop of Armagh; but much of her verse for children was written before she married and had a family of her own. Her small book *Hymns for Little Children*, published in 1848, and dedicated to her godsons, is remarkable in containing no less than three hymns renowned throughout the English-speaking world: 'Once in royal David's city', 'There is a green hill far away', and the lyrical 'All things bright and beautiful', which originally contained the verse suggesting that each individual's place in life was ordained:

The rich man in his castle,
The poor man at his gate,
God made them, high or lowly,
And ordered their estate.

'The Beggar Boy' and 'The Fieldmouse' appeared in her *Moral Songs*, 1849.

ALLINGHAM, WILLIAM (1824–1889), an Irishman of English descent, was born at Ballyshannon in Donegal. For most of his life he was a customs officer; but years in government employ did not undermine his love of literature, nor his affection for the Irish peasantry. 'The Fairies', written at Killybegs in 1840 and published in his *Poems*, 1850, mentions places he had known since his childhood. It is based on an old highland ditty, one that in Scotland was adapted to the Jacobite cause:

'Tis up the rocky mountain and down the mossy glen,
We darena gang a milking for Charlie and his men.

'Riding', the gently humorous account of a turf-cadger, is another piece inspired by a traditional song, the words of which are in *The Oxford Dictionary of Nursery Rhymes*, p. 258. The nursery song 'Wishing' first appeared in *Household Words*, 11 February 1854, and 'Robin Redbreast', written in the autumn of 1856, in his *Fifty Modern Poems*, 1865.

ALMA-TADEMA, LAURENCE (*c.* 1865–1940), was the elder daughter of the Dutch painter Sir Lawrence Alma-Tadema who, early in her life, made his home in England; and it was in England that Laurence (note the spelling) was brought up. 'If No One Ever Marries Me' was published in a collection of her poems *Realms of Unknown Kings*, 1897, and it became a favourite with little girls, particularly in the 1920s and 1930s. Miss Alma-Tadema never did marry. For fifty years an admirer and friend of Paderewski, the Polish pianist and patriot, she was prominent during the First World War in the cause of Polish freedom. A tall, dark, intellectual person, dominant in any social gathering, but patient with children, she ended her days living—as she had predicted—on her own and in a cottage, St. Luke's Cottage, at Wittersham in Kent.

AUNT EFFIE, the author of two much-loved books, *Aunt Effie's Rhymes for Little Children*, 1852, and *Aunt Effie's Gift for the Nursery*, 1854, can now, after more than a century, be pronounced to have been Miss Jane Euphemia Browne (1811–1898). 'Effie' (short for Euphemia) was a lively pretty girl, full of 'curiosity and wit', the daughter of

William Browne of Tallantire Hall, Cockermouth, Cumberland, a background commensurate with the occasional references in her rhymes to butlers and parkland, which will not have been unnoticed by contemporary readers when they wondered who she was. Further, the children for whom she wrote were almost certainly those of her sister Caroline, who had married Lord Teignmouth. She herself did not marry until middle age, when she became Mrs. Stephen H. Saxby, wife of the first vicar of East Clevedon in Somerset.

Barbauld, Anna Laetitia (1743–1825), born Aikin (q.v.), was an outstanding child even in an intellectual family. At two years old she could read short sentences, 'and in half a year more could read as well as most women'. When she was fifteen her father was appointed to Warrington Academy, in Lancashire, and here she was encouraged to write poetry by Joseph Priestley, the discoverer of oxygen, at that time the tutor in classics. The story is that she wrote 'The Mouse's Petition' after finding a mouse in a trap, where it had been confined all night by Dr. Priestley, who was making one of his many experiments with different kinds of air. Her *Poems*, including 'The Mouse's Petition', were published in 1773.

Baring-Gould, Sabine (1834–1924), who was to become one of the most prolific of English authors, wrote 'Now the Day is Over', probably in 1864, for the children of his mission school at Horbury Bridge, in the West Riding of Yorkshire, where he was curate. The children were mostly hands in the local woollen mills, unable to attend school except at night; and sixty or more would come each evening, unless prevented by having to work in the mills at night. The words of the new hymn, which appeared in the *Church Times*, 16 February 1867, and in the supplement to *Hymns Ancient and Modern*, 1868, will thus have had special meaning to them. Another hymn Baring-Gould wrote at this time was 'Onward Christian Soldiers', first sung as the children processed to Horbury at Whitsun. One girl of sixteen, Grace Taylor of Poppleton's Mill, was so poor she is said to have had no clothes thought fit for the occasion. However, in a short while Baring-Gould was to propose to her; and she was to be happily married to him for almost half a century.

Belloc, Hilaire (1870–1953), born in France, of Anglo-French descent, was brought up in England; and at nineteen followed his sister, the future novelist Mrs. Belloc Lowndes, in a literary career. He was a man of immense ability but little known until the publication of *The Bad Child's Book of Beasts*, 1896, in which appeared 'The Yak' and 'The Frog', and which was so immediately popular that the first printing sold out in four days. *More Beasts for Worse Children*, containing 'The Python' and 'The Vulture', followed in 1897; and *Cautionary Tales for Children*, containing 'Jim' and 'Matilda', in 1907, while he was Liberal Member of Parliament for South Salford.

BLAKE, WILLIAM (1757–1827), was the son of a London hosier, and almost all his knowledge was self-acquired, for he left ordinary school at the age of ten to enter a drawing school. Throughout his life he laboured chiefly as an engraver, continuing to the end of his days to be thought of as an artist rather than as a poet, although his verse is some of the purest in the English language. His book *Songs of Innocence*, 1789, in which appear the 'happy songs every child may joy to hear', he literally made himself: writing it, illustrating it, engraving the text and illustrations, printing the book, and selling it. The song now generally known as 'The Piper' was the introduction to the book.

BROWNE, JANE EUPHEMIA. See Aunt Effie.

BROWNE, MATTHEW. See William Brighty Rands.

BROWNING, ROBERT (1812–1889), a Londoner, born in Camberwell, who was a poet almost from birth, attempted in his poetry to represent on the highest intellectual level the complexity of human nature. 'The Pied Piper of Hamelin', virtuoso performance though it is, is not typical of his work, and he was at first reluctant to let it be published. It was written in 1842 to amuse the little son of his friend William Macready, the actor, hence the note at the end of the poem addressed to 'Willie'. The legend of the Pied Piper of Hamelin is an ancient one: older even than Browning supposed. In the earliest known account, itself medieval, the event is stated to have taken place in 1284. One hundred and thirty boys are said to have followed the piper, and to have vanished without trace. The poem was included in Browning's *Dramatic Lyrics*, 1842.

BULLOKAR, WILLIAM (*c.* 1520–*c.* 1590), a Londoner, is notable as being the first man to have written an English grammar, a work published in 1586. He was also deeply concerned by the difficulties that arise from words not always being spelt as they are pronounced, and wished to introduce a revised alphabet of forty letters. His *Aesop's Fabls in tru Ortography*, 1585, was written to show his method; and it was in this work that he addressed himself to his child.

BUNYAN, JOHN (1628–1688), at first followed his father's trade of tinsmith in Bedfordshire, and was a gay young man, though so poor that when he married he and his wife had not, he said, 'so much household stuff as a Dish or Spoon betwixt us both'. However, his wife possessed two religious books which he began to study. He became a preacher and author; was imprisoned for preaching without a licence, and was in prison when he wrote *The Pilgrim's Progress*.

He was clearly gratified by the way children, as well as adults, liked reading *The Pilgrim's Progress*; and his book written specially for the young, *A Book for Boys and Girls: or, Country Rhimes for Children*, 1686, is in its way as remarkable a work. Unlike previous books for the young it consists of 'homely rhimes' about familiar objects and happenings; and Bunyan often added a 'comparison' so that children should understand his allegories more easily.

I do't to shew them how each Fingle-fangle,
On which they doting are, their Souls entangle,
As with a Web, a Trap, a Ginn, or Snare,
And will destroy them, have they not a Care.

BURNS, ROBERT (1759–1796), Scotland's national poet, was the son of a small farmer in Ayrshire, and in his early years could think of poetry only when resting from his labours as a farm hand. He was inspired by the traditional verse of his country; and had he been born a century later he might have produced a score of songs to delight the young, and not felt himself unmanly in doing so. But in Scotland in Burns's day the convention was to admonish children rather than amuse them; and Burns had little inclination to lecture anyone. 'Wee Willie Gray' is unlike his usual verse; and was written to the tune of an old nursery ditty:

Wee Totum Fogg,
Sits upon a creepie;
Half an ell o' gray
Wad be his coat and breekie.

The song was published after his death in the last volume of *The Scots Musical Museum*, 1803.

BURTON, ROBERT. See Nathaniel Crouch.

CARNEY, JULIA A. (1823–1908), a native of Boston, Massachusetts, and a school teacher, whose maiden name was Fletcher, wrote 'Little drops of water' apparently in 1845, the story being that she wrote the lines almost extempore for a Sunday School tract while in class. This tract has not been located. The earliest we have found the words is in the London-published *Juvenile Missionary Magazine*, vol. x (April 1853), but this recording lacks the verse beginning 'So our little errors', which appears in *Hymns and Sacred Songs, for Sunday Schools and Social Worship*, 1855. Both recordings concluded with the missionary verse:

Little seeds of mercy
  Sown by youthful hands,
Grow to bless the nations
  Far in heathen lands.

In the nineteenth century the hymn used to be attributed to the Revd. Dr. E. Cobham Brewer (1810–1897), but it seems his part was simply to write four new verses to follow the first, his version appearing in his little reader *My First Book of Reading and Spelling*, published in 1864.

CARROLL, LEWIS, was the pen-name of Charles Lutwidge Dodgson (1832–1898), mathematical lecturer at Christ Church, Oxford, who wrote several treatises on mathematics under his own name which never achieved the world-wide celebrity of *Alice's Adventures in Wonderland*, and the other books of dream-like nonsense he wrote under his pseudonym. Carrollian humour, however, often arises from Dodgson's application of sound logic to a ridiculous situation: the resulting sense of fitness being one of the reasons his verses and stories are so memorable. What better advice, for instance, could be given to a postage stamp found wandering at night than 'You'd best be getting home . . . the nights are very damp'? Except for the 'Mad Gardener's Song', in which this advice appears, and which was a feature of the two volumes of *Sylvie and Bruno*, 1889 and 1893, the poems we give all appeared in *Alice in Wonderland*, 1865, or in *Through the Looking Glass*, 1872. 'You are old, Father William' parodies Southey's 'The Old Man's Comforts' (q.v.); 'The Lobster Quadrille' uses the metre of Mary Howitt's 'The Spider and the Fly' (q.v.); and 'The Lobster', given in a version published in 1870, burlesques Watts's 'The Sluggard' (q.v.). A tribute to Lewis Carroll by Eleanor Farjeon appears on page 331.

CARRYL, CHARLES EDWARD (1841–1920), was a stockbroker in New York, and director of railroad companies. The great moment in his life came when he read *Alice in Wonderland* by his near-namesake Lewis Carroll (q.v.), and he began writing fantasies in a similar vein. 'The Camel's Complaint' first appeared in the New York children's magazine *St. Nicholas*, April 1892. It was part of the 'ferry tale' he wrote for his daughter Constance, called *The Admiral's Caravan*, which was published in book form in the same year, 1892.

CHAUCER, GEOFFREY (*c.* 1343–1400), the father of English poetry, produced no work especially for the young other than the prose 'Treatise on the Astrolabe', compiled for 'little Lewis my son'. But in his *Canterbury Tales*, when the Manciple (steward) has finished telling the fable of the crow which could imitate the voice of any man, and which spoke once too often—with terrible consequence for his master, and for all crows ever after—he recalls the counsel his mother used to give him about holding his tongue. In this passage Chaucer gives a poetical rendering of advice that was already becoming traditional.

CHEAR, ABRAHAM (died 1668), appears to have been a native of Plymouth, and a Baptist, who wrote some of his poems 'whilst in bonds for the truth of Christ'. Much of his verse employs language which today can produce an effect other than that intended, as in his well-known lines:

'Tis pitty, such a pretty Maid,
as I, should go to Hell.

But he was certainly a writer who was admired by his Puritan contemporaries; and his 'seasonable lessons and instructions to youth', among which was his address to his youngest kinsman, were collected posthumously in *A Looking-Glass for Children*, 1672, and were often reprinted.

CIBBER, COLLEY (1671–1757), a Londoner who was to become poet laureate, showed an aptitude for writing verse while still at school; but began his career as an actor, and only when he could not obtain the parts he wanted did he turn to writing. 'The Blind Boy' appeared in *The British Musical Miscellany*, vol. i (1734), and also on a broadside. Numerous anthologies for children included it in the eighteenth and nineteenth centuries; and a German translation was set to music by Schubert.

COCHRAN, MRS. See Sydney Dayre.

COLERIDGE, SAMUEL TAYLOR (1772–1834), who was at Christ's Hospital with Charles Lamb (q.v.), and who was to become the close friend of Southey and of the Wordsworths (qq.v.), possessed one of the most considerable minds of his day, and indeed of all time. He suggested it was the privilege of genius 'to carry on the feelings of childhood into the powers of manhood', and he exemplified this in some of his verse. His 'Answer to a Child's Question' was written in 1802 when his eldest son Hartley was six; and it was for Hartley, first of all, that he prepared the lesson on metrical feet. 'A Child's Evening Prayer' was written in 1806.

COLERIDGE, SARA (1802–1852), was a 'slender, delicate creature, fair as a snowdrop and almost as pale' when eighteen months old; and when grown to maidenhood was so graceful that it seemed to Wordsworth, 'her foot were loath to crush the mountain dew-drops'. Delightful in person, skilful and intelligent, a lover of books and philosophy, she was just such a one as might be imagined the daughter of a great poet, and perhaps she would have been a considerable writer herself had she not devoted much of her life to the memory of her father S. T. Coleridge (see above). The verses we give come from *Pretty Lessons in Verse for Good Children*, 1834, which she wrote for her three-year-old son Herbert, himself to become a scholar, and first editor of the work now renowned as *The Oxford English Dictionary*.

COOK, ELIZA (1818–1889), was the youngest of eleven children of a London brass-worker. Although almost entirely self-educated, she began to write poetry when she was fifteen; and her first collection was published when she was seventeen. Encouraged by its success, she started sending contributions anonymously to the *Weekly Dispatch*, not even the editor knowing who she was or where she lived. Her poems gave immediate pleasure, and when her identity was revealed she quickly became one of the poets best known to ordinary people. In 1849 she started a periodical called *Eliza Cook's Journal*; and it was in the feature 'Rhymes for Young Readers', on 21 July 1849, that 'The Mouse and the Cake' was published.

COOLIDGE, SUSAN, was the pen-name of Sarah Chauncey Woolsey (1835–1905), member of a moderately well-to-do family in Cleveland, Ohio. She was sent away from home to be educated, to Mrs. Hubbard's Boarding School in Hanover, New Hampshire, and her experiences at the school are undoubtedly reflected in some of her stories. Her best-known books are her Katy books: *What Katy Did*, 1873; *What Katy Did at School*, 1874; and *What Katy Did Next*, 1886. 'Measles in the Ark' comes in *What Katy Did at School*. It is the rhyme Katy wrote at the first meeting of the girls' secret society, the S.S.U.C. (Society for the Suppression of Unladylike Conduct), when they played the game 'Word and Question'; and Katy had to write a rhyme which introduced the word *measles*, and answered the question 'Who was the grandmother of Invention?'

CORBET, RICHARD (1582–1635), born in Surrey, the son of a gardener, was a merry man, a rhymester, and a practical joker who 'loved . . . boy's play very well'—even when he became bishop of Oxford. But his wishes for his son Vincent, which were published among his *Poems* in 1647, were to no purpose. Aubrey was to report that Vincent was 'a very handsome youth' who had become a wastrel. 'He is run out of all, and goes begging up and downe to Gentlemen.'

CORBETT, ELIZABETH T., was a regular contributor to *St. Nicholas*, the outstanding New York magazine for young people; and it was in *St. Nicholas* that the 'Three Wise Old Women' first appeared, in April 1878. The verses were subsequently published in book-form on both sides of the Atlantic, and were soon said to be 'as well established in popular favour as the old woman in Mother Goose that went to sleep in the king's highway'.

CORY, WILLIAM (1823–1892), classical scholar, and one of the great tutors at Eton, where he was an assistant master for twenty-six years, was a man who combined immense knowledge of the past with a sense of personal involvement in its triumphs and tragedies. To the outside world he was little known. His poetry, which includes 'Heraclitus'—a poem often set in schools for recitation—was not immediately appreciated; and he published anonymously until almost the end of his life. 'A Ballad for a Boy', which appeared in the 1891 edition of *Ionica*, was written in 1885.

COTTON, NATHANIEL (1705–1788), was a physician who spent most of his life in St. Albans in Hertfordshire, where he brought up a large family, wrote poetry, and managed a mental home, which he dignified with the name 'Collegium Insanorum'. He was a kindly man who practised what he preached: self-control, self-effacement, and contentment. His *Visions in Verse, for the Entertainment and Instruction of Younger Minds*, published anonymously in 1751, was immensely popular, and was reprinted more than a dozen times during the next half-century. 'To a Child Five Years Old' first appeared in Dodsley's *Collection of Poems*, 1755; and the fable of 'The Bee, the Ant, and the Sparrow' in the enlarged edition of 1763.

CROSSMAN, SAMUEL (1624?–1684), was a Cambridge-educated churchman who, for a period, did not conform with the establishment. His hymn 'My song is love unknown' gained wide circulation in the many editions of *The Young Man's Calling, or The Whole Duty of Youth*, 1678; but first appeared in Crossman's *The Young Man's Meditation*, 1664, a companion work to his *Young Man's Monitor* of the same date, which was written for the children and servants of some friends.

CROUCH, NATHANIEL (1632?–1725?), the son of a tailor in Lewes, Sussex, was one of the first men to make a respectable living by the disreputable practice, now common, of digesting or restyling other people's books, and passing them off as his own. *Youth's Divine Pastime. Containing Forty Remarkable Scripture Stories, turned into common English Verse. With Forty Curious Pictures proper to each Story. Very Delightful for the Virtuous imploying the Vacant Hours of Young Persons, and preventing Vain and Vicious Divertisements*, first published about 1689, is one of the few books for which he wrote anything original, and in it appeared 'David and Goliath'. It went into at least eighteen editions; and a sequel, which was in print by 1710, contained 'The Tower of Babel'. Usually, and perhaps wisely, Crouch wrote under a pseudonym, as Robert Burton, Richard Burton, or the initials R. B.

DAYRE, SYDNEY (fl. 1881), was the pen-name of a Mrs. Cochran who wrote verse for the New York children's magazine *St. Nicholas*, verse that was much in the style that A. A. Milne (q.v.) was later to adopt—expressing children's thoughts in a realistic manner without making the child look ridiculous. In 'A Lesson for Mamma', which appeared in *St. Nicholas*, April 1881, she even foreshadows something of Milne's rhythm and long pauses. 'Morning Compliments' appeared seven years later in January 1888.

DE LA MARE, WALTER (1873–1956), born in Kent, the sixth child of an official in the Bank of England, was a true and life-long poet in the spirit of Blake and Christina Rossetti. Like many great poets he was modest, gentle, haunted. Characteristically, when he began writing, he wrote under an assumed name, Walter Ramal, which was part of his name spelt backwards. His first book *Songs of Childhood*, 1902, contained 'Tartary', 'John Mouldy', and 'Bunches of Grapes'; his best-known book *Peacock Pie*, 1913, included 'Alas, Alack!', 'Old Shellover', and 'The Song of the Mad Prince'; his most influential book, perhaps, was *Come Hither*, a new kind of anthology with notes as special as the poems. A plaque to his memory can be seen in St. Paul's Cathedral, where his ashes are buried.

DEKKER, THOMAS (1572?–1632), a Londoner, a contemporary of Shakespeare, a dramatist, and a lyric poet, seems to have had little benefit from his work. He suffered from poverty, and was long in prison for debt. *The Pleasant Comodie of Patient Grissill*, in which appears 'Golden slumbers kiss your eyes', was written in collaboration with Henry Chettle and William Haughton, apparently in 1599, and published in 1603. In it Janicolo, the grandfather, instructs a servant to rock the cradle, while he charms his daughter's two infants to sleep 'by sweet tunde lullabyes'. It is accepted that the lullaby he sings was Dekker's composition.

DIXON, HENRY (1675–1760), an erudite and enlightened schoolmaster born in London, was master of St. Andrew's School, Holborn, before he was twenty. From there he was appointed to Bath, becoming a master at the Blue Coat School, Bath, on its foundation in 1711; and remaining at the school until his death almost forty years later. His claim to fame lies in his authorship of *The English Instructor; or, The Art of Spelling Improved*, 1728, one of the most influential primers of the eighteenth century. The work was a successful attempt to make the first lessons for children 'easy, profitable, and delightful'; and is interlaced with Dixon's verses, written in the number of syllables appropriate to the lesson. 'The Description of a Good Boy', frequently reprinted in rival reading books, is written in words of one syllable. If *The English Instructor* had not been so popular, Henry Dixon might be better known today. But it was so much used that of the first fifty editions hardly more than a dozen copies are known to have survived.

DODGSON, CHARLES LUTWIDGE. See Lewis Carroll.

DORSET, CATHERINE ANN (1751?–1835), was the younger sister of Charlotte Smith (q.v.), and contributed to her sister's *Conversations Introducing Poetry, for the Use of Children*, 1804. Thereafter, on the death of her husband, an army captain, it was perhaps natural she should think of writing verse for children; and when William Roscoe's shilling booklet *The Butterfly's Ball* was published in 1807 (q.v.), she immediately wrote *The Peacock 'At Home'* as a sequel. Its reception was almost as enthusiastic. Issued in a similar style, 'Price One Shilling plain, and Eighteen-pence coloured', it sold by the thousand, and in five years was reprinted twenty-five times.

ELIOT, THOMAS STEARNS (1888–1965), most influential poet of his day, was born at St. Louis, Missouri, went to Harvard, and then as a young man made England his home, and lived in London for the rest of his life. He was a man of the highest intellectual abilities; critic, editor, and publisher, as well as poet. It was his friend and mentor Ezra Pound who dubbed him 'Old Possum'; and when in 1939 he came to publish a book of verse for children, a book different from anything he had written before, it seemed to him right to use the name in the title: *Old Possum's Book of Practical Cats.*

EWING, JULIANA HORATIA (1841–1885), member of one of the most happy of literary families, was the second of the eight children of Margaret Gatty, who herself was an author, as well as founder, in 1866, of the fine children's monthly *Aunt Judy's Magazine*. 'Aunt Judy' had been the nursery nickname the Gatty children had for their story-telling sister Juliana; and predictably Juliana, who married Major Alexander Ewing in 1867, and subsequently lived mostly at Aldershot, became the magazine's mainstay, contributing both tales and verses. 'The Burial of the Linnet' appeared in the September number, 1866; 'The Willow-Man' in December 1872; 'A Friend in the Garden' in January 1873; 'The Dolls' Wash' in September 1874; and 'Garden Lore' in March 1879. Alfred Scott Gatty (q.v.) was one of her brothers.

FARJEON, ELEANOR (1881–1965), who was the daughter of an English novelist, and grand-daughter of the great American actor Joseph Jefferson, was enchanted throughout her life by fairy tales and nursery songs, and her poems repeatedly echo their language and rhythms; in fact her jingle about the name of the London bridge and tube station, Blackfriars, has itself been taken for a traditional nursery rhyme, and printed anonymously. However, her strength lay in the delineation of character and the telling of a magic tale; and when these accomplishments were combined, as in 'Mrs. Malone', she added wonderfully to the classics of juvenile literature. 'Blackfriars' was included in *Nursery Rhymes of London Town*, 1916; 'The Night will

Never Stay' in *Tunes of a Penny Piper*, 1922; 'Lewis Carroll' in *The New Book of Days*, 1941; and 'Tailor' in *Cherrystones*, 1942. 'Mrs. Malone' appeared as a separate publication in 1950.

FERGUSON, JAMES (1842–*c.* 1910), a native of Stanley in Perthshire, began work in a mill at the age of ten, was apprenticed to a grocer at fourteen, and throughout his life had humble employment, being a labourer, chargehand, shop assistant, and clerk in the dyeing works of Pullar's of Perth. At one time he was a painter of provision-merchants' tickets. Yet from his youth onwards he contributed poems and sketches to local newspapers (under the name of Nisbet Noble) and gained a more than local reputation. 'Auld Daddy Darkness' was composed as a companion-piece to Robert Tennant's 'Wee Davie Daylicht' (q.v.).

FIELD, EUGENE (1850–1895), was a literary columnist in Chicago, and 'Wynken, Blynken, and Nod' appeared in the Chicago *Daily News*, 9 March 1889. 'The little story occurred to me as I was riding on the street cars. I had determined to write a series of lullabies and had begun one which I had meant to entitle a Dutch lullaby . . . When the name Wynken, Blynken and Nod occurred suddenly to me, I abandoned the windmill story and took up with the wooden shoe. I sat up in bed and wrote out the lullaby as it now appears with the exception that I first wrote

"Into a sea of blue"

and this line I changed next morning to

"Into a sea of dew".

The original draft of the poem was made upon brown wrapping paper.' In book form the poem first appeared in *A Little Book of Western Verse*, 1889. 'The Sugar-Plum Tree' was the first poem in *With Trumpet and Drum*, 1892.

FOXTON, THOMAS (*c.* 1695–1740), was one of the first to take up Watts's suggestion that 'some happy and condescending genius' should write verse specially for the young. His *Moral Songs Composed for the Use of Children*, 1728, have not Watts's genius, but most of them are certainly, as he himself says, about 'real occurencies which children daily meet with, and in which they themselves are the principal actors'. The poems were subsequently revised, to some advantage; and a selection were included in *A Choice Collection of Hymns and Moral Songs*, 1781.

FRERE, JOHN HOOKHAM (1769–1846), was a career diplomatist whose career came to an end in 1809 when, as British minister in Madrid, he was partially responsible for Moore's fateful retreat to Corunna. By nature, however, he was a poet, a wit, and a man of letters. As a boy at Eton he was one of the founders of *The Microcosm*, the first successful school-magazine; and the last twenty-seven years of his life, when he lived in Malta, were devoted to literary activities. Here, for the amusement of his nephew in England, he wrote in about 1820 *Fables for Five Years Old* (published 1830); and the Uncle Bartle he suggests the little boy would want to visit was Bartholomew Frere, secretary to the embassy at Constantinople.

FYLEMAN, ROSE AMY (1877–1957), born in a suburb of Nottingham, was the daughter of an unsuccessful but learned immigrant lacemaker (as a child Rose never knew a meal without a dictionary on the table); and she trained to be a singer. She was singing professionally, and teaching in her sister's school, when she was persuaded to send some of her verses to *Punch*. 'Fairies' appeared 23 May 1917, and was greeted with such enthusiasm that five publishers wrote to her within a week. Other verses followed ('A Fairy Went A-Marketing' was the opening item in *Punch* for 1918); and the poems were collected in a succession of books, including *Fairies and Chimneys* (1918), *The Fairy Green* (1919), and *The Fairy Flute* (1921), which mark the peak of the fashion for fairy poetry, soon to give way to the nursery-life verse of A. A. Milne (q.v.), which she herself was instrumental in introducing. In book form the poems we give appeared in *Fairies and Chimneys*, with the exception of 'Mrs. Brown' (*The Fairy Green*), and 'Temper' (*The Fairy Flute*).

GATTY, ALFRED SCOTT (1847–1918), was both a distinguished genealogist who became Garter Principal King-of-Arms, and a prolific writer of humorous and sentimental songs, who often wrote the music as well as the words. Since his mother was Margaret Gatty, the founder of *Aunt Judy's Magazine*, and an elder sister was Mrs. Ewing (q.v.), it was natural that his early songs should be written for the young, and that they should appear in the family's magazine. 'The Three Little Pigs' was published in *Aunt Judy's Magazine*, February 1870.

GRAHAME, KENNETH (1859–1932), a Scotsman and descendant of Robert the Bruce, was secretary of the Bank of England, and wrote essays and poems only in his spare time. In 1907, when his son Alastair was nearly seven, he began telling him a bedtime tale about a mole, a rat, and a toad, who lived on a river bank (the family had just moved to Cookham Dene beside the Thames), and his tale was to become the most wonderful of all tales not so much for seven-year-olds as for those just reaching double figures, *The Wind in the Willows*. 'Ducks' Ditty' is the song Ratty composed as he sat on the river bank in the sun, teasing the ducks.

HALE, SARAH JOSEPHA (1788–1879), was born in Newport, New Hampshire, the daughter of a Revolutionary soldier, Captain Gordon Buell. She lived a quiet rural life until, at the age of thirty-four, she found herself a widow, with scanty means and five children to support. She turned to writing, producing, with extraordinary industry, novels, sketches, poetry, and cookery books, and also editing magazines, *Godey's Lady's Book* among them. 'Mary's Lamb' appeared, above her initials, in *The Juvenile Miscellany*, September–October 1830; and soon afterwards in a volume of her work *Poems for Our Children*. She later stated the poem was based on an actual incident in her childhood when she cared for a lamb on her father's farm.

HART, ELIZABETH ANNA (1822–1888?), was a member of a literary family: daughter of Edward Smedley, a prolific writer; first cousin of Frank Smedley, the novelist; and younger sister of Menella Smedley (q.v.) with whom she collaborated in *Poems written for a Child*, 1868, and *Child-World*, 1869. 'Mother Tabbyskins', which is one of the poems most often recalled by our older correspondents, first appeared in *Good Words for the Young*, 1 November 1868.

HERRICK, ROBERT (1591–1674), son of a London goldsmith, entered the Church when he was thirty-two; and in 1629 became the vicar of Dean Prior, a village on the edge of Dartmoor. Here he lived for the rest of his life, except during the Protectorate when, being a firm royalist (see George Wither, who was on the other side), he was dispossessed of his living. He was a bachelor and a great celebrator of small occurrences. Any incident or creature might become the theme for a song: he wrote about his cat, his dog (a spaniel named Tracy), about country customs, fairies, his servants, and himself. Altogether he wrote more than a thousand short poems, most of them, including the pieces he addressed to children, being published in *Hesperides*, 1648.

HICKSON, WILLIAM EDWARD (1803–1870), was a boot-manufacturer in Smithfield, who retired while still in his thirties to devote himself to good causes, especially the advancement of national education. He was a gifted musician, and, as may be seen from 'We waited for an omnibus', which appeared in *The Musical Gift*, 1859, an understanding and humorous person.

HOFFMANN, HEINRICH (1809–1894), of Frankfurt, was the doctor at a lunatic asylum, who also practised in the City, and often had to visit children. When, in 1844, he wanted a picture-book for his own three-year-old son, he found none to his liking, for none depicted the hazards of life amusingly so that a child might remember the warnings yet not be alarmed by the perils. Dr. Hoffmann had been in the habit of telling stories and drawing pictures to gain the confidence of his young patients; and apparently found little difficulty filling a notebook with the verses and drawings which were to become renowned as *Der Struwwelpeter oder lustige Geschichten und drollige Bilder*. It is not known who made the translation in 1848 entitled *The English Struwwelpeter*, but he or she was an inspired versifier whose rendering has become part of the familiar verse of the English language.

HOGG, JAMES (1770–1835), of Ettrick in Selkirkshire, was a shepherd boy who taught himself to write by copying from a book as he lay on the hillside watching his flock. Both he and Robert Burns were born on 25 January; and Hogg's ambition, when he learnt of Burns's death, was to succeed him in Scottish poetry. 'A Boy's Song' pays tribute more, perhaps, to Gellatley's deerhound song in *Waverley* than to Robert Burns; but the words have the freshness of direct experience that characterizes Hogg at his best. The poem was published in 1831 in the first volume of *The Remembrance*, an annual edited by Thomas Roscoe, son of William Roscoe (q.v.).

HOOD, THOMAS (1799–1845), was born in the City of London at 31 Poultry, the address of the publishing house of Vernor and Hood, a firm—well known for its children's books—in which his father was a partner, his mother being the daughter of the other partner. He lived most of his life in London, a man of cheerful disposition who suffered constantly from ill-health; and a poet who wrote light verse that often conveyed deep feeling. His hints to a girl paying a visit to France were written in 1843 for Henrietta, the daughter of his friend, the artist and engraver William Harvey. They were published after his death by his children in *Fairy Land; or, Recreation for the Rising Generation*, 1861.

HOOK, THEODORE (1788–1841), humorous writer and practical joker: the man who in 1809 perpetrated the Berners Street hoax, when a thousand tradesmen and notables, ranging from undertakers and harpsichord-makers to the Duke of York and the Archbishop of Canterbury, found themselves jammed in Berners Street as a result of urgent summonses, on one pretext or another, to attend a Mrs. Tottenham. Hook's characteristically witty verses on punning were written for a children's annual *The Christmas Box*, 1828. 'Entick's rules' to which he refers, appeared in Entick's *Dictionary*, much used in schools, where a table was included of words alike in sound but different in meaning.

HOSKYNS, JOHN (1566–1638), was a member of parliament who spoke out too freely about the King's Scottish favourites, and was committed to the Tower of London in 1614, where a fellow-prisoner was Sir

Walter Raleigh. According to Aubrey, 'He, with much adoe, obtained at length the favour to have his little son Bennet to be with him,' and it was to Bennet (i.e. Benedict), then aged five, that he addressed his epigram on ruling one's tongue. There are many versions of this epigram. The one we give appears in Louise Brown Osborn's *Life of John Hoskyns*, 1937.

HOUGHTON, LORD. See Richard Monckton Milnes.

HOWITT, MARY (1799–1888), daughter of a strict Staffordshire Quaker, Samuel Botham, was determined to be a writer, although her father disapproved of imaginative literature, and even of pictures. However, in 1821 she married William Howitt (see below) whose ambition was the same as hers; and despite bearing twelve children, she became the author, editor, or translator of more than a hundred works (as a translator she introduced the fairy tales of Hans Andersen to England); and among her voluminous writings for children are poems that have been repeatedly reprinted, notably 'The Spider and the Fly' which first appeared in *The New Year's Gift, and Juvenile Souvenir*, 1829, and subsequently in *Sketches of Natural History*, 1834. 'Buttercups and Daisies' and 'The Seagull' were included in her *Birds and Flowers and other Country Things*, 1838.

HOWITT, WILLIAM (1792–1879), was born at Heanor in Derbyshire, in a Quaker household, but one less austere than that, sixteen miles away, of his future wife Mary (see above). He was a man of wide interests and adventurous spirit; an active humanitarian, who had perhaps more energy even than had Mary. During their industrious and happy life-partnership he produced almost as many books as she did, some of them of great length. 'The Wind in a Frolic' appeared first in *Ackermann's Juvenile Forget-me-not* for 1830, and then in *The Boy's Country Book*, 1839, one of the earliest and best of childhood autobiographies. 'The Migration of the Grey Squirrels', which also appeared in the *Forget-me-not* for 1830, and which tells a legend similar to that in *Squirrel Nutkin*, was added to Mary's *Sketches of Natural History*, 1834.

IDLEY, PETER (died 1473?), wrote 'Instructions to his Son' (a boy named Thomas), in more than 7,500 lines of verse; and although his advice comes, for the most part, from didactic works already current, such as the Latin treatises of Albertanus of Brescia, the work stands as a pleasing monument to a father's concern for his child's welfare at the close of the Middle Ages. Further, the father has almost certainly been identified, by Professor Charlotte D'Evelyn, as an Oxfordshire squire and landowner, Peter Idley, who held several appointments in the reign of Henry VI, among them that of gentleman falconer and under-keeper of the royal mews and falcons. The text is based on Professor D'Evelyn's transcription.

INGELOW, JEAN (1820–1897), one of those authors—the more usual type—who are more praised in their lifetime than afterwards, was born at Boston in Lincolnshire, the daughter of a banker. She was strictly brought up, so strictly that she is said not to have been allowed writing paper when a child, and to have written her poems on the white shutters of her bedroom window. Such restriction, however, did not stunt her imagination. Her children's story *Mopsa the Fairy* (1869), inspired by *Alice in Wonderland*, is fantasy from start to finish. 'One morning, oh, so early!' is the song Jack sang at the fairy feast, one he had heard his nurse sing. ' "A very good song too," said the dame, at the other end of the table; "only you made a mistake in the first verse. What the dove really said was, no doubt, 'Give us peas.' All kinds of doves and pigeons are very fond of peas." '

JEWSBURY, MARIA JANE (1800–1833), the eldest daughter of a Manchester businessman, had looked after her brother Frank all his life, for their mother had died when he was an infant. She had also, as a young woman, begun sending her poems to local newspapers, and had attracted attention by her personality as well as her writing. Wordsworth, who addressed his poem 'Liberty' to her, said he knew no one whose mind had her quickness; and it was generally believed that a great future lay before her. In 1832 she married the Revd. William Fletcher, a chaplain with the East India Company. This led to her having to leave Manchester, to accompany her husband to Bombay. Within a year of writing the poem for her young brother she had died in India, a victim, like so many of her countrymen, of cholera. 'Partings' and 'To a Young Brother' both appeared in *The Juvenile Forget Me Not*, the first in the volume for 1831, the other in the volume for 1833.

KEATS, JOHN (1795–1821), the son of a London livery-stable keeper, had little education, but in his short life wrote poems as perfect as Shakespeare's sonnets. While on a walking tour in Scotland, in July 1818, he wrote 'Meg Merrilies' and 'There was a naughty boy' to amuse his young sister Fanny, who was kept at home by her guardian. The poem about Meg Merrilies (the gipsy in Scott's *Guy Mannering*) was written at Auchencairn while having breakfast; and 'There was a naughty boy'—referring to himself—when he reached Kirkcudbright. Both were included in the same letter which, despite his tiredness after walking twenty miles, was as joyous a piece of nonsense as ever a young girl received from a grown-up brother. 'I am ashamed of writing you such stuff,' he told her, 'nor would I if it were not for being tired after my day's walking, and ready to tumble into bed so fatigued that when I am asleep you might sew my nose to my great toe and trundle me round the town, like a Hoop, without waking me.'

KEN, THOMAS (1637–1711), was a scholar at Winchester College, who entered the Church, became well known as a forthright preacher, and several times returned to live in Winchester. It was at Winchester, probably in 1683, that he refused, on moral grounds, to open his house to the king's favourite, Nell Gwyn; an action which, contrary to expectations, did no harm to his career. Not long afterwards, when a new bishop of Bath and Wells had to be chosen, Charles II declared, it is said, that no man should have the bishopric but 'the little black fellow that refused his lodging to poor Nelly'. 'An Evening Hymn' was one of the hymns Ken had written, sometime before 1674, for the use of Winchester scholars, directing them to be sure to sing it in their rooms at night. The precise form in which they did so is not known. When published in 1692, without authorization, there were thirteen stanzas; and when Bishop Ken included it in *Three Hymns*, 1694, there were twelve stanzas. The hymn is usually considerably shortened. The three beautiful verses we give were stanzas one, two, and four.

KILNER, DOROTHY (1755–1836), who lived at Maryland Point in the north-east environs of London, was a prolific writer of stories for and about children in the 1780s, and almost certainly was responsible for *Poems on Various Subjects, for the Amusement of Youth*, published about 1783, price one shilling, by John Marshall and Co. of Aldermary Church Yard, Bow Lane, in the City of London. Possibly Southey was one of the boys who read this book. The style of 'You are old, Father William' (p. 93) is highly reminiscent of 'Henry's Secret'.

KINGSLEY, CHARLES (1819–1875), Devon-born, Cambridge-educated, was for more than thirty years rector of Eversley in Hampshire. A man of wide sympathies, athletic, an enthusiastic naturalist, a friend to the poor, a controversialist, an inspiring tutor (he himself had four children), and a follower of the scientific and intellectual developments of his day, he was for some years Professor of Modern History at Cambridge, yet he was a novelist rather than a scholar, and above all he was a poet. 'I do feel,' he remarked, 'a different being when I get into metre.' 'A Farewell' was written in 1856 for his niece Charlotte Grenfell. The other poems appeared in his best-known tale *The Water-Babies*, 1863. 'Clear and cool, clear and cool' was the song the river sang; the doll song was sung by Mrs. Doasyouwouldbedoneby; and 'Young and Old' was the old song the school dame used to sing as she sat spinning what she called her wedding dress. The children could not understand the song, 'but they liked it none the less for that; for it was very sweet, and very sad, and that was enough for them'.

KIPLING, RUDYARD (1865–1936), who was born in India and educated in England, was undistinguished at school except for having one trait, common among people who are to become great, a passion for reading. Through his reading and observation he became wonderfully conscious of the past being a part of the present; and could, as in 'A Smuggler's Song', evoke the excitement of times past as vividly as if he himself had experienced it. He loved England, and was proud of her history. He liked reminding people that the ground they stand on is the same their ancestors trod; and he believed that the steadfastness of the men who made England great continues, likewise, in the blood of their descendants, if they are willing to recognize it. In 'If—', which first appeared in *Rewards and Fairies*, 1910, he gave some of the best rules to live by that have ever been penned. Thirty years later, in the bitter days of the Second World War, Winston Churchill bade the nation take heart from Kipling's words:

> If you can dream—and not make dreams your master;
> If you can think—and not make thoughts your aim:
> If you can meet with Triumph and Disaster
> And treat those two impostors just the same.

'The Hump' came in *Just So Stories*, 1902; 'Puck's Song' (here in its expanded version) and 'A Smuggler's Song' in *Puck of Pook's Hill*, 1906; and 'The Way through the Woods', like 'If—', in *Rewards and Fairies.*

LAMB, CHARLES (1775–1834), and MARY (1764–1847), brother and sister, lived together in London, chiefly in the City, where Charles was a clerk. They came from a humble family, and had to face appalling difficulties. Charles was a life-long friend of S. T. Coleridge, with whom he was at school; and a close friend of Southey and the Wordsworths (qq.v.); but he was somewhat on the fringes of literature until he wrote *The Essays of Elia* in middle life. In the first decade of the nineteenth century much of his and Mary's spare time was taken up writing children's books for William Godwin, who published their *Poetry for Children, entirely original* in 1809. The majority of the poems were by Mary, about a third being by Charles (one of them was 'Choosing a Name'). They wrote them to supplement their meagre income. 'You must read them, remembering they were task-work,' Charles told Coleridge; 'and perhaps you will admire the number of subjects, all of children, picked out by an old Bachelor and an old Maid. Many parents would not have found so many.'

LANDOR, WALTER SAVAGE (1775–1864), author of *Imaginary Conversations of Literary Men and Statesmen*, was well-to-do, opinionated, self-willed, and forever quarrelling with his neighbours—so much so he kept having to move house; but he loved animals, flowers, pictures, the classical writers (who much influenced his poetry), and, above all, his children. 'Before a Saint's Picture', which was addressed to his second son Walter, appeared in his *Works*, 1846.

LEAR, EDWARD (1812–1888), was born at Highgate, the twentieth of twenty-one children of a stockbroker, who went to prison for debt when Edward was thirteen. By profession an artist, and by temperament a nervous, unprepossessing 'old cove', Lear was happiest when amusing children with his 'nonsenses' as he called them; and it was while he was at Knowsley Hall, drawing the animals in the Earl of Derby's menagerie, that he made friends with the Earl's grandchildren and wrote the character verses that were to become his first *Book of Nonsense*, 1846. Numerous rhymes and comic alphabets followed, mostly written for individual child-acquaintances who invariably seem to have enjoyed his company, despite his bulbous appearance. As he himself wrote on hearing that a young lady had said how pleasant it must be to know Mr Lear:

> 'How pleasant to know Mr Lear!'
> Who has written such volumes of stuff!
> Some think him ill-tempered and queer,
> But a few think him pleasant enough.

'Nonsenses' i–vi were published in 1846, and vii–viii in *More Nonsense*, 1872. The other pieces were all published in *Nonsense Songs, Stories, Botany, and Alphabets*, 1871, except for 'The Pobble who has No Toes' which appeared in *Laughable Lyrics*, 1877.

LONGFELLOW, HENRY WADSWORTH (1807–1882), the most popular American poet of his day, is said to have composed 'There was a little girl' on an occasion in the late 1850s when his daughter Edith refused to have her hair curled. The attribution is very uncertain, and appears to rest largely on the single testimony of one of his friends, Mrs. Blanche Macchetta (see *The Oxford Dictionary of Nursery Rhymes*). However, it must be said that at the time of the poet's death, or soon afterwards, the lines were generally held to be by Longfellow, and his publisher supported the belief.

LOWELL, JAMES RUSSELL (1819–1891), was well qualified to give the advice that he wrote in a child's album, for he himself was not one to let the ring slip from between his fingers. He was successful in life as well as in literature. In addition to being a humorist, literary critic, and poet of enduring quality, he was outstanding as an editor, as a professor at Harvard for twenty years, and, in the latter part of his life, as a diplomat representing the United States in Spain and in Great Britain. 'Birthday Verses' appeared in the *Atlantic Monthly*, January 1877.

LYDGATE, JOHN (1370?–1450), recalled that when he was at school (probably at Bury St. Edmunds) he was at first 'loth to lerne' and 'lovid no besynesse sauf pley or merthe'. Soon, however, his great desire was to write poetry like Chaucer, whom he met, and whose son was a friend. *Stans Puer ad Mensam*, a description of how a boy should conduct himself when waiting at table, had wide circulation in the fifteenth century, was printed by Caxton, and was much used by advisers on deportment in the sixteenth century. The evidence for Lydgate's authorship lies in a comment, at the end of some versions of the treatise, that if any fault is found John Lydgate should be blamed. The text is a blending of Lambeth MS. 853 and Harleian MS. 2251 transcribed by F. J. Furnivall, Early English Text Society, no. 32, with reference also to Jesus College MS. 56 f. 77, transcribed by J. O. Halliwell, *Reliquae Antiquae*, vol. i, p. 156.

MACDONALD, GEORGE (1824–1905), was born at Huntly in Aberdeenshire. He was educated locally and at Aberdeen University, where, his family being in straitened circumstances, he had to maintain himself while a student. After graduating he came south to make a living, eventually winning recognition and many friends as a poet, but earning little money to support his wife and family. Even so, he was a man so fond of children he referred to the eleven mouths he had to feed as 'the wrong side of a dozen'. It was he who urged C. L. Dodgson (Lewis Carroll, q.v.) to publish *Alice in Wonderland*, after his wife had read the first draft of it to their children. His own best-known book *At the Back of the North Wind*, a story of strange otherworldliness, was published in 1871, having been serialized in *Good Words for the Young*. 'Where did you come from, baby dear?' appeared, as part of the story, in the number for August 1870.

MARCHANT, JOHN (fl. 1751), wrote, among other works, two little books of verse for children: *Puerilia; or, Amusements for the Young*, 1751, and *Lusus Juveniles; or, Youth's Recreation*, 1753. The pieces about the girl and her parrot and about the boy's visit to the puppet show appeared in the first of these. Marchant describes youthful pleasures and anxieties with some exactness; and the little 'masters and misses' of the eighteenth century often come to life as they play with marbles and dolls, and learn to swim or to stitch their samplers. But he felt it necessary, as did others in his day, to give each sketch a meaning, and his moralizing is seldom either apt or poetic.

MARTIN, SARAH CATHERINE (1768–1826), was still in her teens when Prince William Henry (the future William IV) was a visitor to her home, lost his heart to her, and proposed marriage. Their elders quickly separated them, and Sarah remained a spinster all her life. 'The Comic

Adventures of Old Mother Hubbard' were prepared for publication in 1804 when she was staying at Kitley, a fine house near Yealmpton in Devon; and the story is that the original Mother Hubbard was the housekeeper there. But the first three verses were already traditional. Sarah Catherine Martin's achievement was to extend the story so that it could be made into a booklet; and this little booklet, published in 1805, not only became a bestseller, but started a new trend in fanciful verse for the young.

MIDLANE, ALBERT (1825–1909), was an ironmonger on the Isle of Wight who, as he himself admitted, preferred studying his hymnbook to listening to the sermon. He was seventeen when his first hymn was printed; and by the end of his life he had written more than eight hundred hymns. 'There's a friend for little children' was published in December 1859, in a small Evangelical magazine *Good News for the Little Ones*, the third verse of six being:

There's a Friend for little children,
  Above the bright blue sky—
A Friend who never changeth,
  Whose love can never die.
Unlike our friends by nature,
  Who change with changing years,
This friend is *always* worthy
  The precious name He bears.

The pessimistic view of human relationships which this expresses was softened in *Hymns Ancient and Modern*; and the *A. & M.* version has been the best known now for more than a century.

MILLER, THOMAS (1807–1874), an orphan who taught himself to read and write, was a basket-maker in Nottingham when the success of his first book of poems enabled him to go to London. Here he combined his talents to good purpose when he put some of his verses into fancy baskets he had made, and sent them to the Countess of Blessington, then at the height of her fame as a beauty and hostess. She approved the verses, and Miller's success was assured. His well-known descriptions of 'Evening' and 'The Watercress Seller' appeared in *Original Poems for My Children*, 1850.

MILLER, WILLIAM (1810–1872), a native of Glasgow, a wood-turner by trade, and a poet by nature, sent the manuscript of 'Willie Winkie' to the editors of *Whistle-Binkie; a Collection of Songs for the Social Circle*, who nearly rejected it as 'a cantie bit Cock Robin lilt'. However, when, happily, the song was published in 1841 it was immediately popular, appealing to the young as an expression of mischief, while recognized by the mature to be a personification of sleep.

MILNE, ALAN ALEXANDER (1882–1956), was well established as a journalist and playwright when Rose Fyleman (q.v.) asked him to write some verse for a children's magazine she was starting, *The Merry-Go-Round.* He had written a play for children, but had not hitherto written verse for the young. However, his son Christopher Robin (born 1920) was now three, and memories of his own childhood were being reawakened. He took the challenge seriously: giving his verse, which is always technically excellent, as much attention as if he was writing for the Queen (indeed 'Vespers' is in the library of the Queen's Dolls' House); and by the end of the year he had written enough to fill a book. *When We Were Very Young*, published in 1924, was an instant success; and was followed in 1927 by *Now We Are Six*. The pieces here are from *When We Were Very Young*, except for 'Us Two' which is from *Now We Are Six*.

MILNES, RICHARD MONCKTON, LORD HOUGHTON (1809–1885), poet, critic, politician, book-collector, landowner, and a socialite who befriended many men of talent, was a man who himself seems to have been incapable of sustained effort, and never fulfilled his early promise. 'Lady Moon', published in *Poems of Many Years*, 1838, was written long before he had children of his own; but he made certain his daughter Amicia should learn it when three years old. 'Good Night and Good Morning' which he had produced on its own in a sumptuous quarto volume in 1859, was one of the poems most frequently included in children's poetry books at the end of the century.

MOORE, CLEMENT CLARKE (1779–1863), an accomplished and well-to-do professor of Biblical learning in New York, and one of the founders of the General Theological Seminary, composed 'A Visit from St. Nicholas' in 1822 for the amusement of his six children, Margaret, Charity, Benjamin, Mary, Clement, and Emily. A relative copied the verses into her album, showed them to a friend, and they were published anonymously the following year in the *Troy Sentinel*, 23 December 1823. Although the poem was immediately popular, and frequently reprinted, Moore did not acknowledge his authorship before its appearance in *The New York Book of Poetry*, 1837. The tradition of St. Nicholas or Santa Claus (i.e. the Dutch *Sant Nikolaas* or *Sinterklaas*) filling children's stockings with presents on Christmas Eve was already strong in New York; but Moore added touches to the story, principally it seems the idea that Santa Claus arrives by air, a fancy he may have had from Washington Irving's burlesque *History of New York*, 1809. The subsequent unwaning popularity of 'A Visit from St. Nicholas' is undoubtedly largely responsible for the present-day characterization of Father Christmas, in Britain as well as in America.

NASH, OGDEN (1902–1971), a New Yorker, who had intended to be a serious poet, but who for forty years produced sophisticated and witty verse about the American social scene. While his verse is light-hearted it is, in fact, never light; but carefully worked out, metrically ingenious, and often philosophically shrewd. He worked as hard at his verse as if it was serious poetry, returning to a poem, as he once told us, again and again to see if more could be made of it; and he thus raised humorous verse to a new level. 'Morning Prayer' was one of the verses written to accompany piano pieces in Tchaikovsky's *Children's Album*. It was published in *The New Nutcracker Suite and Other Innocent Verses*, 1962.

NESBIT, EDITH (1858–1924), who was born in Kennington, the youngest of six children of an agricultural scientist, was a warm-hearted, impetuous person, who liked outrageous clothes, new enterprises, going on excursions, and filling her house with guests. She always felt she ought to be a poet; but rarely wrote poetry that gives the continuing pleasure of the 'Child's Song in Spring', which has been a favourite poem with anthologists ever since it appeared in *A Pomander of Verse* in 1895. Her fame rests on her story-telling, and on the child characters she portrayed in, for instance, *The Story of the Treasure Seekers*, *The Wouldbegoods*, and *The Railway Children*.

NEWBERY, THOMAS, was probably a member of the celebrated publishing family who issued books in London almost continuously from the sixteenth century to the beginning of the nineteenth century. He is only known, however, as the author of *A booke in Englysh metre, of the great Marchaunt man called Dives Pragmaticus, very preaty for children*, 1563, a book whose agreeable aim was to bring together 'the Names of all kynd of wares' so that children might become familiar with them, a feat he accomplished in seventy-four verses.

NOBLE, NISBET. See James Ferguson.

OAKMAN, JOHN (1748?–1793), a Londoner, born at Hendon, seems to have lived a somewhat shiftless life as an engraver, print-seller, and hack-writer; but to have met with success as a song-writer and versifier, writing, for instance, a continuation to Cowper's tale of 'John Gilpin'. It is not known whether 'The Glutton', which is in imitation of Watts's poem 'The Sluggard' (q.v.) appeared earlier than in *Moral Songs for the Instruction and Amusement of Children*, 1802. It was reprinted in 1806 in *Rural Scenes; or, A Peep into the Country, for Good Children.*

O'KEEFFE, ADELAIDE (1776–1855), was the daughter of John O'Keeffe, a prolific writer of farces and comic operas, who had come to London from Dublin about 1770. In 1797 he became totally blind;

and Adelaide, who was his only daughter, looked after him with devotion. She was one of the 'young persons' who contributed, along with the Taylors (qq.v.), to *Original Poems for Infant Minds*, and 'The dog will come when he is called' appeared in the second volume, in 1805. 'The Kite' appeared in a book, entirely of her own verse, with the derivative title *Original Poems: Calculated to Improve the Mind of Youth*, 1808.

PARRY, EDWARD ABBOTT (1863–1943), was County Court Judge, Manchester (where he had a reputation for the rapid despatch of cases), when he wrote the fairy tale books *Katawampus*, 1895, and *Butterscotia*, 1896, in which his best-known verses appear. These compositions were referred to as 'Pater's Rhymes', for His Honour Judge Parry was a family man, and family jokes and personalities form the basis of his books. To read them is to learn something of the spirit of a Victorian family:

Oh, I have four children, three girls and one boy.
The laddie can whistle, the girlies can sing,
And when they are jolly the life we enjoy,
Is better than that at the Court of the King.
But when they are snarly, or when they are cross,
Or the dread Katawampus is having its fling,
I pack them all up, as a matter of course,
And consign them *with care* to the Court of the King.

'Pater's Bathe' and 'I would like you for a Comrade' came in *Katawampus*; and 'The Jam Fish' in *The Scarlet Herring*, 1899.

PENKETHMAN, JOHN (fl. 1630), advertised himself as being able 'to translate old manuscripts or bookes in any kind of Latin into English, Prose or Verse', and *The fairest Fairing for a Schoole-bred Sonne; Whereby Praise, Ease, and Profit may be wonne*, *c.* 1630, is an example, since it is a version of *Carmen de moribus* at the beginning of Lily's Latin grammar.

PRIOR, MATTHEW (1664–1721), English diplomat and, according to his own words, 'poet by accident', addressed his poetic letter to Lady Margaret Cavendish Holles-Harley when she was five and he was fifty-five. Prior died the next year; while Lady Margaret, who was to become Duchess of Portland, lived for another sixty-five years. Although she was so young when he died—while a guest at her father's house—she remembered the deaf and ailing poet with affection, recalling, long afterwards, that he 'made himself beloved by every living thing in the house,—master, child, and servant, human creature or animal'.

RAMAL, WALTER. See Walter de la Mare.

RANDS, WILLIAM BRIGHTY (1823–1882), the son of a small shopkeeper in Chelsea, and largely self-educated, gained his knowledge by reading at the stalls of second-hand booksellers. Most of his best poems, such as 'The Pedlar's Caravan' and the three succeeding pieces, occur not in the first edition of *Lilliput Levee*, 1864, but in the enlarged second edition of 1867. His splendid lines 'Great, wide, beautiful, wonderful World' first appeared in *Good Words for the Young*, December 1868, under the pseudonym Matthew Browne; 'The Cat of Cats' came in the same magazine, March 1870, being a passage in his *Lilliput Revels*; and 'Winifred Waters' in the posthumous collection *Lilliput Lyrics*, 1899

RHODES, HUGH (fl. 1540), born and bred in Devonshire, became a gentleman of the king's chapel in Henry VIII's time; and, probably for the benefit of the children of the chapel, prepared *The Boke of Nurture, or Schoole of good Maners*, a work published before 1540 and described as being 'very utile and necessary unto all youth'. The book seems to have been a popular one in the second half of the sixteenth century: it was much revised, and went into not less than six editions.

RICHARDS, LAURA ELIZABETH (1850–1943), born in Boston, Massachusetts, the daughter of Julia Ward Howe who wrote 'The Battle Hymn of the Republic', was one of six children. She lived most of her life in Gardiner, Maine; and did not 'commence author' until after her marriage, when she began to make up jingles for the newly-founded *St. Nicholas Magazine*, using the back of her first-born for a writing-desk, as the baby lay prone on her knees. She became a prolific author, most of her books being for children, among them the much-loved *Queen Hildegarde* and *Captain January*. Her verses often have a lively nursery-rhyme quality which keeps them at the forefront of the memory. 'Mrs. Snipkin and Mrs. Wobblechin' appeared in *Sketches and Scraps*, 1881; 'My Uncle Jehoshaphat' in *In My Nursery*, 1890; and 'Eletelephony', more than forty years later, in *Tirra Lirra*, 1932.

RILEY, JAMES WHITCOMB (1849–1916), poet of the Hoosier folk, born at Greenfield, Indiana. He seldom went far from home, and if he did usually took the wrong train or got off at the wrong station. Yet he not only became officially 'the most beloved citizen' of Indiana, but on 7 October 1912 children in schools throughout the United States celebrated his birthday. 'Little Orphant Annie', at first called 'The Elf Child', appeared in the Indianapolis *Journal*, 15 November 1885, Annie's name then being 'Allie'. 'The Raggedy Man' was printed in the *Century Magazine*, December 1890. In book form the poems appeared in, respectively, *Character Sketches*, 1886, and *Rhymes of Childhood*, 1891.

RONKSLEY, WILLIAM (fl. 1712), wrote verse because he observed that verse appealed to young minds more readily than did prose. His book *The Child's Weeks-work*, 1712, which also contains traditional rhyming riddles and proverbs, was intended to 'allure and lead' little children into the way of reading; and his own verses, some of them written in words of one syllable, are of a simplicity unusual for their time.

ROSCOE, WILLIAM (1753–1831), a historian and man of business, was Member of Parliament for Liverpool when 'The Butterfly's Ball'—written for one of his younger sons—was published: first in *The Gentleman's Magazine*, November 1806, and then on its own as an illustrated booklet in 1807. Its success was immediate and continuing. The king and queen admired it, and requested it should be set to music; the writing of imitations became something of a literary craze; and by 1808 the words could be purchased even at fairs, printed on pocket handkerchiefs. For its sequel, 'The Peacock "At Home"' by Mrs. Dorset, see pp. 132–6.

ROSS, CHARLES HENRY (*c.* 1842–1897), was one of those people who spend their lives amusing others, whose jokes and rhymes become proverbial in their lifetime, yet who are forgotten as soon as they die. Ross was a clerk at Somerset House, aged about twenty, when he produced *Ye Comical Rhymes of Ancient Times, Dug up into Jokes for Small Folks*, 1862. Thereafter he wrote books with titles such as *The Eldest Miss Simpson, her haps and mishaps* and *The Contra-Dictionary of London*; he also wrote dramas, a burlesque, an operetta, and a pantomime. When still a young man he became editor of *Judy*, the great rival to *Punch*, and one of his cartoonists was Marie Duval, an eighteen-year-old governess, who had just arrived from France, and was to become an actress on the English stage. Ross proposed to her, and not only married her, but adopted her name for the cartoons he himself drew for his magazine.

ROSSETTI, CHRISTINA GEORGINA (1830–1894), born in London of Italian parentage, was the youngest of four brilliant children. Her ability was evident at the age of twelve when a nosegay for her mother's birthday was accompanied by the message:

Today's your natal day;
Sweet flowers I bring:
Mother, accept I pray
My offering.

And may you happy live,
And long us bless;
Receiving as you give
Great happiness.

Brought up at home, she helped her mother teach in a school, and was ardent in helping others though herself often ill. Throughout her life she was devoted to poetry, particularly to the writing of religious verse. All the compositions here are from *Sing-Song*, 'a nursery rhyme book', as she termed it, published in 1872.

SAXBY, MRS. JANE EUPHEMIA. See Aunt Effie.

SCOTT, SIR WALTER (1771–1832), who more than anyone made England conscious of the history and romance of Scotland, produced the 'Lullaby of an Infant Chief' for Daniel Terry's dramatization of his novel *Guy Mannering*, performed at Covent Garden on 12 March 1816. The words—the first and last stanzas only—were sung by Miss Bertram with the refrain:

> Oh! rest thee, babe; rest thee, babe; sleep on till day!
> Oh! rest thee, babe; rest thee, babe; sleep while you may.

Scott had originally written the lullaby to the air 'Cadil gu lo'; and in his *Poetical Works*, vol. x (1820), he gives the refrain:

> O ho ro, i ri ri, cadil gu lo,
> O ho ro, i ri ri, cadil gu lo.

SEAGER, FRANCIS (fl. 1550), translator and petty poet, was probably Devonshire-born. His *The Schoole of Vertue, and booke of good Nourture for chyldren and youth to learne theyr dutie by*, of which a revised edition appeared in 1557, enjoyed a remarkably long life. More than a hundred and twenty-five years after its publication Anthony à Wood observed the book still being 'commonly sold at the stalls of Ballad-singers'.

SHARPE, RICHARD SCRAFTON (*c.* 1775–1852), kept silent about his authorship of comic verses for children until 1837, thirty years after the first publication of *Old Friends in a New Dress*. He is known to have produced several similar booklets of verse, among them probably *Dame Wiggins of Lee* (see pp. 153–4), and *Anecdotes and Adventures of Fifteen Gentlemen* (see p. 154); but he was so self-effacing that these attributions cannot be made with any certainty. By trade he is said to have been a grocer, and to have kept a shop in Bishopsgate, London.

SMART, CHRISTOPHER (1722–1771), was confined in the King's Bench Prison for debt when his little book *Hymns for the Amusement of Children*, 1771, was published; and almost certainly he was in prison when he wrote some of the hymns. He had, however, written one hymn for children twenty years earlier, for when the contents of the second number of *The Lilliputian Magazine* was announced, on 29 June 1751, 'A Morning Hymn for all little good Boys and Girls' was described as 'by Mr. Kitty Smart'. 'Kit' Smart, who at this time was in the employment of John Newbery, the children's-book publisher, and enjoying the most tranquil period of his tormented life, can thus be seen to be one of the most significant of early writers for the young. His verses have an unaffectedness that lead the way to William Blake.

SMEDLEY, MENELLA BUTE (1820–1877), Lewis Carroll's 'dear cousin', contributed her 'North Pole Story' to the first number of *Aunt Judy's Magazine* which appeared in May 1866. Most of the stirring verse-tales of the nineteenth century, such as are contained in Henley's *Lyra Heroica* (1892), were not written specially for children, however much children were subsequently induced to recite them. But 'A North Pole Story', which is said to be based on fact, was undoubtedly addressed to the young, a fact which may account for the one or two weaknesses in the verse. Nevertheless the tale vividly reflects nineteenth-century enthusiasm for exploration and adventure, and was very popular. It was republished in *Poems written for a Child*, 1868, a book, produced in conjunction with her sister Mrs. Hart (q.v.), which Lewis Carroll used to present to his child friends.

SMITH, CHARLOTTE (1749–1806), found herself at the age of sixteen married to a spendthrift husband; and subsequently having to support a large family (she had twelve children) by writing. Nevertheless she did not let the struggle to make ends meet depress her spirit. She was deeply fond of the Sussex and Hampshire countryside, which were her homelands, and was unusually knowledgeable about plants and birds. *Conversations Introducing Poetry, for the Use of Children*, 1804, in which appeared her 'Invitation to the Bee', shows this clearly; and her verse is always interesting and warm-hearted. But she was constantly short of time—she once complained a poem had cost her 'near an hour' to compose—and she seldom polished her verse as she might have done. Mrs. Dorset (q.v.) was her younger sister.

SMITH, ROBERT (died 1555), a man of high intellect who, after being in the service of the Provost of Eton College, was given office with the clergy at Windsor Castle, an appointment of which he was deprived on the succession of Queen Mary, for he was a man who stuck to his principles; and in consequence was burnt at the stake, on 8 August 1555. His 'Exhortation', of which we give an extraet, written in prison a few days before his martyrdom, has been an inspiration to subsequent generations, for no trace of self-pity is admitted, nor of indignation on behalf of his children. On the contrary he exhorts his children, who are to be orphaned in the most horrible manner, to care for those who are less well off than themselves; and he himself practised as he preached, devoting his last days to the welfare of fellow-prisoners. The

'Exhortation', first printed in 1559 (when it was incorrectly ascribed to Mathewe Rogers) reached a vast audience: in Britain through its inclusion in Foxe's *Actes and Monuments* ('The Book of Martyrs'), 1563; and in America through *The New-England Primer*, which was published towards the end of the seventeenth century and became in the eighteenth century one of the books best known to children after the Bible.

SOUTHEY, ROBERT (1774–1843), the precocious son of a Bristol linen-draper, was commissioned, when in his early twenties, to write verses for *The Morning Post* at a guinea a week, and 'The Old Man's Comforts' appeared 17 January 1799. It was quickly welcomed by the children's anthologists, e.g. by Lucy Aikin in *Poetry for Children*, 1801, and remained popular until outshone by the brilliance of Lewis Carroll's parody (see p. 242). 'The Cataract of Lodore' was originally conceived as an amusement for Edith, Southey's eldest daughter, then five years old; but was not developed into a poem until twelve years later, when Southey was poet laureate (hence the reference in lines 22–3) and was writing for the benefit of his youngest child, Cuthbert. Lodore Falls are in Cumberland, at the foot of Derwent Water.

STEVENSON, ROBERT LOUIS (1850–1894), excelled in almost everything he wrote, whether ethical essays for adults, or adventure stories for schoolboys such as *Treasure Island*; and no man has conveyed more directly the experience of being young than he did in *A Child's Garden of Verses*, published in 1885. Partially, perhaps, because he was often lying ill in bed when he wrote these verses—sometimes being as helpless as a child, and having to write in the dark with his left hand—he seems to have relived the sensation of being young, while possessing the mature humour of an adult. In particular he recalled holidays spent with young cousins at Colinton Manse, his grandfather's home in the south-western outskirts of Edinburgh on the Water of Leith, which is the scene of most of these poems.

TAYLOR, ANN (1782–1866), the eldest child in a hard-working family of engravers, won a prize, when seventeen, with her rhymed answer to an enigma in the only annual then published for children, *The Minor's Pocket Book*. She became a regular contributor; and in 1804–5 a collection of poems chiefly by herself and her sister Jane (q.v.) was published in two small volumes, *Original Poems for Infant Minds*, which became one of the most popular children's books ever published. Other small volumes followed ('The Baby's Dance' appeared in *Rhymes for the Nursery*, 1806); but she wrote little after her marriage to the Revd. Joseph Gilbert in 1813. She did, however, revise her poems a number of times, not always to their advantage, and we have tended to follow the first of her revised texts. In her eighty-fifth year, with more success, she rewrote, by request, what had been the last verse of 'My Mother':

For God, who lives above the skies,
Would look with vengeance in His eyes,
If I should ever dare despise
My Mother.

'Vengeance', she agreed, 'is not a word I should now employ.'

TAYLOR, JANE (1783–1824), the lively but delicate sister of Ann Taylor (q.v.), became the better known of the two during her lifetime since, after Ann's marriage, she continued to write, and began signing her writings. Although 'My Mother' was the most-loved of the Taylor poems in its day, Jane's 'Twinkle, twinkle, little star', which appeared in *Rhymes for the Nursery*, 1806, has proved more memorable. However, the sisters lived in such close company at their father's home in Angel Lane, Colchester, that it is sometimes difficult to distinguish their work apart, and it is uncertain which of them wrote 'The Cow' and 'The Sheep' (both published in 1806). What can be said is that no two young women aroused more affection in the nineteenth century through their work; and that their admirers ranged from the humble purchasers of farthing sheets at country markets to literary giants such as Walter Scott and Robert Browning.

TENNANT, ROBERT (1830–1879), a native of Airdrie, was orphaned at ten, and most of the education he received was through his own efforts. All his adult life he was a postman, chiefly in Glasgow. 'I have had many *ups* and *downs* during my life,' he wrote, 'for I have been tramping up and down stairs in this great city every working day for about twenty-three years.' A man of gentle, guileless nature, he often wrote for the Glasgow newspapers, but produced only one book of poems, *Wayside Musings*, 1874. 'Wee Davie Daylicht' was his most-loved poem during his lifetime, and has remained so.

TENNYSON, ALFRED, LORD (1809–1892), poet laureate in succession to Wordsworth (q.v.), and the most substantial poet of his day, was a man of retiring disposition who lived much of his life on the Isle of Wight or in the then remote country near Haslemere. 'Sweet and Low', which was inserted in the 1850 edition of *The Princess*, and 'Cradle Song' which was incorporated in 'Sea Dreams', 1860, are specimens of child-song rather than verses written directly for children; but Tennyson seems to have thought of them as being for children as appears from the circumstance that when, many years later, the editor of the children's magazine *St. Nicholas* asked Tennyson for a contribution, he sent 'The City Child' and 'Minnie and Winnie' which he had originally written, like 'Sweet and Low', for insertion in *The Princess*. They were published in the February number of *St. Nicholas*, 1880.

THACKERAY, WILLIAM MAKEPEACE (1811–1863), the author of *Vanity Fair* and *The Rose and the Ring*, was fond of going out with his young daughters and their friends; and it was on a visit to the London zoo that he composed the joke rhyme about the animals' characteristics. Anne, his eldest daughter, was later to recall, in his *Works*, vol. xii (1899), that her playfellows on this occasion, as on many others, were the children of Sir Henry Cole, 'and the youngest boy caught up the rhyme, and ran about repeating the last verse with its various readings, sometimes preferring one, sometimes the other'.

THAXTER, CELIA (1835–1894), was born in Portsmouth, New Hampshire, and her best poetry reflects the strange circumstance of her upbringing. Her father, Thomas B. Laighton, was a prosperous businessman and politician who expected, when Celia was four years old, to be elected State governor. Disappointed in his ambition, he had himself appointed a lighthouse-keeper; and retired with his family to the desolate Isles of Shoals, ten miles out to sea, determined never again to set foot on the mainland. Here Celia and her two younger brothers were brought up, with little company but the seabirds and the sound of the sea. When seventeen she married a Browning enthusiast, Levi Lincoln Thaxter, one of her parents' visitors; but she continued to live with her family, and it was not until 1860, when she moved inland with her husband and their three children, that a poem (expressing her unhappiness at being away from the sea) was shown to J. R. Lowell (q.v.), and published in the *Atlantic Monthly*. In 1866 she returned to the sea; and spent much of the rest of her life on or near the Islands. 'The Sandpiper' appeared in her *Poems*, 1872, and thereafter in her *Poems for Children*, 1884.

THOMAS, EDWARD (1878–1917), lived in the Hampshire village of Steep, which is on a steep wooded hill (known locally as a 'hanger' from the trees hanging to its side), a hill that rises above our own home in deep and haunting country. During the First World War, when Thomas became a soldier and was soon to die, he recalled the happiness the countryside had given him in verses that detail the common experience of those who love the wild dog-rose rather than, say, the *Gloire de Dijon*. 'If I should ever by chance grow rich' was written early in April 1916 for his daughter Bronwen, with whom he used to compete in searching for the first white violet of the year. 'What shall I give?' was written soon afterwards for his younger daughter, Baba, then aged five. And the person to whom from his military camp he sent these poems to be typed (if she thought them 'not too bad') was the coming children's poet Eleanor Farjeon (q.v.).

THOMPSON, D'ARCY WENTWORTH (1829–1902), was a Greek scholar, and classical master at Edinburgh Academy where one of his pupils was Robert Louis Stevenson (q.v.). His young wife died in 1860, a week after giving birth to his only son, who in consequence was brought up by a grandmother; and it was for his son that the bereaved father wrote *Nursery Nonsense; or, Rhymes without Reason*, 1864. The son, who was to become a distinguished naturalist, was given the names D'Arcy Wentworth (when his grandmother took him to be christened she said, 'I'll call him after his Father, that can't hurt anyone'); but the little boy, unable to pronounce 'D'Arcy', called himself Dadu, hence the line 'Granny and I with dear Dadu'. And a possible outcome of their 'rambling on the shore' was that marine biology became the young D'Arcy's speciality.

THOMPSON, FRANCIS (1859–1907), born in Preston, was unsuccessful in Manchester as a medical student, and unsuccessful in London at making a living. He was destitute and addicted to opium when a bootmaker near Leicester Square gave him light work in his shop, and paper to write on. He sent two poems to the editor of *Merry England* and they were published. When the editor requested him to present himself at his office Thompson had 'no shirt beneath his coat and bare feet in broken shoes'. But such were the poems that Browning (q.v.), shortly before his death, recognized their author to be a poet capable of achieving 'whatever ambition might suggest'. 'Ex Ore Infantium' appeared first in *Merry England*, May 1893, and then in *New Poems*, 1897.

TROWBRIDGE, JOHN TOWNSEND (1827–1916), born on his father's farm in Monroe County, New York state, was a Bostonian by adoption, and a writer by trade: author of some forty novels for boys (the *Jack Hazard* series among them). His love of a good story and ability to depict character is also apparent in his verse. He was at one time joint-editor of the magazine *Our Young Folks*; and 'Darius Green and his Flying-Machine' appeared in the number for March 1867. At this time the only way men were able to travel in the air was in balloons, or in airships such as those Henri Giffard was making.

TURNER, ELIZABETH (1775?–1846), lived at Whitchurch in Shropshire, and was one of the more successful of the writers who were inspired by the Taylors (q.v.), her popularity stemming not so much from the depth of her sentiments as from the almost mesmerizing precision of her rhythm and rhyme. Each of her books bore the name of a flower: *The Daisy; or, Cautionary Stories in Verse*, 1807; *The Cowslip*, 1811; *The Pink*, 1823; *The Blue-Bell*, 1838; *The Crocus*, 1844. 'The Canary', a poem which became almost proverbial in the first half of the nineteenth century, appeared in *The Daisy*. The three other poems appeared in *The Crocus*.

WATTS, ISAAC (1674–1748), the composer of hundreds of hymns ('O God, our help in ages past' and 'Jesus shall reign where'er the sun' among them) is said, when a child, to have had such a propensity for speaking in rhyme that he could not avoid it even when he wished. On his father threatening to whip him for this habit, the child burst into tears and on his knees cried:

Pray father, do some pity take,
And I will no more verses make.

Happily this incident, if true, did not impair Watts's love of song; and he became especially earnest that children should be encouraged to enjoy the pleasures of verse and harmony. In *Divine Songs Attempted in Easy Language for the Use of Children*, 1715, he wrote verses that were to be familiar to hundreds of thousands of children during the next two centuries. Further, he recommended that other authors should write for children, and that their verses should be 'flowing with cheerfulness, and without the solemnities of religion, or the sacred names of God and holy things; that children might find delight and profit together'. The 'Cradle Hymn' appeared in an edition after 1715.

WESLEY, CHARLES (1707–1788), younger brother of John Wesley, the evangelist, with whose life his own was closely bound, became one of the most inspired and prolific hymn-writers of all time. He is credited with 6,500 hymns: 'Jesu, lover of my soul' and 'Hark! the herald-angels sing' among them. 'Gentle Jesus, meek and mild' first appeared in the collection issued by the two brothers in 1742, *Hymns and Sacred Poems*; and subsequently, among 'Hymns for the Youngest', in Charles's *Hymns for Children*, 1763.

WHITTIER, JOHN GREENLEAF (1807–1892), America's 'Quaker poet', was the son of a Massachusetts farmer, and attended the local country school. He began writing poetry when a teacher lent him the poems of Robert Burns (q.v.). He was then about fourteen; and he continued to write for the rest of his long life, championing humanitarian causes, especially the abolition of slavery; and portraying the rural New England scene he knew so well. His poem 'In School-Days' first appeared in *Our Young Folks*, January 1870. The name of the golden-haired girl was Lydia Ayer. She died when she was fourteen.

WILSON, JOHN (1588–1677), a Puritan minister, born at Windsor and educated at Cambridge, wrote *A Song, or Story, for the lasting Remembrance of diuers famous works, which God hath done in our time* in 1626, when he had a living at Sudbury in Suffolk. The work, consisting of versified accounts of the Armada, the Gunpowder Plot, and other events which, at the time he wrote, were within living memory, was composed expressly for the young:

> But come, ye children, ye of tender age,
> This vnto you I write, and thus in verse,
> That ye might best conceaue, learne, and reherse.

Subsequently he emigrated to America; and was pastor of the newly-founded First Church in Boston for more than thirty years.

WITHER, GEORGE (1588–1667), a Hampshire man, poet, pamphleteer, and a captain on the Parliamentary side in the Civil War. He claimed to be the first man to write personal hymns for the comfort of different types of people, as rich men, poor men, soldiers, servants, lovers, inn-keepers, the old, and the young. The hymns appeared in *Haleluiah or Britans Second Remembrancer*, 1641; and he included the 'Rocking Hymn', because, he said, 'Nurses usually sing their children asleep'; but 'through want of pertinent matter, they oft make use of unprofitable (if not worse) songs. This was therefore prepared, that it might help acquaint them, and their nurse-children, with the loving care and kindness of their heavenly Father.'

WOOLSEY, SARAH CHAUNCEY. See Susan Coolidge.

WORDSWORTH, DOROTHY (1771–1855), saw the country and country folk with the same poetic eyes as her brother, William Wordsworth (q.v.), whose constant companion she was; but she knew that he was the poet, not herself. A writer of wonderful prose, whose letters and journals are the perfect complement to her brother's poetry, she seldom attempted verse unless to please children, such as her nephews and nieces. 'The Cottager to her Infant' was composed in 1805, when her niece Dora was an infant. 'What way does the Wind come?' was written at Dove Cottage, Grasmere, in 1806—'Edward' (in the last line) being her nephew Johnnie. 'Loving and Liking' was apparently written in consequence of the casual expression of a child, visiting her at Rydal Mount in 1832.

WORDSWORTH, WILLIAM (1770–1850), who became poet laureate after the death of Southey (q.v.), has left individual accounts of how many of his poems were written. Thus 'Lucy Gray' was composed in 1799, founded on the story of a little girl who lived near Halifax in Yorkshire; the heroine of 'We are Seven' was a girl he met in Herefordshire in 1793; and Barbara Lewthwaite, named in 'The Pet Lamb', was one of two lovely sisters who lived near his home at Grasmere in the Lake District. All three poems appeared in the second volume of *Lyrical Ballads, with Other Poems*, 1800. The publication of 'The Pet Lamb' had, however, an unfortunate sequel. Within a few months

Lindley Murray included it in his new schoolbook, and the book came into use at Grasmere School where Barbara was a pupil. 'Alas, I had the mortification,' Wordsworth recalled, 'of hearing that she was very vain of being thus distinguished.' He took this as a warning not to give the names of living people in his poetry; for though he had used her name she had not, in fact, been the child he had overheard talking to the lamb. The fourth poem, the quatrain, was written extempore in the album of his god-daughter Rotha Quillinan, 3 July 1834.

WYNNE, JOHN HUDDLESTONE (1743–1788), was one who preferred writing and penury to regular work and plenty. On leaving St. Paul's School he was apprenticed to a printer, but even while an apprentice he contributed to the periodicals. However, he seems to have had little originality. Most of his life was spent writing books to the orders of the booksellers, among them the two books for children which proved to be his most popular works: *Choice Emblems for the Improvement and Pastime of Youth*, 1772, in which appeared the lines 'Time's an hand's-breadth'; and *Tales for Youth: in Thirty Poems*, published in 1794 after his death, in which came 'The Horse and the Mule'.

ANONYMOUS

'A was an Archer', the most renowned of rhyming alphabets, is given here as it appeared in *A Little Book for Little Children* by T. W., published in London in the time of Queen Anne. This is the earliest known recording of the lines; but almost certainly they were not original here, and date from the seventeenth century. Innumerable children have been brought up on this alphabet, and have recalled the rhyme with pleasure. One, who put the letters to good use, was Charles Dickens.

'Anecdotes of Four Gentlemen'. These verses appeared in a brightly coloured booklet *Anecdotes and Adventures of Fifteen Gentlemen* issued by John Marshall about 1821. The booklet was clearly a rival to that containing the 'Three Wonderful Old Women' (q.v.); and reputedly was written by Richard Scrafton Sharpe (q.v.). 'There was a sick man of Tobago' is notable in nonsense literature for being the rhyme which a friend recited to Edward Lear (q.v.), and which gave him the idea for the verses in his *Book of Nonsense*, 1846, the book which was to popularize the limerick verse-form.

'The Babes in the Wood'. This résumé of the old ballad of the children in the wood (registered 1595) has been attributed to Michael Aislabie Denham, but in *Folk-Lore of the North of England*, 1851, Denham says he learnt his version 'from the recitation of a female relative'; and the song appears to have been well known since early in the century. The composite version we give benefits from the further recordings in *The Illustrated Book of Songs for Children*, 1863, and in *Notes and Queries*, 22 February 1873.

'The Bald Cavalier', 'The Father and his Children', and 'The Star-gazer' (under the title 'The Astrologer'), were included in a little book *Fables in Verse, for the Improvement of the Young and the Old*, given as being by 'Abraham Aesop, Esq.' and 'Woglog the great Giant', and in fact probably assembled and part-written by John Newbery, the leading children's-book publisher of his time, together with his employee Christopher Smart (q.v.). The book was 'printed for the Booksellers of all Nations' in 1757; and the booksellers continued to need reprints for the next twenty-five years.

'Customs Change'. See 'A Goodly Child'.

'Dame Wiggins of Lee' was first published in 1823 as a shilling booklet. It was said to have been written 'principally by a lady of ninety'; and it has subsequently been stated that this lady was a Mrs. Pearson who kept a toyshop in Fleet Street, while her helpmate may have been the practised writer of light verse, R. S. Sharpe (q.v.). 'Dame Wiggins' was taken up by the wits of the day and enjoyed extraordinary popularity. It then gained a fresh lease of life when Ruskin recommended the verses, added some more of his own, and had the story reprinted in 1885 for the unexceptionable reason that 'it relates nothing that is sad, and pourtrays nothing that is ugly'.

'Demeanour' appeared in a commonplace book made by Richard Hill, a London tradesman and father of seven children, who lived in the reign of Henry VIII. The verse was probably not new even when Richard Hill noted it. The text is as transcribed by Roman Dyboski for the Early English Text Society, Extra Series no. 101, 1908.

'The English Succession' comes from *The History of England* by Thomas Thumb, Esq., 1749, the earliest of history books to be written especially for juvenile reading, rather than for memorizing as a text book. One great advantage children might appear to have had in George II's time was that there were fewer kings and queens to remember than there are now. But in Georgian days children were often expected to remember the succession of rulers long before the Norman Conquest.

'Epitaph on a Dormouse' appears in the renowned *History of Little Goody Two-Shoes*, 1765, a small book with the large claim to being the first novel written specially for the amusement of young children.

It was frequently reprinted; and the 'Epitaph on a Dormouse' was also published separately, set to music as a glee.

'The Father and his Children'. See 'The Bald Cavalier'.

'A Goodly Child' and 'Customs Change' are observations from *The Book of Curtesye* which was a 'lytyl newe Instruccion' addressed to a child, and written 'acordynge vnto your age playne in sentence but playner in langage'. It was among the first books printed by Caxton at Westminster, about 1477–8. The author, according to one text, was a disciple of John Lydgate.

'Greedy Jane' seems to have first appeared in E. V. Lucas's anthology *Another Book of Verse for Children*, 1907, where the jingle is assigned to Anon who, as Blanche remarks in *The Daisy Chain*, 'writes so much poetry'.

'A Guinea-pig Song' appeared in *A Poetical Description of Beasts, with Moral Reflections for the Amusement of Children*, published by Thomas Carnan in 1773. The humour is much in the vein of Goldsmith's 'Elegy on Mrs. Mary Blaize' and 'Elegy on the Death of a Mad Dog'.

'The Happy Nightingale' appeared in the first number of the first periodical for children, *The Lilliputian Magazine: or the Young Gentleman & Lady's Golden Library*, which commenced publication, according to advertisements, in March 1751; and a poet who had a hand in it was Christopher Smart (q.v.). The magazine was issued by the children's-book publisher John Newbery, under the name of his young stepson Thomas Carnan. In a similar playful manner, 'The Happy Nightingale', with its splendid encouragement to be unafraid in the dark, is ascribed to Polly Newbery, his eldest daughter, then no more than eleven years old.

'The Maiden's Best Adorning'. These precepts appeared with others on a broadside entitled *The Maidens Best Adorning: or, A Directory for the Female-Sex; being A Fathers Advice to his Daughter*, printed in London in 1687. They were reprinted a number of times during the next hundred years, in America as well as in Britain. In 1698, when they were included in William Caton's *Abridgement of Eusebius Pamphilius's Ecclesiastical History*, they were given as being by Greshon Boate (presumably Gershon Boate), who is otherwise unknown, unless, as is very possible, Gerard Boate or de Boot is denoted, a Dutch physician and writer who settled in London and died in 1650.

'Manners at Table when away from Home' comes from Harleian MS. 541, of about 1480, supported by Egerton MS. 1995 (as printed by F. J. Furnivall for the Early English Text Society, in 1868), with the spelling and some phrases modernized. The advice is addressed to the children, mostly boys, who at this time were sent away at the age of seven or eight to live and learn in a greater man's house. Several similar sets of maxims are extant. In them the instruction that the meat should not be dipped into the salt-cellar is recurrent, as also the importance of washing the hands after eating, which was a social ritual customarily performed in pairs.

'Pussy' appeared anonymously in a miscellany, *The Child's Song Book, for the Use of Schools and Families*, published in Boston in 1830. Whether or not the song was original to this volume, which attempted 'to combine pure religious and moral sentiment with innocent hilarity', is uncertain. The words have often been attributed to Jane Taylor, as has so much other unclaimed verse, but evidence for this is wanting; and since the version in *The Child's Song Book* is earlier and superior to any other, and is better known in the United States than in Britain, the song is probably of American origin.

'A Schoolmaster's Admonition' probably dates from the reign of James I. It was printed in black-letter on a broadsheet so that it could be pasted on a school wall for every child to see and remember. The only known copy is in the British Museum. It is headed: 'A Table of good Nurture: wherein is contained a Schoole-masters admonition to his Schollers to learne good manners'.

'The Song of the Reed Sparrow' and 'The Wren' come in *A Poetical Description of Song Birds* which was published 'for the Amusement of Children' by Thomas Carnan in 1773. No copy of the first edition is known, and only two copies (one of them in our collection) seem to have survived of subsequent editions: which shows that children know a good book when they find one and read it to extinction. Whoever wrote these verses piped a new note for the young, and may be looked upon as an immediate forerunner to William Blake.

'The Stargazer'. See 'The Bald Cavalier'.

'Symon's Lesson of Wisdom for all Manner of Children' is from a manuscript in the Bodleian Library, Oxford, Bodl. MS. 832, f. 174, as printed by F. J. Furnivall for the Early English Text Society, 1868, but with the spelling modernized. The suggestion has been made that the lines are addressed to a boy who is familiar with the Bishop's presence, perhaps a cathedral chorister, such a one who would appreciate the sentiment that he must learn fast if he is to take the Bishop's place.

'Table Rules for Little Folks'. These rules were printed on cards and hung on the walls of Victorian nurseries and dining-rooms, in much the manner that notices were hung in bathrooms in the 1930s beginning:

Please remember, don't forget,
Never leave the bathroom wet.

Several versions of 'Table Rules' exist. The one we give is from *My Poetry Book*, issued by the Religious Tract Society in 1858; and it can be compared with the 'Manners at Table' of medieval days (pp. 7–8). The precept 'Children should be seen and not heard' was in fact not new even when given by Aristophanes.

'The Ten Commandments' have often been given to children in rhyme for their easier remembrance. Bunyan commenced his *Book for Boys and Girls*, 1686, with a metrical rendering; and Watts copied it, with little improvement, for his *Divine Songs*, 1715. The most felicitous wording we have seen was known to a child, Mary Vining, in 1731 when she stitched her sampler, now in our possession.

'Three Wonderful Old Women' have the distinction of being characters in the earliest known publication to consist of what are now known as limericks. This was *The History of Sixteen Wonderful Old Women, illustrated by as many Engravings; exhibiting their Principal Eccentricities and Amusements*, which was a 'novelty for the nursery' issued by John Harris in 1820. The booklet was quickly followed by one consisting of 'Anecdotes' of certain gentlemen (see pp. 152–3).

'To Theodora' was added to the 1708 edition of Fénelon's *Instructions for the Education of a Daughter*, a translation from the French, edited by George Hickes; but it is unknown who wrote the verses, or from where they come. What is fairly certain is that they are not by Dean Hickes himself, whose chief writings are theological or antiquarian, and who seems to have become editor of *The Education of a Daughter* only by chance.

'Tumbling' is from *Nancy Cock's Pretty Song Book for all Little Misses and Masters*, a small illustrated rhyme-book advertised for sale in 1744, but of which no copy is known earlier than one of about 1781.

'Two Little Kittens' almost became traditional in the early years of this century, when many children learnt it; and, in fact, it turns up as a 'folksong from Vermont', together with a tune, in *Songs of the Americas*, 1943. It was first published, it seems, in the *Parish Magazine*, July 1859, where it appeared above the initials M.L.R. Subsequently it was included in *Songs for Our Little Friends*, 1868, with a tune by E.R.B., and was frequently anthologized in America as well as Britain.

'The Unhappy Schoolboy' is another piece from Richard Hill's commonplace book compiled early in the sixteenth century (see 'Demeanour'). When the unhappy schoolboy says pertly he has been 'milking ducks' as his mother told him, he speaks with the same tongue that schoolboys do today, when they send a new boy on a fool's errand to buy 'pigeon's milk'. The humour in the last verse is also traditional, occurring in the old Scots ballad 'Fair Annie':

O gin my sons were seven hares,
  Rinnin' owre yon lily lea,
And I mysell a good greyhound,
  Soon worried they a' should be!

Few schoolboy colloquial songs are known as early as this. The text, taken from F. J. Furnivall's transcription, Early English Text Society, no. 32, 1868, has been slightly modernized.

'What Became of Them?' appealed to children particularly, it seems, in the early decades of the present century, when it was frequently reprinted in Britain as well as in the United States. Its first appearance seems to have been in that repository of so much good writing for the young, the New York magazine *St. Nicholas*, in the number for September 1880.

'The Wren'. See 'The Song of the Reed-Sparrow'.

INDEXES

INDEX OF AUTHORS

INDEX OF AUTHORS

INDEX OF FIRST LINES AND FAMILIAR TITLES

INDEX OF FIRST LINES

INDEX OF FIRST LINES

INDEX OF FIRST LINES

INDEX OF FIRST LINES

MORE OXFORD PAPERBACKS

This book is just one of nearly 1000 Oxford Paperbacks currently in print. If you would like details of other Oxford Paperbacks, including titles in the World's Classics, Oxford Reference, Oxford Books, OPUS, Past Masters, Oxford Authors, and Oxford Shakespeare series, please write to:

UK and Europe: Oxford Paperbacks Publicity Manager, Arts and Reference Publicity Department, Oxford University Press, Walton Street, Oxford OX2 6DP.

Customers in UK and Europe will find Oxford Paperbacks available in all good bookshops. But in case of difficulty please send orders to the Cash-with-Order Department, Oxford University Press Distribution Services, Saxon Way West, Corby, Northants NN18 9ES. Tel: 01536 741519; Fax: 01536 746337. Please send a cheque for the total cost of the books, plus £1.75 postage and packing for orders under £20; £2.75 for orders over £20. Customers outside the UK should add 10% of the cost of the books for postage and packing.

USA: Oxford Paperbacks Marketing Manager, Oxford University Press, Inc., 200 Madison Avenue, New York, N.Y. 10016.

Canada: Trade Department, Oxford University Press, 70 Wynford Drive, Don Mills, Ontario M3C 1J9.

Australia: Trade Marketing Manager, Oxford University Press, G.P.O. Box 2784Y, Melbourne 3001, Victoria.

South Africa: Oxford University Press, P.O. Box 1141, Cape Town 8000.

THE WORLD'S CLASSICS

THE WIND IN THE WILLOWS

Kenneth Grahame

The Wind in the Willows (1908) is a book for those 'who keep the spirit of youth alive in them; of life, sunshine, running water, woodlands, dusty roads, winter firesides'. So wrote Kenneth Grahame of his timeless tale of Toad, Mole, Badger, and Rat in their beautiful and benevolently ordered world. But it is also a world under siege, threatened by dark and unnamed forces—'the Terror of the Wild Wood' with its 'wicked little faces' and 'glances of malice and hatred'—and defended by the mysterious Piper at the Gates of Dawn. *The Wind in the Willows* has achieved an enduring place in our literature: it succeeds at once in arousing our anxieties and in calming them by giving perfect shape to our desire for peace and escape.

The World's Classics edition has been prepared by Peter Green, author of the standard biography of Kenneth Grahame.

'It is a Household Book; a book which everybody in the household loves, and quotes continually; a book which is read aloud to every new guest and is regarded as the touchstone of his worth.' A. A. Milne

OXFORD BOOKS

THE NEW OXFORD BOOK OF IRISH VERSE

Edited, with Translations, by Thomas Kinsella

Verse in Irish, especially from the early and medieval periods, has long been felt to be the preserve of linguists and specialists, while Anglo-Irish poetry is usually seen as an adjunct to the English tradition. This original anthology approaches the Irish poetic tradition as a unity and presents a relationship between two major bodies of poetry that reflects a shared and painful history.

'the first coherent attempt to present the entire range of Irish poetry in both languages to an English-speaking readership' *Irish Times*

'a very satisfying and moving introduction to Irish poetry' *Listener*

OXFORD BOOKS

THE OXFORD BOOK OF ENGLISH GHOST STORIES

Chosen by Michael Cox and R. A. Gilbert

This anthology includes some of the best and most frightening ghost stories ever written, including M. R. James's 'Oh Whistle, and I'll Come to You, My Lad', 'The Monkey's Paw' by W. W. Jacobs, and H. G. Wells's 'The Red Room'. The important contribution of women writers to the genre is represented by stories such as Amelia Edwards's 'The Phantom Coach', Edith Wharton's 'Mr Jones', and Elizabeth Bowen's 'Hand in Glove'.

As the editors stress in their informative introduction, a good ghost story, though it may raise many profound questions about life and death, entertains as much as it unsettles us, and the best writers are careful to satisfy what Virginia Woolf called 'the strange human craving for the pleasure of feeling afraid'. This anthology, the first to present the full range of classic English ghost fiction, similarly combines a serious literary purpose with the plain intention of arousing pleasing fear at the doings of the dead.

'an excellent cross-section of familiar and unfamiliar stories and guaranteed to delight' *New Statesman*

ILLUSTRATED HISTORIES IN OXFORD PAPERBACKS

THE OXFORD ILLUSTRATED HISTORY OF ENGLISH LITERATURE

Edited by Pat Rogers

Britain possesses a literary heritage which is almost unrivalled in the Western world. In this volume, the richness, diversity, and continuity of that tradition are explored by a group of Britain's foremost literary scholars.

Chapter by chapter the authors trace the history of English literature, from its first stirrings in Anglo-Saxon poetry to the present day. At its heart towers the figure of Shakespeare, who is accorded a special chapter to himself. Other major figures such as Chaucer, Milton, Donne, Wordsworth, Dickens, Eliot, and Auden are treated in depth, and the story is brought up to date with discussion of living authors such as Seamus Heaney and Edward Bond.

'[a] lovely volume . . . put in your thumb and pull out plums' Michael Foot

'scholarly and enthusiastic people have written inspiring essays that induce an eagerness in their readers to return to the writers they admire' *Economist*

THE CONCISE OXFORD DICTIONARY OF OPERA

New Edition

Edited by Ewan West and John Warrack

Derived from the full *Oxford Dictionary of Opera*, this is the most authoritative and up-to-date dictionary of opera available in paperback. Fully revised for this new edition, it is designed to be accessible to all those who enjoy opera, whether at the opera-house or at home.

* **Over 3,500 entries on operas, composers, and performers**
* **Plot summaries and separate entries for well-known roles, arias, and choruses**
* **Leading conductors, producers and designers**

From the reviews of its parent volume:

'the most authoritative single-volume work of its kind'
Independent on Sunday

'an invaluable reference work'
Gramophone

THE CONCISE OXFORD DICTIONARY OF MUSIC

New Edition

Edited by Michael Kennedy

Derived from the full *Oxford Dictionary of Music* this is the most authoritative and up-to-date dictionary of music available in paperback. Fully revised and updated for this new edition, it is a rich mine of information for lovers of music of all periods and styles.

* **14,000 entries on musical terms, works, composers, librettists, musicians, singers and orchestras.**
* **Comprehensive work-lists for major composers**
* **Generous coverage of living composers and performers**

'clearly the best around . . . the dictionary that everyone should have'
Literary Review

'indispensable'
Yorkshire Post

THE CONCISE OXFORD COMPANION TO ENGLISH LITERATURE

Edited by Margaret Drabble and Jenny Stringer

Derived from the acclaimed *Oxford Companion to English Literature*, the concise maintains the wide coverage of its parent volume. It is an indispensable, compact guide to all aspects of English literature. For this revised edition, existing entries have been fully updated and revised with 60 new entries added on contemporary writers.

* **Over 5,000 entries on the lives and works of authors, poets and playwrights**
* **The most comprehensive and authoritative paperback guide to English literature**
* **New entries include Peter Ackroyd, Martin Amis, Toni Morrison, and Jeanette Winterson**
* **New appendices list major literary prize-winners**

From the reviews of its parent volume:

'It earns its place at the head of the best sellers: every home should have one'
Sunday Times